ILLUSTRATED
WORLD OF
THE BIBLE
LIBRARY

ILLUSTRATED

WORLD OF

LIBRARY

McGRAW-HILL BOOK COMPANY, INC.

THE BIBLE

2. THE FORMER PROPHETS

NEW YORK · TORONTO · LONDON

First published in Jerusalem — Ramat-Gan, Israel,
under the title, VIEWS OF THE BIBLICAL WORLD: Volume 2

Library of Congress Catalogue Card number 59— 43080

41168

PRINTED IN ISRAEL

INTRODUCTION

THE second part of "Illustrated World of the Bible Library" contains the books of the Former Prophets: Joshua, Judges, Samuel and Kings. Like its predecessor, this volume too consists of plates illustrating selected passages from these books each accompanied by a short explanatory text. The Editors have once again been at pains to choose for reproduction objects as close as possible in time and place to the text which they are meant to illustrate. Preference has been given to subjects which have the greatest illustrative and aesthetic value.

While stressing that this volume and its predecessor together form a continuous whole, the Editors would draw attention to several distinguishing features of this second part of "World of the Bible Library", that arise from its different subject-matter. The Former Prophets, which comprise the bulk of the historical writing of the Bible, provide us with a continuous record of the history of Israel in its own land, from the tribal conquest and occupation of Canaan down to the destruction of the First Temple and the Babylonian exile — in all a period of something over six hundred years. Their contents and style are thus rich and varied. These books represent different types of ancient Israelite literature: stories about tribal heroes (such as the daring deeds of Ehud the son of Gera and of Samson), war-songs (Deborah's Song), laments over the dead (David's Lament over Saul). Elsewhere we find administrative lists, such as that of Solomon's districts; fragments of chronicles, such as the record of Ahab's building activities; and temple archives, such as the descriptions of the journeyings of the Ark and the building of Solomon's Temple. Other, quite different, elements are provided by the acts of the prophets — as in the stories of Elijah and Elisha, and by parables such as those of Jotham, Nathan the prophet and of the woman from Abel-Beth-Maachah. Side by side with the variegated mosaic of stories in the Book of Judges we find long self-contained, homogeneous units of historical writing, such as the record of the conquest of Canaan or of the reigns of David and Solomon.

Since nearly all the events described in the Former Prophets took place on the soil of ancient Israel, the reader will find in this volume a large number of maps and views of sites or landscapes, together with many photographs of the animal and plant life characteristic of the country. The archaeological exhibits have also been chosen, as far as possible, from the finds yielded by excavations in this country: the remains of walls and buildings, weapons and domestic utensils at various stages of their development, and objects connected with the cult of the idols against which the prophets fought with so much fervour. The reader will find here inscriptions in Hebrew from the Land of Israel, beside documents in cognate languages from the neighbouring countries. The establishment of the People of Israel in its land and its emergence as a sovereign nation, with all the trappings of statehood, are clearly reflected in the reproductions included in this volume. In this period Israel entered into close relations with its neighbours, and also with more distant states, especially those in the north and north-east of the Fertile Crescent. The volume opens with the Israelite tribes fighting with the inhabitants of Canaan, and a little later struggling against new invaders from among the "Sea Peoples", such as the Philistines. In the beginning of this era Egypt is still the main source of pictures illustrating Israel's contact with these peoples, since Canaan was either still under Egyptian domination or had but recently emerged from it. With the crumbling of Egyptian rule, the political centre of gravity moved northwards. David's and Solomon's relations with Tyre and Sidon left their mark on the cultural and economic life of Israel in various ways, among them in the development of joint commercial enterprises in the Red Sea. The wars between Israel and Aram in the time of the Divided Monarchy, and more particularly the rise of, first, the Assyrian and then the Babylonian empires, make Syria and Mesopotamia the chief source of material illustrating the history of Israel in the second half of the period of the First Temple. Wherever possible, the Editors have used the archaeological finds from this region to give the reader trustworthy pictures of historical events (such as Sennacherib's capture of Lachish) and portraits of historical figures mentioned in the Bible (such as Jehu, King of Israel, and the Pharaoh Tirhaka of the Kushite Twenty-fifth Dynasty).

It is the Editors' hope that, like its predecessor, this volume will assist both the student and the general reader to gain a deeper understanding of the literature and history of biblical times.

CREDITS

The work of preparing this volume has once more been entrusted to the editors of the previous volume: Professor Michael Avi-Yonah and Dr. Abraham Malamat, who were joined by Dr. Shemaryahu Talmon.

It is the Editors' pleasant duty to express their gratitude to the Editorial Board, the Editorial Advisory Council, and the Assistants (whose names are given in the additional list) and to all those who have helped them in their work.

We also wish to thank those who helped us in obtaining the plates reproduced here, or who have given us the benefit of their comments on the contents of this volume: Professor W. F. Albright; Dr. R. D. Barnett, London; Professor N. Glueck, Cincinnati; Professor A. Parrot and Professor C. F. A. Schaeffer, Paris; Professor G. E. Wright, Harvard; Father R. North, S.J., of the Pontifical Biblical Institute of Jerusalem; Mr. R. W. Hamilton, Oxford; Dr. M. Dothan, Professor M. Stekelis and Mr. S. J. Schweig, of Jerusalem.

We further wish to express our appreciation to all the distinguished public figures and scholars, in Israel and abroad, who have given this project their whole-hearted support from the outset, and above all to H.E. The President of Israel, Mr. Izhak Ben-Zvi; the Prime Minister, Mr. David Ben-Gurion; the former Minister of Education and Culture, Mr. Z. Aranne; and the Minister of the Interior, Mr. M. H. Shapira.

Once again it is our pleasant duty to thank the Israel Ministry for Foreign Affairs, the Ministry of Education and Culture, the Ministry of Commerce and Industry, the Ministry of Finance and the Ministry of Defence, as well as the Jewish Agency and "Malben" for their encouragement and ready assistance.

Our thanks are also due to the museums, individuals and photographers who assisted us in obtaining the plates required. Those in Israel include the staff and library of the Archaeology Department of the Hebrew University; the Department of Antiquities (museum and library) of the Ministry of Education and Culture, and its former director, Dr. S. Yeivin; the National and University Library, Jerusalem; the Bezalel National Museum, Jerusalem; the Haaretz Museum, Tel-Aviv; the James de Rothschild Expedition at Hazor; the collection of Mr. J. Leibovitch; the Clark Collection at the Jerusalem Y.M.C.A.; the collection of Dr. R. Hecht, Haifa; that of the Ben-Zvi Institute for the Study of the Oriental Jewish Communities at the Hebrew University; The Shrine of the Book, Jerusalem; the Tell Qasile Collection, Tel-Aviv; the permanent exhibition on the site of the Megiddo excavations; the Nautical Museum, Haifa; the Pontifical Biblical Institute, Jerusalem; the Israel Aero Club.

Contributions from abroad have been provided by the Metropolitan Museum, New York; the Oriental Institute of the University of Chicago; the archives of Professor N. Glueck; Professor G. Reed; the collections of the Marburg and Alinari Photographic Institutes; the Museum of Fine Arts, Boston; the Detroit Art Museum; the University Museum, Philadelphia; the Brooklyn Museum; the Baltimore Museum; the British Museum, London; the Museum of the Ancient Orient, Istanbul; the Hittite Museum, Ankara; the National Museum, Rome; the Vatican Museum, Rome; the Staatliche Museen, Berlin; the Archaeological Museum, University of London; the Ny-Carlsberg Glyptothek, Copenhagen; the collection of A. Goitein, U.S.A.; the Louvre, Paris; and the Rijksmuseum, Leiden.

The Editorial Board also wishes to thank the following authors, editors and publishers for their kind permission to use plates published by them: W. F. Albright, W. Andrae, N. Avigad, D. Baldi, R. D. Barnett, P. Berger, A. M. Blackman, H. Bonnet, E. Douglas van Buren, M. Burrows, E. Chiera, Ch. Chipiez, F. M. Cross, G. Dalman, W. R. Dawson, N. de G. Davies, A. Deimel, J. Dossin, M. Dunand, G. R. Driver, A. Erman, C. S. Fisher, H. Frankfort, A. Furman, S. J. Gadd, K. Galling, A. H. Gardiner, P. C. Gau, A. J. Gayet, H. Gressmann, H. Grimme, L. H. Grollenberg, U. Hölscher, L. Klebs, S. N. Kramer, P. Lemaire, A. Lhote, G. Loud, D. G. Lyon, R. A. S. Macalister, M. J. L. Mallowan, Ch. McCown, B. Meissner, A. Mekhiterian, J. T. Milik, P. Montet, S. Moscati, H. H. Nelson, P. E. Newberry, J. Nougayrol, A. T. Olmstead,

M. Oppenheim, M. Pallottino, R. A. Parker, A. Parrot, A. T. Peet, G. Perrot, W. M. Flinders Petrie, K. Pflüger, W. Phillips, H. Ranke, G. A. Reisner, P. Rost, A. Rowe, H. W. P. Saggs, A. H. Sayce, C. F. A. Schaeffer, H. Schmökel, O. Schröder, C. Schumacher, W. Stevenson-Smith, C. Steuernagel, E. L. Sukenik, F. Thureau-Dangin, J. Trever, O. Tufnell, N. H. Tur-Sinai, B. Ubach, C. Watzinger, R. Weill, M. Werbrouck, J. G. Wilkinson, H. E. Winlock, L. Woolley, W. Wreszinski, G. E. Wright;

American Schools of Oriental Research, E. J. Brill, Ltd., British Museum, British School of Archaeology in Iraq, F. A. Brockhaus, Constable & Co., W. de Gruyter & Co., Editions Cahiers d'Art, Editions Ides et Calendes, Egypt Exploration Fund, Egypt Exploration Society, Folkswang Verlag, Fondation égyptologique Reine Elizabeth, M. P. Geuthner, V. Gollancz, Hachette, Harvard University Press, J. C. Hinrichs, Imprimerie nationale, G. Klipper, Marietti, Metropolitan Museum, J. C. B. Mohr-Paul Siebeck, Monestir de Montserrat, John Murray Ltd., Oriental Institute — University of Chicago, Oxford University Press, Palestine Exploration Fund, Penguin Books, Ltd., Presses universitaires de France, Routledge & Kegan Paul, Ltd., Ferdinand Schöningh, A. Skira, Society of Antiquaries, University Museum — University of Pennsylvania, The Trustees of the Late Sir Henry S. Wellcome, Yale University Press.

In addition we have made full use of the comprehensive studies of R. Lepsius, A. Layard and P. E. Botta. The photographs in Israel were taken mainly by Z. Kluger, B. Rotenberg and A. Allon. Use has also been made of photographs taken by M. Bar-Am, A. Hirschbein, A. Volk, J. Lister and Professor D. Amiran, and also of photographs from the U.S.A. whose owners wish to remain anonymous.

Finally, we express our warm appreciation to the management and workers of the Schwitter A.G., Zürich; to the A. Levin-Epstein Ltd.

Press, Bat-Yam; to the Haaretz Press Ltd., Tel-Aviv; to the Hakorech Binders' Cooperative, Holon (supported by "Malben"); and to the Tel-Aviv Bindery — for their care and devotion in making the plates, setting up the text, and printing and binding this volume.

The English translation of the biblical text used in this publication is mainly that of the *Revised Standard Version of the Bible,* copyrighted 1946 and 1952 by the Division of Christian Education, National Council of Churches, and used by permission.

THE EDITORS

JOSHUA

The plate on the right is a reproduction of the first page of the Book of Joshua from Aharon ben Asher's *Keter Hatorah*. This, one of the earliest and most important of all biblical manuscripts, was written at the end of the 9th or the beginning of the 10th century A.D.

(col 3)		(col 2)		(col 1)

אשר נתן לכם משה עבד
יהוה בעבר הירדן מזרח
השמש ויענו את יהושע
לאמר כל אשר צויתנו נעשה
ואל כל אשר תשלחנו נלך
בכל אשר שמענו אל משה
כן נשמע אליך רק יהי יהוה
אלהיך עמך כאשר היה
עם משה כל איש אשר
ימרה את פיך ולא ישמע
את דבריך לכל אשר תצונו
יומת רק חזק ואמץ ׃

וישלח יהושע בן נון מן
השטים שנים אנשים מרגלים
חרש לאמר לכו ראו את
הארץ ואת יריחו וילכו
ויבאו בית אשה זונה ושמה
רחב וישכבו שמה ויאמר
למלך יריחו לאמר הנה
אנשים באו הנה הלילה
מבני ישראל לחפר את
הארץ וישלח מלך יריחו
אל רחב לאמר הוציאי
האנשים הבאים אליך
אשר באו לביתך כי לחפר
את כל הארץ באו ותקח
האשה את שני האנשים

תשכיל הלוא צויתיך חזק
ואמץ אל תערץ ואל תחת כי
עמך יהוה אלהיך בכל אשר
תלך ׃
ויצו יהושע את שטרי העם
לאמר עברו בקרב המחנה
וצוו את העם לאמר הכינו
לכם צידה כי בעוד שלשת
ימים אתם עברים את הירדן
הזה לבוא לרשת את הארץ
אשר יהוה אלהיכם נתן לכם
לרשתה ׃
ולראובני ולגדי ולחצי שבט
המנשה אמר יהושע לאמר ׃
זכור את הדבר אשר צוה
אתכם משה עבד יהוה לאמר
יהוה אלהיכם מניח לכם
ונתן לכם את הארץ הזאת
נשיכם טפכם ומקניכם ישבו
בארץ אשר נתן לכם משה
בעבר הירדן ואתם תעברו
חמשים לפני אחיכם כל
גבורי החיל ועזרתם אותם
עד אשר יניח יהוה לאחיכם
ככם וירשו גם המה את
הארץ אשר יהוה אלהיכם
נתן להם ושבתם לארץ
ירשתכם וירשתם אותה ׃

ויהי אחרי מות משה עבד ׃
יהוה ויאמר יהוה אל יהושע
בן נון משרת משה לאמר ׃
משה עבדי מת ועתה קום עבר
את הירדן הזה אתה וכל העם
הזה אל הארץ אשר אנכי נתן
להם לבני ישראל כל מקום
אשר תדרך כף רגלכם בו לכם
נתתיו כאשר דברתי אל משה ׃
מהמדבר והלבנון הזה ועד
הנהר הגדול נהר פרת כל ארץ
החתים ועד הים הגדול מבוא
השמש יהיה גבולכם ׃ לא
יתיצב איש לפניך כל ימי חייך
כאשר הייתי עם משה אהיה
עמך לא ארפך ולא אעזבך ׃
חזק ואמץ כי אתה תנחיל את
העם הזה את הארץ אשר
נשבעתי לאבותם לתת להם ׃
רק חזק ואמץ מאד לשמר
לעשות ככל התורה אשר
צוך משה עבדי אל תסור
ממנו ימין ושמאול למען
תשכיל בכל אשר תלך ׃ לא
ימוש ספר התורה הזה מפיך
והגית בו יומם ולילה למען
תשמר לעשות ככל הכתוב
בו כי אז תצליח את דרכך ואז

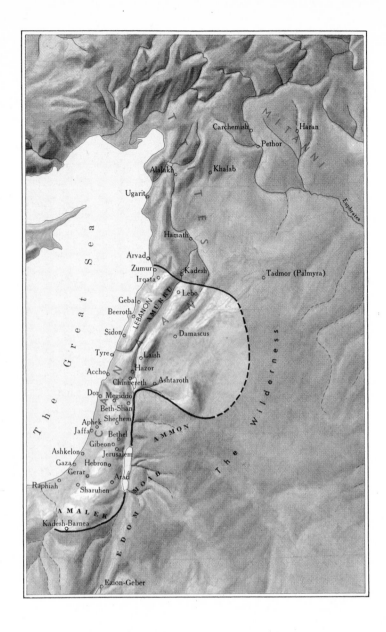

FROM the wilderness and this Lebanon as far as the great river, the river Euphrates, all the land of the Hittites to the Great Sea toward the going down of the sun shall be your territory. (Josh. 1 : 4)

Before his death, Moses had, from Mount Nebo, seen the Promised Land which it was not vouchsafed him to enter. Now, after his death, God renews His promises to Moses' servant, Joshua: "Every place that the sole of your foot will tread upon, I have given to you" (Josh. 1 : 3). The boundaries described here correspond roughly to those promised to Abraham in the Covenant Between the Pieces (Gen. 15 : 18) and redefined in Deut. 11 : 24.

It is hard to say precisely what geographical reality lay behind the delineation of the boundaries given here. Possibly they reflect the limits of the Egyptian province of Canaan and of the Hittite domain in Syria. As a result of the peace treaty signed between the two powers in the first third of the 13th cent. B.C., the northern frontier of the Egyptian province of Canaan was re-established to the north of the Lebanon. The Syrian territory beyond was controlled by the Hittite kings until close to the end of the 13th cent., shortly before the collapse of the Hittite Empire. The boundaries between the Hittite Empire and Egypt (see map) would appear to have been known to the Israelites. While the conquests of Joshua did not reach the limits outlined here, the Kingdom of David and Solomon stretched over almost the full extent of the promised territory (see p. 209; and compare Vol. I, p. 239).

AND Joshua the son of Nun sent two men secretly from Shittim as spies . . .   (Josh. 2 : 1)

The task of the two spies who came to the house of Rahab was to reconnoitre the Land of Canaan, and especially Jericho, which was the gateway to the country (Josh. 2:1—2). Both from the stories in the Bible and from non-biblical sources we learn that reconnaissance played an important part in the military operations of antiquity. Thus, the reconnaissance of the twelve spies in the time of Moses had a strategic, political and economic purpose. Their orders were to obtain information about the nature of the country, the character of its inhabitants, their economic conditions and the like (see Vol. I, pp. 210—212). Sometimes, however, such reconnaissance had the limited, purely tactical, purpose of collecting information required for a specific military operation (Nu. 21:32; 2 Sam. 10:3; and elsewhere). Such were Joshua's reconnaissances at Jericho and Ai (Josh. 7:2 ff.).

The methods of espionage employed at the time of the Conquest can be inferred from the Annals of Ramses II (first half of the 13th cent. B.C.). In his description of his battle with the Hittites at Kadesh-on-the-Orontes, the Pharaoh relates that the Hittite king sent two spies to trick him into revealing his whereabouts. The spies were caught. The way in which they were interrogated is shown on the Egyptian reliefs depicting the battle. In the picture reproduced here, from the rock-temple at Abu Simbel, the Egyptian "interrogators" are seen beating the two spies with rods, until they confess.

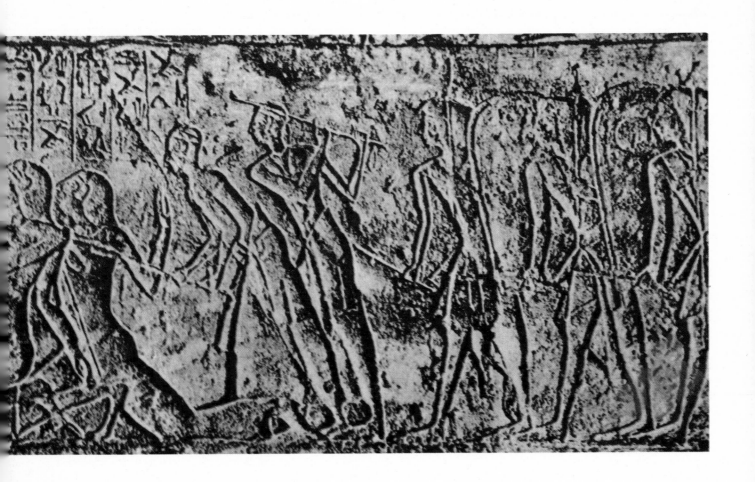

FOR her house was built into the city
wall, so that she dwelt in the wall.

(Josh. 2 : 15)

Jericho, the first of the Canaanite cities to be conquered by the Israelites, is the most ancient city that has so far
been brought to light (see Vol. I, p. 24). Recent excavations show that the city was surrounded by a wall as
early as the seventh millennium B.C. At the end of the Middle Bronze Age it was encircled by a stone glacis
(see picture on left) as an additional strengthening to the brick wall built on top of it. Of the settlement of the
Late Bronze Age (the city conquered by Joshua) virtually nothing remains today: the wall that was formerly
assigned to this period is probably of an earlier date. Some scholars maintain that the Late Bronze city made use
of the Middle Bronze Age glacis shown here, and that this was the wall which collapsed in the time of Joshua.
There is archaeological evidence that the inhabitants of Jericho used occasionally to build their houses onto the
city wall. Although this evidence antecedes the time of Joshua by hundreds of years, it nevertheless serves to
illustrate the verse in which Rahab's house is described as "built into the city wall", with its windows facing
outwards.
The right-hand picture-plan shows the northern section of the walls of Jericho with their adjacent buildings
as unearthed in 1907—1909.

AND he will without fail drive out from before you the Canaanites, the Hittites, the Hivites, the Perizzites, the Girgashites, the Amorites, and the Jebusites.   (Josh. 3 : 10)

Before the Israelites crossed the Jordan, Joshua strengthened their morale by reminding them of God's promise to drive out the seven Canaanite peoples from before them. Only a few of these peoples are known to us, from other biblical verses and non-biblical sources. Of the Girgashites nothing at all is known. The Perizzites apparently lived in the hill country (Josh. 17:15; Judg. 1:4—6). The Jebusites held Jerusalem right down to David's conquest of the city. The Hivites were located in Gibeon and the neighbouring cities to the west (see p. 35), and also in the north of Canaan (see Josh. 11:3; Judg. 3:3). The Hittites alone are well known from non-biblical sources. In the second half of the second millennium B.C. they established a great empire in Anatolia; some of them actually settled in Canaan itself (see p. 20 and Vol. I, pp.68, 77). In the list of the peoples of Canaan, the Canaanites and the Amorites are mentioned as separate entities; but usually their names are used in the Bible as a collective term to describe the early inhabitants of the country in general.

The distinguishing physical characteristics of the Canaanite peoples are clearly marked in Egyptian representations, such as the relief from the tomb of Horemheb at Thebes (second half of the 14th cent. B.C.) which depicts prisoners-of-war from Canaan, mostly bearded Semites, being led at the end of a rope. Among the heads on the lower register the fourth and fifth figures from the right are different from the rest: one has a shaven crown with pigtails, the other long hair which partly covers a large ear-ring in his ear. These are almost certainly Hittites.

THE waters coming down from above stood and rose up in a heap far off, at Adam, the city that is beside Zarethan . . .   (Josh. 3 : 16)

The Jordan stopped flowing for the Israelites at harvest time when its waters even flood "the Pride of the Jordan"—the wooded belt along the river. This miraculous cutting off of the waters of the Jordan can be explained by the topography of the region. "Adam, the city" is to-day Tell ed-Damiya close by some fords on the eastern bank of the river, near the confluence of the Jabbok with the Jordan. The potsherds found on the tell (see picture), show that the site was occupied in the period of Joshua, the Judges and the Kings. To the north of this tell stands Tell Umm Hamad, presumably the site of Zarethan.

The Jordan flows here in a deep channel, bordered to the east by high almost perpendicular valley-slopes. As the material that builds up this slope is highly erodible, its lowermost part is constantly being undercut by the riverflow. The consequent sliding down of this mass into the riverbed occasionally dams up the channel, temporarily stopping the flow of water. Such occurrences are recorded for A.D. 1267, 1906, and 1927 (after an earthquake).

COMMAND the priests who bear the Ark of the Covenant . . .   (Josh. 4 : 16)

According to the Book of Joshua, the Ark of the Covenant played a vital part in the crossing of the Jordan. The priests carried it on their shoulders in front of the whole host, and as soon as their feet touched the brink of the river its waters were cut off "and the people passed over opposite Jericho" (Josh. 3:3—17). The ark was regarded as the most sacred of all ritual objects. It was built by God's command at the time of the Giving of the Law on Mount Sinai (Ex. 25 : 10—22). Throughout the wandering in the wilderness it went before the Israelite host to guide them (Nu. 10 : 33). After the Conquest the ark was set up in Shiloh together with the tabernacle (Josh. 18 : 1, also see pp. 113, 120, 173).

The ark was carried on the shoulders of the priests and Levites by means of long poles passed through rings attached to its sides (Ex. 25:14). These poles were not detached from the ark even when it reached its final resting place (1 Ki. 8:7—30). The picture is of a detail from the stele of Meri-meri, the Treasurer of Thebes (Nineteenth Dynasty), which shows an ark being carried in a ritual procession by his servants. They are preceded by other retainers carrying water-jars on their shoulders (also, apparently, for some ritual purpose).

WHEN all the kings of the Amorites that were beyond the Jordan to the west, and all the kings of the Canaanites that were by the sea, heard . . . their heart melted, and there was no longer any spirit in them, because of the people of Israel.

(Josh. 5 : 1)

The loosely federated army of the Israelite tribes commenced its conquest of Canaan with religious fervour. Even earlier, after their first victories over the Amorite kings east of the Jordan, they had gained renown as warriors (Nu. 22:4—5). No wonder, then, that when the victorious tribes surged forward onto the west bank of the Jordan, the people of Canaan were overcome by terror and capable of offering only a feeble resistance: "And as soon as we heard it, our hearts melted, and there was no courage left in any man, because of you" (Josh. 2:11).

Helplessness of this kind is forcibly portrayed in a relief from the reign of Seti I (end of the 14th century B.C.) which was found at Karnak. With a few powerful strokes the artist has recreated the deadly terror which paralyzed the Canaanites in the face of the Pharaoh. Yanoam, a Canaanite fortress close to the Sea of Galilee, encircled by what may be either the waters of the Jordan or a moat, is seen yielding to the Egyptian forces. The population, whose features are typically Semitic, are standing on the wall with their hands raised in submission. A few of them have fled outside and are hidden among the trees in a nearby wood. Some are hugging the earth in a desperate attempt to conceal themselves, while others are peeping out from between the trees with their hands on their heads in a gesture of supplication or expression of grief.

AT that time the LORD said to Joshua, "Make flint knives . . ."
(Josh. 5 : 2)

When the Israelites reached Canaan, Joshua was commanded to remove the shame of Egypt from them by circumcising those that had been born in the wilderness, "for they were uncircumcised, because they had not been circumcised on the way" (Josh. 5 : 7). Thereby was renewed the sign of the covenant between God and Abraham (Gen. 17 : 9-14), and the whole people sanctified before the struggle for the conquest of Canaan. Just as Zipporah had circumcised her son with a flint (Ex. 4 : 25), so Joshua used flint knives, even though by this time — the end of the Bronze Age and beginning of the Iron Age — the use of metal instruments was widespread. It is characteristic of ritual implements that they continue to be used for sacred purposes even after they have become obsolete in daily life. The practice of circumcision with flint knives was known also in ancient Egypt (see Vol. I, p. 57).

In the upper picture — three flint knives from the Early Bronze Age which were found in Palestine.

The lower picture shows a detail from the tomb of an Egyptian official of the Twelfth Dynasty at Beni Hasan, depicting the manufacture of flint instruments. In the bottom register the craftsman on the left is lifting up an instrument that he has roughly fashioned on an anvil standing on the floor in front of him. The other craftsmen are holding flint knives in their left hand and retouching their blades with a chisel which seems to be made of bone.

A ND behold, a man stood before him with his drawn sword in his hand . . .

(Josh. 5 : 13)

Just before the attack on Jericho, the Captain of the Hosts of the Lord appeared to Joshua in the guise of a man of war. The divine messenger brought Israel the assurance that God would give them victory in their battles with the Canaanite kings (Josh. 5 : 14). The Captain's words, with their echo of God's words to Moses from the burning bush, are meant to indicate that Joshua, too, no less than Moses, was found worthy of a theophany (Ex. 3 : 5; Josh. 5 : 15). The conception of a god in the guise of a warrior (as in the appellation "the God of Hosts"), with a drawn sword in his hand, also occurs in Canaanite tradition.

The figurine reproduced here was discovered at Megiddo in a tomb from the Late Canaanite period (the time of Moses and Joshua). It is made of bronze and is about 5 in. high. The god, who is wearing a high crown, holds in his left hand a square shield of the kind which was characteristically Canaanite in the 14th, and to some extent also in the 13th cent. (see Vol I, p. 150). In his right hand there is a drawn sword (on the sword see below, p. 33).

N OW Jericho was shut up from within and from without because of the people of Israel; none went out, and none came in.

(Josh. 6 : 1)

The site of the ancient city of Jericho, beside the spring of Elisha (see p. 254), is now known as Tell es-Sultan (pictured here), about one mile north-west of modern Jericho. Because of its abundant supply of water and rich soil the surrounding area was, from the earliest times, a flourishing oasis which attracted settlers from the neighbouring arid regions. As it was close to the fords of the Jordan, its conquest would lay open the approaches of Canaan to the Israelite tribes who were bearing down upon it from beyond the river.

The inhabitants of the city were greatly alarmed by the approach of the Israelites and took precautions against spies from without (see p. 21) and enemies from within. They closed their gates and prepared for a siege (cf. Josh. 2:5,7). Presumably they relied upon the walls of their city to withstand Joshua's attacks; the Bible implies that at first they actually fought against the Israelites (Josh. 24:11). It is doubtful whether the nomadic Israelite tribes could have taken a well-fortified Canaanite city like Jericho by storm. Indeed, according to the biblical story, the walls of the city miraculously collapsed at the sound of the Israelite trumpets and the shouts of the Israelite host.

The horns (Heb. *shofar*, usually translated "trumpet") play an important part in the story of the fall of Jericho. The priests' blast on the horn gives the people the sign to shout: "As soon as the people heard the sound of the horn, the people raised a great shout, and the wall fell down flat" (Josh. 6 : 20). The purpose of both the horn-blast and the shouting (apart from the miraculous event connected with them in this particular instance) was to create as much noise as possible and thereby to spread confusion in the enemy's ranks. This practice was followed in other biblical battles, as for example, during the war of Gideon (Judg. 7 ; see p. 88).

A similar description of the use of rams' horns and trumpets as a psychological weapon is found in the Dead Sea Scroll of "The War of the Sons of Light Against the Sons of Darkness". In the seventh column of the Scroll there is a detailed description of the duties of the priests and Levites on the battle-field. In the eigth column (see the lower picture) the use of trumpets in battle is described as follows: "The priests shall blow on the six trumpets (Heb. *hazozeroth*) of assault a high-pitched intermittent note to direct the fighting, and the Levites and all the band of horn-blowers shall blow in unison a great battle fanfare to melt the heart of the enemy". Here it is the Levites who blow the horns and not the priests, as at Jericho. But here too, just as biblical times, the principal function of the horns is to demoralize the enemy.

The upper picture is a detail of a relief from the 9th or 8th cent. B.C. discovered a Carchemish, showing the blowing of a horn. The man who is standing and blowing the ram's horn is one of a troupe of musicians.

THE priests blowing the trumpets.

(Josh. 6 : 4)

ＡND they burned the city with fire, and all within it; only the silver and gold, and the vessels of bronze and of iron, they put into the treasury of the house of the LORD. (Josh. 6 : 24)

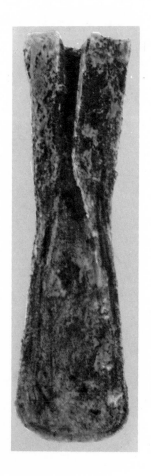

The metal objects from Jericho were dedicated to "the treasury of the house of the Lord" (Josh. 6 : 24) by Joshua's special order (Josh. 6 : 19). In the same way David dedicated to the Lord vessels of silver, gold and bronze from the booty taken in his wars, or from the gifts presented to him by his allies (compare 2 Sam. 8 : 10—11). Objects made of metal were the currency of the ancient Orient and were highly valued as such in the international exchange mart of the second and first millennia B.C. It was customary for the vanquished to present such objects as peace-offerings or tribute to their conquerors, as was done, for example, in the reigns of Rehoboam (1 Kings 14 : 26) and Hezekiah (2 Kings 18 : 15—16).

The upper picture shows articles of gold from Tell el-Ajjul (ancient Beth Eglayim), south of Gaza, belonging to the Middle Bronze Age (the patriarchal period). The other two pictures are of bronze objects from Megiddo: a Late Bronze adze (bottom left), and an Early Iron Age bowl (Period of the Judges and the early Monarchy).

"WHEN I saw among the spoil a beautiful mantle from Shinar . . . and a bar of gold weighing fifty shekels . . ."

(Josh. 7 : 21)

Achan, the son of Carmi, of the tribe of Judah, was put to death for defying the solemn ban (Heb. *herem*) by laying sacrilegious hands on the booty taken at Jericho (Josh. 6 : 24). The goods appropriated by Achan and hidden in his tent were a mantle from Shinar, twenty shekels of silver and a "bar of gold".

The lower picture shows a strip ("bar") of gold with embossed ornamentation, used as a headband. It was discovered at Tell el-Ajjul in a Middle Bronze Age tomb. "A mantle of Shinar" is, literally, a mantle made in the land of Shinar (Babylonia). This must have been a mantle of outstanding quality, if it was worth bringing to Jericho from such a distance.

The statue of a woman reproduced here provides an example of a Mesopotamian wool-mantle made in imitation of natural ram's fleece. It was found at Khafaja in the middle Tigris region and belongs to the second half of the third millennium B.C. There is, of course, no means of knowing whether the biblical mantle of Shinar was like the ancient Sumerian one illustrated here, or resembled rather Babylonian mantles of a kind that were in use in later periods.

A<small>LL</small> Israel returned to Ai, and smote it with the edge of the sword.

(Josh. 8 : 24)

The expression of smiting or killing "by the edge of the sword" is found mainly in those sections of the Bible that describe the wanderings in the wilderness and the conquest and occupation of Canaan. In those times the sword in common use throughout the Middle East was the "slashing sword" with its curved blade and single cutting edge. On account of its shape this sword has sometimes been mistakenly described as a "sickle-sword". In fact, it differs from the sickle in the position of its single cutting edge, which is on the convex side of the sword and not on the concave side as is the case in the sickle. Originating in Sumer in the patriarchal period, the curved sword spread thence to the Fertile Crescent (see Vol. I, p. 76). In the Late Bronze Age (approximately the time of the Exodus) it was commonly used in Canaan and Egypt alike. In Egypt it was called *hepes*, because of its resemblance to the foreleg of an ox. The "sickle-sword" was, of course, not used for thrusting: it was a slashing weapon, as is clearly shown by the Egyptian relief reproduced here in which Ramses III is shown smiting his Canaanite enemies "with the edge of the sword" (cf. p. 41). The relief is roughly of the same period as the conquest of Canaan.

SO Joshua burned Ai, and made it for ever a heap of ruins, as it is to this day.

(Josh. 8 : 28)

The next city to fall to the Israelites, after Jericho, was Ai, to the east of Bethel (Gen. 12:8; Josh. 7:2). This city, too, was totally destroyed; but, in contrast to Jericho, the Israelites were explicitly commanded by the Lord to despoil it first (Josh. 8:27). The site of Ai still remains uncertain. According to the biblical text, Ai was burnt down and turned into a heap of ruins; in other words, it was never rebuilt as a large, fortified city. "An everlasting heap" of this kind has been excavated among the ruins of an ancient city close to Bethel (see the accompanying picture). The place is called by the Arabs et-Tell, meaning "the mound", a name reminiscent of Ai, which means in Hebrew "heap of ruins". However, the excavations carried out at et-Tell show that this ancient city was destroyed about a thousand years before Joshua. If we continue to identify it with Ai in spite of the archaeological evidence, we shall be obliged to assume that the tradition of a much earlier destruction has found its way into the story about Joshua's conquests. Some scholars hold that the biblical story really refers to the taking of nearby Bethel which is not properly described in the Book of Joshua (Josh. 8:17).

N OW their cities were Gibeon, Chephirah, Beeroth, and Kiryath-Yearim.
(Josh. 9 : 17)

Unlike the Amorite kings who formed a military
alliance against the Israelites (Josh. 9 : 1), the Gibeonites made a covenant with Joshua and "the
leaders of the congregation" (Josh. 9 : 15, 19). The
Bible relates in detail how the Gibeonites had
recourse to trickery in order to save themselves.
The Gibeonites referred to here are presumably
the confederation of Hivite cities, with their centre
at Gibeon (see p. 37); they were situated in the
hill-country to the west of the watershed. Gibeon
is the modern el-Jib, north-west of Jerusalem (see
p. 37). Chephirah has been identified with Tell
Kefira (shown in the picture), north of Kiryath
Anavim; Kiryath-Yearim with Deir el-Azhar near
to Abu-Ghosh. The identification of Beeroth is
disputed: some scholars locate it at the modern
village el-Bira near Ramalla, while others sug-
gest Nebi Samwil, north of Jerusalem (see the
accompanying map). The Gibeonites differed from
the Canaanites not only ethnically, but also politi-
cally and socially: their rulers were not to be
called kings, but elders (Josh. 9 : 11). It may well
have been their conflicts with the Canaanites that
induced the Gibeonites to come to terms with the
Israelites (cf. p. 37).

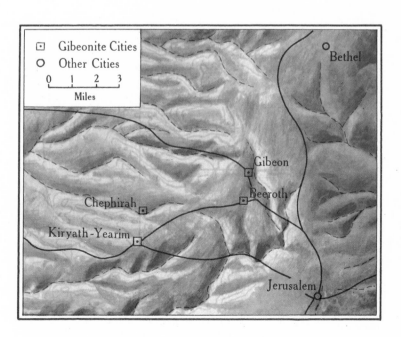

Bᴜᴛ Joshua made them that day hewers of wood and drawers of water for the congregation and for the altar of the Lᴏʀᴅ . . .

(Josh. 9 : 27)

"Hewers of wood and drawers of water" were the most menial of all the Temple ministrants (Josh. 9 : 23). They were recruited from the various Gentile groups subjugated by the Israelites: the Gibeonites also belonged to this category. They may at first have ministered at the great High Place in Gibeon (cf. 1 Kings 3 : 4). In the reign of Saul they were almost exterminated (2 Sam. 21 : 1—5). The remnant which survived must have been placed by Solomon among the slaves of the Temple at Jerusalem and have lost their national identity there. Their descendants returned to Jerusalem from the Babylonian Exile with Zerubbabel (Ezra 2 : 55; Neh. 7 : 57). The picture above shows a wooden model of a bakery from the Middle Kingdom of Egypt. On the left is a "water-drawer" bringing water in two buckets suspended from a yoke, while the one next to him is carrying a jar on his head.

Below is a reproduction of a potsherd from Megiddo (Middle Bronze Age) portraying water-drawers carrying water by means of buckets and a yoke.

BECAUSE Gibeon was a great city, like one of
the royal cities . . .   (Josh. 10 : 2)

The site of ancient Gibeon is an ancient mound within the confines of the modern village of el-Jib (shown above),
about six miles north-west of Jerusalem. The city was thus situated close to the routes from the hill country to
the coastal plain, the chief of which ran from Jerusalem to the coast via Beth-Horon. On account of its geographical position and its strategic advantages, Gibeon was many times in its history a military encampment and
fiercely fought over. Hence the surrender of the Gibeonites to Joshua stirred the Kings of the South, led by the
King of Jerusalem, into making a combined attack upon Gibeon. For, indeed, with the surrender of Gibeon,
the way to the Valley of Aiyalon and the cities of southern Canaan lay open to the Israelites (Josh. 10:28—35).
It is worth remarking that the Pharaoh Shishak also passed through Gibeon on his campaign against Judah and
Israel. In the neighbourhood of Gibeon there are abundant wells. The Bible especially mentions the pool of
Gibeon (see 2 Sam. 2:13) and also "the great pool which is in Gibeon" (Jer. 41:12). The city later became part
of the territory of Benjamin (Josh. 18:25; 21:17) and was included amongst the Levitical cities. It enjoyed special
reverence on account of the "Great High Place" which was still there in Solomon's time (1 Kings 3:4). According
to the Book of Chronicles the Tent of Meeting had once rested there (1 Chron. 16:39; 2 Chron. 1:3).
The excavations carried out at el-Jib have brought to light archaeological relics from the Middle and Late Bronze
Ages (just before the Israelite conquest) and especially from the Israelite period. The name "Gibeon" has been
found stamped on jar-handles from the time of the Israelite Kings. Other discoveries include a tunnel (see p. 164)
of the Late Canaanite period (the eve of the Israelite conquest), by which the ancient inhabitants could make
their way down to the well to draw water without going outside the city walls.

" SUN, stand thou still at Gibeon, and thou Moon
in the valley of Aiyalon".

(Josh. 10 : 12)

Hastening to the aid of Gibeon by a secret night march from his main base at Gilgal (Josh. 10:9), Joshua suddenly
fell upon the five Amorite kings who were besieging the city and sent them fleeing down the main route from
the hill-country to the coast: Gibeon—Beth-Horon—Aiyalon. The Amorite kings retreated down "the ascent
of Beth-Horon", i.e. the narrow track from Upper Beth-Horon to Lower Beth-Horon, and on this rocky and
perilous slope their retreat became a rout. The Bible quotes part of an ancient song from the Book of Yashar
extolling the victory won for Israel by Joshua's prayer on the day of the battle. The day was supernaturally
lengthened in order to give the Israelites time to complete their destruction of the enemy: "And the sun stood
still, and the moon stayed, until the nation took vengeance on their enemies" (ibid. 13). According to the biblical
story, the miracle occured when Joshua was pursuing the enemy "by the way of the ascent of Beth-Horon"
and indeed from this point, at dawn, the sun can be seen rising in the east above Gibeon while the moon
is setting to the west in the direction of the Valley of Aiyalon.
The photograph shows the Valley of Aiyalon from the west. This valley, which is referred to in the el-Amarna Letters as "the field of Yaluna", was so called after the city of Aiyalon in the territory of Dan. The name is
still preserved in the modern Arab village of Yalu nearby.

AND the LORD gave Lachish into the hand of Israel, and he took it on the second day, and smote it with the edge of the sword, and every person in it . . .   (Josh. 10 : 32)

Joshua did not advance into the coastal plain from Beth-Horon beyond Aiyalon, but continued in pursuit southwards toward Azekah, Makkedah, Libnah and Lachish. Founded in the Early Bronze Age (third millennium B.C.), Lachish was a flourishing fortified city in the Late Bronze Age, on the eve of the Israelite conquest.

The remains of the Canaanite city excavated at Lachish (Tell ed-Duweir) provide clear evidence of its destruction. The Canaanite temple at the foot of the mound (see the picture on the right) and the Canaanite settlement on the mound itself were found covered by a layer of ashes. An indication of the date of the sacking of Lachish by the Israelites (c. 1220 B.C.) is provided by an Egyptian inscription on a pottery bowl found in the last Canaanite stratum. On it amounts of wheat were registered, apparently by a tax-collector, together with the data — "the fourth year" (see the picture on the left) almost certainly the fourth year of the Pharaoh Merneptah (1224—1214 B.C.).

AND they came out, with all their troops, a great host, in number like the sand that is upon the seashore, with very many horses and chariots. And all these kings joined their forces, and came and encamped together at the waters of Merom, to fight with Israel. (Josh. 11 : 4-5)

At the battle of the Waters of Merom, Joshua, by a lightning assault, routed the Canaanite kings of Galilee who had taken up arms against him at the summons of Jabin, king of Hazor. Some scholars identify the Waters of Merom with the spring next to the village of Meron; others find the site of the settlement of Merom in Tell el-Khirba near Jebel Marun, close to which there rises a plateau suitable for chariot warfare. This city would appear to be mentioned also in Egyptian lists from the reigns of Thutmose III and Ramses II. In a relief, discovered in the temple of Ramses II, it is depicted as surrounded by a double wall (see illustration on p. 40 above).

In this battle the Israelite tribes met a well-organized army which was equipped with chariots. The Canaanite chariots, which had already reached a very high stage of development by the second third of the second millennium B.C., were the most formidable weapon that the Israelites had to face. The Canaanite chariot was brought to Egypt by the Hyksos tribes, was adopted by the Egyptians and finally became the pride of the Egyptian army. In its typically Canaanite form it was a very light vehicle, almost entirely unarmoured, with four-spoked wheels. The Egyptian army, however, developed the chariot by adding armour — and thus weight — and strengthening the wheels which now had six spokes. By the time of Joshua the Canaanite chariot had already been influenced, in its turn, by the Egyptian. This is shown by the ivory reliefs from Megiddo which contain many representations of such chariots (see the reproduction below, and p. 80). In these ivory carvings from the 13th or the beginning of the 12th cent. B.C. we find Canaanite chariots with six-spoked wheels. Every chariot is drawn by two horses. To one side of the chariot is fastened the quiver of arrows and the bow-case of the bowman, the fighting partner of the charioteer who holds the reins (the bow cannot be seen in the picture). The chariots are escorted by foot-soldiers armed with weapons characteristic of the Canaanites of this period: the round shield (which replaces the square one) and the "sickle-sword" (see p. 33).

ND Joshua turned back at that time, and took
Hazor, and smote its king with the sword; for
Hazor formerly was the head of all those kingdoms.

(Josh. 11 : 10)

The commanding position of Hazor at the junction of several international trade routes gave it great strategic importance and made it the most powerful of the Canaanite cities of the north. Hence the biblical description of it as "the head of all those kingdoms". From cuneiform documents it is clear that, as early as the first third of the second millennium B.C., Hazor had become a famous commercial centre and that its renown had spread as far as Mari in Mesopotamia. Egyptian records and the el-Amarna Letters indicate that in the second half of the second millennium B.C. Hazor was the centre of an important kingdom which had extended its sway as far as the region of Ashtaroth in Bashan. In the time of the Israelite Kingdom it was once more an important fortified centre (1 Kings 9:15) and remained as such until the destruction of the cities of Galilee by Tiglath-Pileser III (see pp. 280—281).

The tell of Hazor, Tell el-Qadah, (see the illustration), is one of the largest and most imposing in the Middle East. The citadel rises 120 feet above its surroundings and covers 25 acres. At its foot lay the lower town which covered an area 3000 feet long by 2100 feet wide. This city was protected by a wall and earth-rampart built in the first half of the second millennium B.C. The excavations on the site have shown that the lower city flourished in the Canaanite period only, while the Israelite settlement was confined to the tell itself. The defeat of Jabin, king of Hazor, sealed the fate of the Canaanites in the north of the country.

So Joshua took all that land, the hill country and all the Negeb and all the land of Goshen and the lowland and the Arabah and the hill country of Israel and its lowland.

(Josh. 11 : 16)

In the Bible, Joshua is portrayed as an outstanding military leader who inflicted a series of crushing defeats on the Canaanites by the skilful use of such tactics as feint retreats to draw them out into the open field, ambushes, surprise attacks and night operations. These stratagems were well suited to the military capacities of nomad tribesmen in their engagements with an organized and well-equipped army operating from strongly fortified cities. Chapters 2—11 of the Book of Joshua list the victorious campaigns of the Israelites from the south to the north of Canaan. From his base at Gilgal Joshua advanced into the country around Bethel. His main engagements were fought in the hill country: the battle at Ai and down the road Gibeon — Beth-Horon—Aiyalon and then southwards through the foothills to Lachish and Debir; and the battle at the Waters of Merom in Galilee. Of all the protracted wars against the Canaanites, the Book of Joshua gives a detailed description only of the decisive battles in the mountains of Judah, of Ephraim and of Galilee (see map). "Joshua made war a long time with all those kings ... They took all in battle" (Josh. 11 : 18—19). At the end of the fighting the following districts had fallen to the Israelites: 1) the hill-country (Heb. *Har*), i.e. the mountain-of Judah; 2) the Negeb, i.e. the southern desert of Judah; 3) the land of Goshen, i.e. the region south of Hebron, so named from the city of Goshen (see Josh. 10:41; 15 : 51); 4) the lowland (Heb. *Shephelah*), i.e. the lower slopes of the Judean mountains along the edge of the coastal plain; 5) the *Arabah,* i.e. the Jordan Valley; and 6) "the hill-country of Israel" (Heb. *Har Yisrael*), a collective term for the mountains of Ephraim and Galilee. From other passages in the Bible it is clear that many Canaanite cities, among them some of the most important ones, both in the hill-country and in the plain, were not taken by the Israelites (see pp. 46—47).

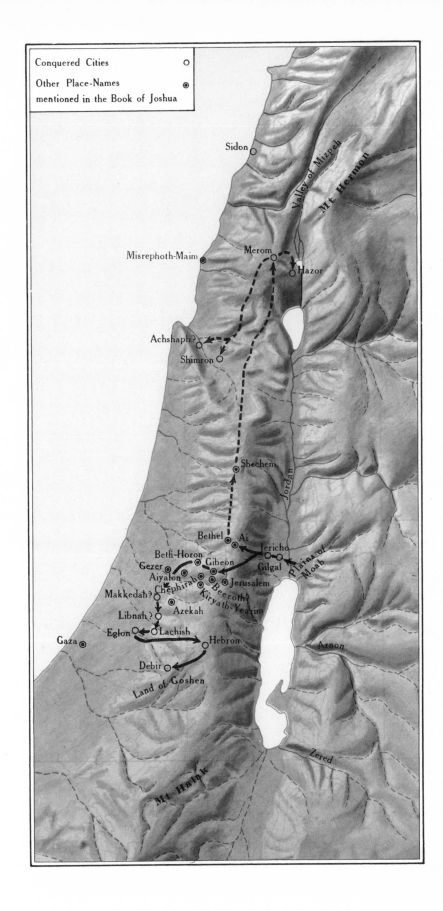

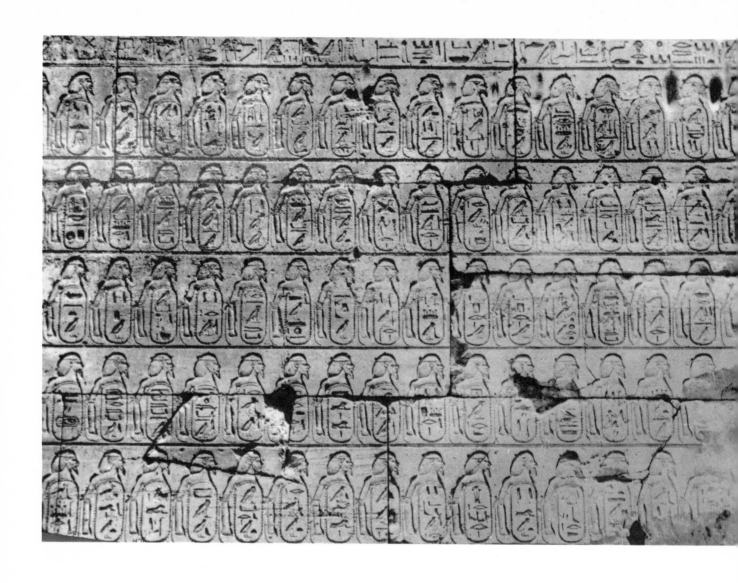

AND these are the kings of the land whom Joshua and the people of Israel defeated on the west side of the Jordan . . .

(Josh. 12 : 7)

To the west of the Jordan thirty-one kings, whose names are listed in Joshua, chapter 12, were conquered by Joshua. Twelve of them are not mentioned in the earlier chapters, namely the kings of Hormah, Arad, Adullam, Geder, Tirzah, Tappuah, Hepher, Aphek, Lasharon (Aphek of the Sharon?), Kedesh, Taanach and Megiddo. This list apparently sums up the results of various campaigns against the Canaanites, some of which were fought out after Joshua's time. The list itself shows that Canaan was divided into small city-kingdoms which fought the Israelites one by one and allied themselves together only on rare occasions. The list begins with the cities of the south in the order of their conquest (vv. 9—12) and continues with a group of cities in Galilee (vv. 19—20). This list bears some resemblance to the ancient Egyptian custom of incising on the walls of their temples the names of conquered cities. Our picture shows one of the walls of the temple of Amon at Karnak on which are inscribed the places taken by Thutmose III in Palestine and Syria in the 15th cent. B.C. The name of each city is engraved in hieroglyphics in an oval frame topped by the head of a Canaanite captive representing its king.

THE king of Megiddo, one.   (Josh. 12 : 21)

Among the Canaanite kings defeated by the Israelites (see p. 44) was the King of Megiddo, whose city is mentioned in the list together with Taanach, Yokneam in Carmel and Dor in Naphath-Dor (Josh. 12 : 21—23). From both archaeological evidence and non-biblical sources it is clear that Megiddo was one of the most important cities in Canaan, occupying a key position on the "Sea Road" that connected Egypt with Syria and Mesopotamia (see p. 296). Megiddo was founded in the Chalcolithic period, in the fourth millennium B.C. Its king is frequently mentioned in Egyptian records of the second millennium B.C. as an Egyptian vassal. In the 15th cent. B.C., Thutmose III, in the course of his punitive expedition against the revolted kings of Canaan, besieged Megiddo and captured it. After the Israelite conquest Megiddo was allocated to the territory of Manasseh; but the members of this tribe were unable to reduce it (Josh. 17 : 11; Judg. 1 : 27). Apparently it was not conquered till the reign of David.

The excavations at Megiddo have brought to light a collection of ivories from the end of the Late Canaanite period (the time of Joshua). These ivories are incised with scenes depicting, among others, the life at the court of a Canaanite king (cf. pp. 41, 80, 210). The illustration here shows one such ivory, depicting a scene of court life, apparently an inlay from a piece of wooden furniture. On the right the king is seen returning from battle riding in his chariot to which two captives are tied: he is preceded by an armed soldier and followed by his armour-bearer. On the left he is seen sitting on his cherubim-flanked throne; he is raising a drinking cup in his right hand and holds a lotus-flower in his left. A woman in gorgeous Syrian raiment (apparently the queen) is waiting upon him, while another woman plays on the lyre. Behind the king stand two of his attendants, beside a jar and offerings.

Unconquered Territory

Tribal Boundaries

0   5   10   15   20
        Miles

Sidon

Iyon

Tyre

Kanah

Dan

Kedesh

N A P H T A L I

D A N

M A A C H A H

Abdon

Hazor

G E S H U R

Accho

Ramah

A S H E R

Chinnereth

Aphek

Golan?

Ashtaroth

Cabul

Aphek

Hannathon

Achshaph

Yabneel

Z E B U L U N

Shimron

Tabor

Dor

Carmel

Yokneam

Chesulloth

Tabor

Anaharath

I S S A C H A R

Yarmuth

Edrei

Megiddo

Jezreel

Lo-Debar

M A N A S S E H

Aron

Beth-Shan

Ham

Ibleam

Ramoth-Gilead

Hepher?

Bezek

Yabesh-Gilead

Socoh

M A N A S S E H

Zaphon

Shechem

Succoth

Mahanaim

Tappuah

Penuel

A M M O N

Aphek

Shiloh

G A D

Gath-Rimmon

Adam

Yogbehah

Jaffa

Yehud

E P H R A I M

Rabbath-Ammon

Lod

Bethel

Beth-Nimrah

Beth-Horon

D A N

Gibeon

Ramah

Gezer

B E N J A M I N

Jericho

Heshbon

Ekron

Kiryath-Yearim

Jerusalem

Beth-Yeshimoth

Ashdod

Beth-Shemesh

Medeba

Azekah

Bethlehem

Ashkelon

J U D A H

R E U B E N

Lachish

Hebron

Dibon

Gaza

Gath?

En-Gedi

Aroer

Debir

Carmel

Gerar

Eshtemoa

Ziklag?

M O A B

Sharuhen

Arad

S I M E O N

Beersheba

Hormah?

Aroer

Kir of Moab

Zoar

Tamar

E D O M

Sela

Bozrah

Kadesh-Barnea

Punon

Hazar Addar

AND these are the inheritances which the people of Israel received in the land of Canaan... Their inheritance was by lot...   (Josh. 14 : 1-2)

Joshua was not only a victorious general: he is also portrayed as a political leader and spiritual guide of the Israelite tribes during their settlement in Canaan. He it was who allocated the land to the west of the Jordan among the nine and a half remaining tribes, after two and a half of the twelve tribes had already received from Moses their portions on the eastern side of the river (see the map and the following pages). Like Moses Joshua did not live to complete his mission: "and there remains yet very much land to be possessed" (Josh. 13 : 1). Although the whole country was apportioned by lot among the different tribes, as is clear from various biblical passages, most of them managed to establish themselves in only a part of their territories (Josh. 17 : 18; Judg. 1 : 27 ff.). The complete occupation of the areas still held by the Canaanites took a long time, and in some places was never accomplished at all.

In this chapter the Bible gives a concise and clear description of the extent of "the land that yet remains", i.e. those parts of Canaan which withstood the pressure of the land-hungry tribes. They comprised the country of the Philistines with its five principal cities; the whole of "the land of the Canaanites", i.e. the coastal plain from Gezer in the south to the valley of Accho in the north; and the Valley of Jezreel. Also listed here are the northern districts of Canaan, most of which were outside the limits of the Israelite occupation: the Phoenician coastal cities; the land of the Amorites, which stretched from the Lebanon range to Gebal on the Phoenician coast; and the eastern end of the Lebanon and the Lebanon plain "from Baal-Gad below Mount Hermon to the entrance of Hamath *(Lebo-Hamath)*" (Josh. 13 : 1—5).

AND Moses gave an inheritance to the tribe of the Reubenites according to their families . . .
Heshbon, and all its cities that are in the tableland; Dibon, and Bamoth-Baal, and Beth-
Baal-Meon.
(Josh. 13 : 15, 17)

The territory allotted to the tribe of Reuben stretched from Aroer on the banks of the Arnon river to the tableland
of Medeba. The precise borders are not recorded, presumably because they were constantly changing, since the
Reubenites were nomadic cattle-rearers (see 1 Chron. 5 : 8—10). Among the principal centres in the tribe's
territory are Heshbon (cf. Vol. I, p. 224) and Dibon. The latter was situated on a plateau to the north of the
river Arnon, beside the "King's Highway" from Kir-Moab (Kerak) to Rabbath-Ammon. The excavations
near the modern village of Diban (see the illustration) have shown that the site was first occupied in the Early
Bronze Age (third millennium B.C.). At the beginning of the Iron Age it was resettled by the Moabites (Nu.
21 : 30), from whom it was reconquered by the Amorites and who lost it to the tribes of Gad and Reuben.
According to Nu. 32 : 34 "the sons of Gad built Dibon", and for this reason it was also known as Dibon-Gad
(Nu. 33 : 45), while in Josh. 13 : 17 Dibon is included amongst the cities of Reuben. This shows that between
the Conquest and the occupation of the conquered territory changes occured in the tribal boundaries. Still later
Dibon again became Moabite; King Mesha was born here and, on his stele found there, he styles himself "the
Dibonite" (see p. 256).

ND half Gilead, and Ashtaroth, and Edrei, the cities of the kingdom of Og in Bashan; these were allotted to the people of Machir the son of Manasseh . . . (Josh. 13 : 31)

The Kingdom of Og of Bashan, with its cities "fortified with high walls, gates and bars" (Deut. 3 : 5), was allotted to half of the tribe of Manasseh. This territory comprised Bashan and half of Gilead, in which were situated the important cities of Ashtaroth and Edrei (see Vol. I, p. 249). Ashtaroth (Tell Ashtara), so called in honour of the goddess Ashtoreth (Astarte), stood on the "King's Highway" that ran the whole length of the Trans-Jordan plateau. It is mentioned in the Egyptian execration-texts of the 19th cent. B.C., and then in the list of Canaanite cities captured by Thutmose III and in the Amarna Letters. Shortly before the Israelite conquest, Ashtaroth was the chief city in the Amorite Kingdom of Og (Josh. 12 : 4). It became one of the Levitical cities (Josh. 21 : 27; 1 Chrqn. 6 : 71) and was the birthplace of David's great warrior, Uzziah the Ashterathite (1 Chron. 11 : 14). In the 9th and 8th cent. B.C. it was an important strong-point in Bashan and a bone of contention between the Kingdom of Israel and the Aramaean Kingdom of Damascus: only in the reign of Jeroboam II was it set free from Aramaean pressure. In the year 733/2 B.C. Ashtaroth was taken by Tiglath-Pileser III and its capture is commemorated on a relief which was found in the city of Calah on the Tigris.

Reproduced here is a section of this relief showing the city of Ashtaroth standing on an eminence and surrounded by a double wall, as befits a fortified frontier city. The inner wall has high towers crowned by battlements.

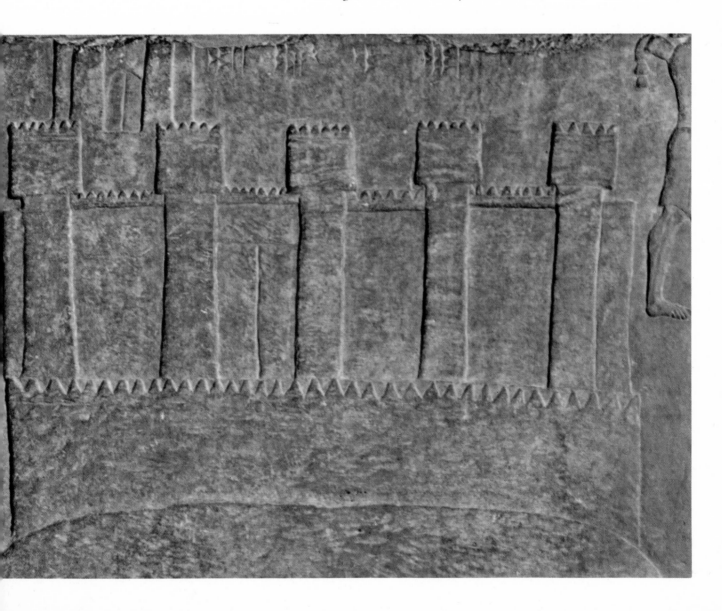

THE lot for the tribe of the people of Judah according to their families . . . And the east boundary is the Salt Sea, to the mouth of the Jordan.

(Josh. 15 : 1, 5)

The description of the territory of Judah is the most detailed of all those given in the Book of Joshua, as befits the special place held by this tribe in Israelite history. The frontier lines are described from south-east to north west. The points of reference chosen are either frontier cities or geographical landmarks, such as the top, shoulder or slope of a mountain; a valley, a spring or a river. The description begins with the southern border; this border line, however, cannot be reconstructed with any certainty. Most probably, it ran south-westwards from the Dead Sea, then, turning west, crossed the Negeb and, circling to the south of Kadesh-Barnea (Ein Qudeirat), ran along the "Brook of Egypt" (Wadi el-Arish) to the Mediterranean. The Dead Sea provided a natural border for the tribe of Judah, as it did later for the Kingdom of Judah. At the point where the Jordan flows into the Dead Sea the frontiers of three tribal portions met: that of Reuben on the Trans-Jordanian side, that of Judah to the south-west and that of Benjamin to the northwest.

The illustration is an aerial view of the mouth of the Jordan where it flows into the Dead Sea, seen from the north.

THEN the boundary
extends from the top of
the mountain to the
spring of the Waters of
Nephtoah . . .

(Josh. 15 : 9)

The northern border of the territory of Judah is described from east to west (see the map). It ran from Beth-Hoglah (Deir Hajla) by way of the ascent of Adummim and skirted Jerusalem to the south (Jerusalem belonged to the portion of Benjamin — see p. 57). On reaching the watershed, the border turned north-westwards to the Waters of Nephtoah (Lifta) and then westwards. Near to Kiryath-Yearim the borders of Judah, Benjamin and Dan met. The territory of Judah had a common border with that of Dan north of Chesalon and along the Sorek Valley (Wadi Sarar and Wadi Rubin). Here the border passed close by Beth-Shemesh, Timnah (Tell el-Batashi), Ekron (Tell el-Muqanna) and Yabneel (Yavneh) until it reached the Mediterranean. In theory, the territory of Judah comprised all the coastal plain from the Sorek in the north to the "Brook of Egypt" in the south; but in actual fact most of this area was never conquered. It would appear that the tribe of Judah advanced to the out-skirts of Gaza, Ashkelon and Ashdod (Josh. 15 : 45—47; Judg. 1 : 18), but was not able to overcome these strongly fortified cities.

The view above shows the modern village of Nephtoah (Lifta) and the valley below it containing the spring of the Waters (*Me*) of Nephtoah. Some scholars maintain that the spring was named in honour of the Pharaoh Me(r)neptah who campaigned in Canaan at the end of the 13th cent. B.C., as there is Egyptian evidence for the naming of wells in the hill-country in his honour.

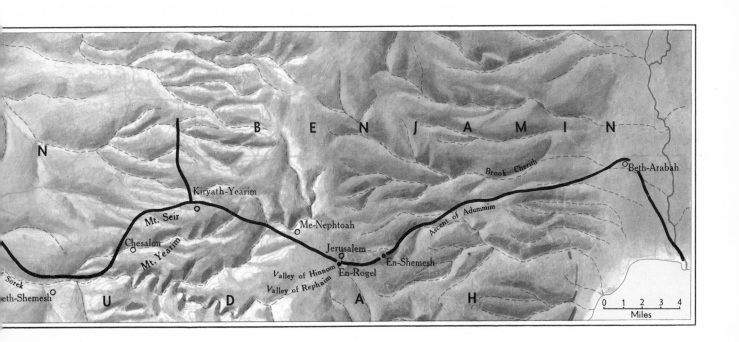

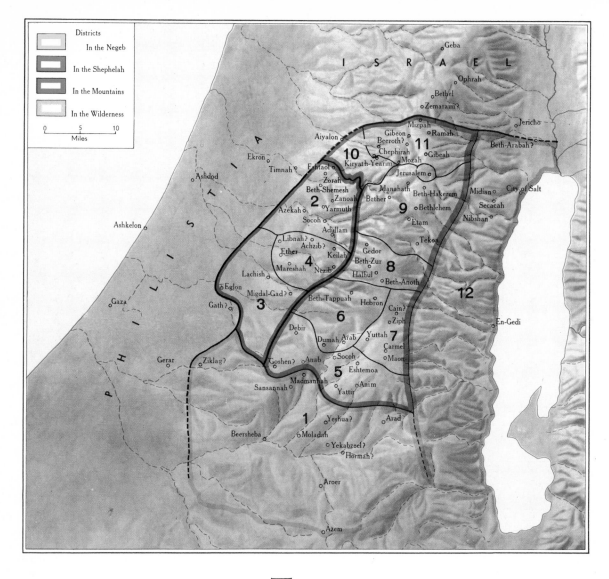

THIS is the inheritance of the tribe of the people of Judah
according to their families.   (Josh. 15 : 20)

The description of the borders of Judah is followed by a detailed list of its cities, arranged topographically and
according to administrative districts. The list is divided into four geographical groups, each under a different
regional heading: the *Negeb* (south) (Josh. 15 : 21); the *Shephelah* (lowland), i.e. the lower slopes between the
hill-country and the coastal plain (v. 33); the *Har* (Mountain), i.e. the hill-country of Judah (v. 48); and the
Midbar (Wilderness), i.e. the Judaean desert (v. 61). Within this geographical framework there are signs of a
further sub-division into twelve administrative districts. It is generally assumed that this list presupposes the later
administrative division of the country under the Kingdom of Judah, which also included a district from the
territory of Benjamin.
The map illustrates this division of the territory of Judah into twelve districts.
The Negeb
1) The district of Beersheba — Arad (Eder) (Josh. 15 : 21—32).
The Shephelah
2) The district of Zorah — Azekah (vv. 33—36).   3) The district of Lachish — Eglon (vv. 37—41)
4) The district of Lebonah — Mareshah (vv. 42—44).
The Mountain
5) The district of Debir — Goshen (vv. 48—51).   6) The district of Hebron (vv. 52—54)
7) The district of Maon — Ziph (vv. 55—57) 8) The district of Halhul — Beth-Zur (vv. 58—59). 9) The district
of Bethlehem (according to the Septuagint translation).   10) The district of Kiryath-Yearim — Rabbah (v. 60)
11) The district of Gibeon — Mizpah (Josh. 18 : 25—28)
The Wilderness
12) The district of Beth-Arabah — En-Gedi (Josh. 15 : 61—62).

THEN the boundary went down to the brook Kanah. The cities here, to the south of the brook, among the cities of Manasseh, belonged to Ephraim. Then the boundary of Manasseh goes on the north side of the brook . . . (Josh. 17 : 9)

The territories of Ephraim and Manasseh were the two parts of the single portion allotted to the house of Joseph (Josh. 16). Their limits are not described in the same detail as those of Judah. The southern border of Ephraim—and of the whole house of Joseph — was in part identical with the northern border of Benjamin (Josh. 16 : 1—4; 18 : 12—14) The western border is not mentioned, but the territory occupied by Ephraim certainly did not stretch as far as the Mediterranean. The northern border of Manasseh (and of the Joseph tribes as a whole) is also not fully delineated, apparently because of fluctuations in the tribal territory. On the other hand, the southern border of Manasseh, which is also the northern border of Ephraim, is given in great detail. It ran from Michmetath, opposite Shechem, to the country of Tappuah (the region around Yasuf, south of Shechem) and thence to the Brook Kanah "and ended at the sea" (Josh. 16 : 8; 17 : 7—10).

The Brook Kanah (Arabic Wadi Qana, see the illustration) rises to the west of Mount Gerizim, twisting and turning through the hills and runs out to the plain near Jaljuliya. After a course of about 21 miles it flows into the River Yarkon. Its channel to the west of the watershed forms a natural dividing-line in the hill-country; it served to demarcate the tribal territories. (See also the map of the tribes, pp. 46—47).

THEN Joshua said to the house of Joseph, to Ephraim and Manasseh "... but the hill country shall be yours, for though it is a forest, you shall clear it and possess it to its farthest borders ..."   (Josh. 17 : 17-18)

The territory allotted to the Joseph tribes — Ephraim and half Manasseh — was in the centre of Canaan. The description in the Book of Joshua of their portion faithfully reflects the reality of the period, as can be seen from the emphasis laid on the fact that the cities in the valleys remained Canaanite (see Josh. 17 : 11—12 ; Judg. 1 : 27—28). The Joseph tribes were therefore compelled to confine their occupation to the hill-country that was subsequently called the Mountain of Ephraim. These hills, being thickly wooded, required clearing to make them fit for agriculture. That is why, when the Joseph tribes complain of being cramped in their portion, Joshua exhorts them to "Go up to the forest, and there clear ground for yourselves in the land of the Perizzites and the Rephaim" (Josh. 17 : 15). To-day the natural conditions of the hill-country are very different from what they were in Joshua's time. The forests have all been cut down and the rains have washed away the rich top-soil, leaving only bare rock on the summits and slopes of the hills (as seen in the accompanying aerial view of the Mountains of Ephraim).

The clearance of forests to make way for agriculture was customary in other parts of the ancient Orient. Below is a reproduction of an Egyptian painting from the second half of the 15th cent. B.C., which was found in the tomb of Nakht at Thebes. It depicts agricultural work being carried out in an unpopulated region, starting with the felling of trees and ending with hoeing and sowing (see also Vol. I, p. 100).

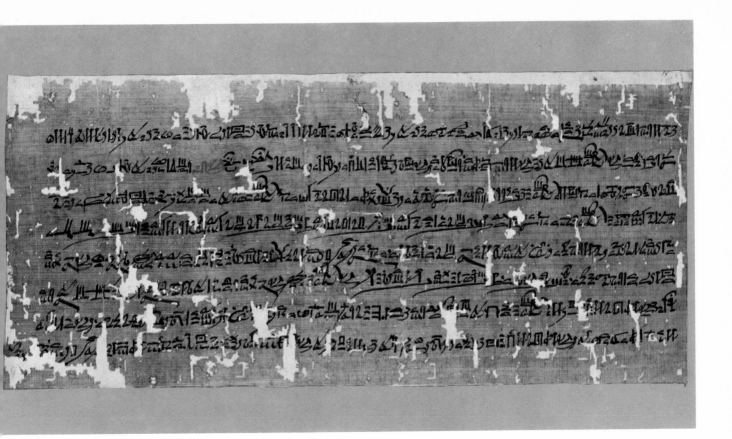

"AND you shall describe the land . . ."
(Josh. 18 : 6)

After the tribes east of the Jordan and Judah and Joseph to the west of it had been allotted their territories, there remained seven tribes "whose inheritance had not been apportioned" (Josh. 18 : 2). The Bible relates that Joshua sent three men from each tribe to survey the Land and divide it into seven portions. Writing a description of the land means the collection of information about its geography and population. Only when these men had completed their task did Joshua cast lots before the Lord at Shiloh and divide up the Land among the people of Israel (Josh. 18 : 10). Such collecting of information about foreign lands was a common practice in the ancient Orient. An instructive example relating to Canaan at the time of the Israelite occupation has been preserved in an Egyptian source from the 13th cent. B.C. The Papyrus Anastasi I contains a satirical letter from an Egyptian scribe to his rival. The writer ridicules his rival for his ignorance and tests him with questions about the geography of Canaan. In the course of this test he gives us a humorous description of the natural features of Canaan with its hills and streams, its animal and plant life, and its cities and their inhabitants. There can be no doubt that the writer of this letter had travel led widely in Canaan and had observed with his own eyes its scenery and the way of life of its population. (A section of the papyrus is reproduced above).

T HE lot of the tribe of Benjamin according to its families came up, and the territory allotted to it fell between the tribe of Judah and the tribe of Joseph.   (Josh. 18 : 11)

The tribe of Benjamin was traditionally associated with the other Rachel tribes, Ephraim and Manasseh; their ethnic kinship and the contiguity of their territories made of them a single tribal bloc. Some scholars maintain that the actual name of the tribe — Benjamin (meaning in Hebrew "son of the South") — refers to the position of its territory to the south of the Joseph tribes. According to the biblical text, Benjamin received its portion after Judah and Joseph had already occupied theirs. This sequence reflects the intermediate position of Benjamin between the other two tribes. The Benjaminites occupied a narrow strip of land running from east to west, from the Jordan to a line drawn from Kiryath-Yearim to Beth-Horon, and separating Judah to the south from Ephraim to the north (see the map). On the west, the territory of Benjamin had a short stretch of common border with the territory of Dan. The widest part of this territory was the centre, along the line of the watershed from Jerusalem to Bethel; an ancient highway ran there, now followed by the modern Hebron-Jerusalem-Nablus road. Along this road lay the most densely populated area, due to the economic advantages afforded by a stable agriculture and commercial exchange. The Book of Joshua lists the cities of Benjamin in two groups: first, those in the north (some of which were even outside the portion of the tribe) and in the east, including the cities of the Jordan Plain (Josh. 18 : 21—24); and, secondly, those in the west, including the four Hivite cities (Josh. 18 : 25—28). This list presumably contains only the most important cities of the territory.

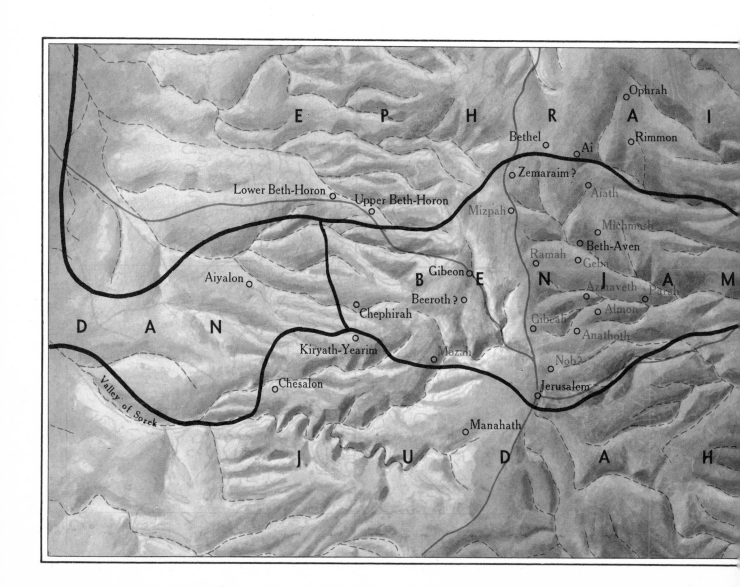

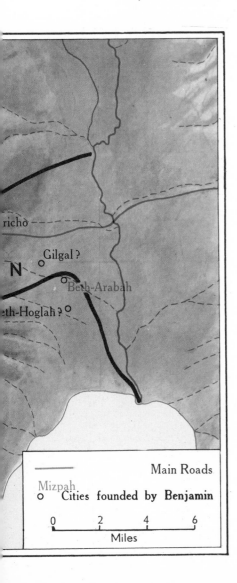

Main Roads

o Cities founded by Benjamin

```
0        2        4        6
            Miles
```

THEN the boundary goes down to the border of the mountain that overlooks the valley of the Son of Hinnom . . . and it then goes down the valley of Hinnom, south of the shoulder of the Jebusites . . .

(Josh. 18 : 16)

The southern border of Benjamin ran eastwards from Kiryath-Yearim to the Waters of Nephtoah and thence along the valley of the Son of Hinnom. From there the border ran below the southern end of the eastern hill of ancient Jerusalem to "south of the shoulder of the Jebusites", ("shoulder" signifying the side of a hill); hence the border passed through the side of a mountain south of the Jebusite city. Jerusalem itself was accordingly included in the territory of Benjamin, as may also be implied from the Blessing of Moses (Deut. 33 : 12).

In the view above, taken in the valley of the son of Hinnom in Jerusalem, looking south-east, the slope of the western hill, to-day called Mount Zion, is seen on the left, with the "shoulder" of the hill opposite it on the right.

THE second lot came out for Simeon . . . And it had for its inheritance Beersheba . . . and Sharuhen — thirteen cities with their villages.

(Josh. 19 : 1, 2, 6)

The borders of the tribe of Simeon are not specified, for the reason explicitly given in the text: "and its inheritance was in the midst of the inheritance of the tribe of Judah" (Josh. 19 : 1). It would seem, therefore, that the list of the cities of Simeon reflects the situation at a time when, although the borders between the two tribes were no longer clearly defined, Simeon still preserved its own territory and its tribal identity. The most outlying of the cities listed is Sharuhen which is mentioned by this name only here in the Bible. Sharuhen, (apparently Tell el-Farah) stood at the south-western limit of the area of permanent Canaanite settlement. It served as a strong-point in the chain of Canaanite fortifications that stretched along the Besor and Beersheba Valleys, from Gaza in the west to Hormah and Arad in the east. In Egyptian records it is stated that the Pharaoh Ahmose besieged Sharuhen for three years, after his expulsion of the Hyksos from Egypt (first half of the 16th cent. B.C.). In the reign of Thutmose III an Egyptian garrison was stationed at Sharuhen. The excavations at Tell el-Farah have brought to light the remains of fortifications from the Hyksos period and an Egyptian citadel. Pharaoh Shishak also took Sharuhen on his Palestinian campaign and apparently sacked it.

The illustration is an aerial view of Tell el-Farah which stands out from the surrounding region (see also Vol. I, p. 264).

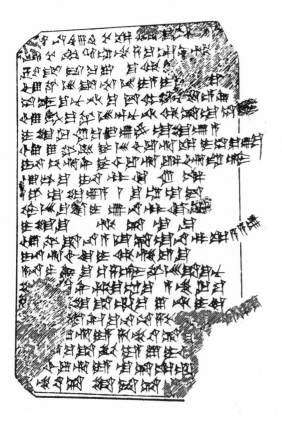

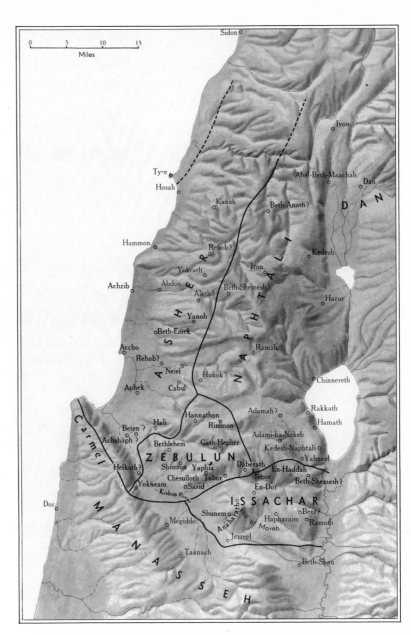

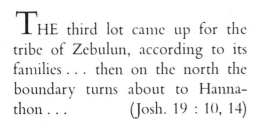 HE third lot came up for the tribe of Zebulun, according to its families ... then on the north the boundary turns about to Hanna-thon ... (Josh. 19 : 10, 14)

After the description of the territory of Simeon at the southern extremity of the Land of Israel, the Bible goes on to mark out the area occupied by the four tribes of the north: Zebulun, Issachar, Asher and Naphtali (see map). The territory of Zebulun comprised the western part of the Valley of Jezreel and the central section of Lower Galilee. Its northern border apparently ran along the ridges to the north of the Beth-Netopha Valley, which was crossed by an important lateral highway connecting the region of the Sea of Galilee with the Plain of Accho. Zebulun too was unable to take possession of two Canaanite cities — Kitron and Nahalol — in its territory (Judg. 1 : 30). Included in the cities of Zebulun is Hannathon (Tell Bedawiya) at the western end of the Valley of Beth-Netopha; this city is known also from the el-Amarna Letters (14th cent. B.C.). In one of these letters the King of Babylon informs Amenhotep IV of Egypt that, when a caravan of his merchants passed through Canaan on their way back from Egypt, they were murdered and stripped of their money near the city of Hannathon by men from Accho and Samhuna — which is, apparently, Shimron in the territory of Zebulun (Josh. 19 : 15). The Babylonian ruler demands that the Egyptian king should have the robbers put to death and in future take more vigorous measures to ensure the safety of the international trade-routes that passed by way of Canaan.

The picture shows the letter of the King of Babylon to the King of Egypt, written in Akkadian in cuneiform characters.

THE fourth lot came out for Issachar, for the tribe of Issachar, according to its families. Its territory included Jezreel, Chesulloth, Shunem.

(Josh. 19 : 17-18)

The tribe of Issachar occupied the south, and particularly the south-east, of Lower Galilee. To the north it had a common border with Naphtali in the Valley of Yabneel and Mount Tabor, the latter being also one of the border-points of Zebulun. Included, too, in Issachar was the eastern part of the Valley of Jezreel; and the eastern border of the tribe apparently ran along the River Jordan. The southern border was constantly shifting. Beth-Shan and the region around it were allotted to the tribe of Manasseh which made inroads into the territory of Issachar (Josh. 17 : 11; see map on p. 59). Issachar did not succeed in driving out the Canaanite inhabitants of the valley and actually became tributary to them, as is implied in the Blessing of Jacob: "Issachar is a strong ass, crouching between the sheepfolds; . . . so he bowed his shoulder to bear, and became a slave at forced labour" (Gen. 49 : 14—15).

The territory of Issachar was partly flat and partly hilly. It contained two valleys, that of Jezreel to the south, and to the north that of Chesulloth, pictured here with the hill of Moreh (1550 ft.) in the background. The photograph was taken from the mountains of Nazareth looking south.

THE fifth lot came out for the tribe of Asher according to its families. (Josh. 19 : 24)

The description of the borders of the territory of Asher is couched in such vague terms that many of the places listed have not yet been definitely identified. The area controlled by the tribe apparently changed in the course of time, as a result of the pressure of outside foes (Judg. 1 : 31) and the expansion of neighbouring tribes (cf. as related of Manasseh in Josh. 17 : 11). The territory of Asher consisted almost entirely of a strip of land with an average width of 12 miles, running from the tip of Mount Carmel in the south to "the fortified city of Tyre" and to Sidon. The northern border of this strip is not specified in the Book of Joshua and can only be drawn conjecturally (see map, p. 59). The Bible gives a poetical description of Asher's abundant produce and also of its fortified cities: "Asher's food shall be rich . . . And let him dip his foot in oil. Your bars shall be iron and bronze." (Gen. 49 : 20; Deut. 33 : 24—25). A territory named Asher occurs in the records of the campaigns of the Egyptian kings Seti I and Ramses II; in Papyrus Anastasi I (see p. 55) there is also mention of a chieftain of Asher (all these documents belong to the thirteenth cent. B.C.).

The conquests of Ramses II in Canaan are portrayed in relief on the walls of the temple at Karnak, near Thebes (reproduced here). Amongst the cities listed as taken are Accho and a city called Gath-Asher. The latter has been identified with an ancient mound on which stands the Arab village of Jatt in the hills of Western Galilee.

THE sixth lot came out for the tribe of Naphtali,
for the tribe of Naphtali, according to its families.
(Josh. 19 : 32)

The territory occupied by the tribe of Naphtali
lay next to that of Asher, covering Eastern Galilee
as far as the Jordan Valley and the Sea of Galilee
and down to Mount Tabor and the Valley of
Yabneel in the south. The "fortified cities" (Josh.
19 : 35) in this territory fall into two groups:
those of the Jordan Valley, and those of Upper
Galilee including Hazor and Kedesh (see map on
p. 59). However, at the time of the Israelite conquest Naphtali was not able to occupy Beth-
Shemesh and Beth-Anath (Judg. 1 : 33). The archaeological survey carried out in Upper Galilee
makes it clear that the Israelites had already
begun to infiltrate into this region at the beginning
of their occupation of Canaan. Several Israelite
sites were brought to light by the survey in hilly
regions, previously uninhabited.

The illustration above shows Tell Harashim
(Khirbet et-Tuleil), the site of one of the settlements established by the Israelites. Below is a photograph of a pottery vessel, one of the characteristic finds from this site.

THE seventh lot came out for the tribe of Dan, according to its families. And the territory of its inheritance included Zorah, Eshtaol, Ir-Shemesh . . . and Me-Yarkon and Rakkon with the territory over against Jaffa.
(Josh. 19 : 40, 41, 46)

The territory occupied by the tribe of Dan lay between the borders of Judah, Ephraim and Benjamin. From Kiryath-Yearim its southern boundary ran down to Beth-Shemesh and from there followed the line of the Sorek Valley. In the north the tribal portion stretched as far as the Yarkon "with the territory over against Jaffa", but Jaffa itself was not taken. Similarly, Gezer and the western slopes of the central mountains were not allotted to Dan but to Ephraim. Dan's portion thus comprised the strip of coastal plain between the Yarkon and the Sorek Valley and a small area in the western foothills (see map on p. 47). The tribe contested the possession of this territory with the Amorites who sought to drive it back into the hills, "for they did not allow them to come down to the plain" (Judg. 1 : 34). It would seem that, like other tribes, Dan was powerless against the Canaanite chariots of the plain and, unable to maintain itself in the cities of Aiyalon and Shaalbim (Judg. 1 : 35), was eventually forced to look for another territory for itself (see p. 106). With the descent of the Philistines upon the coast, the tribal area of Dan was squeezed tighter and tighter, despite the determined resistance offered by the tribe to this new enemy, as is implied in the Samson stories.
The view shows the River Yarkon, the border of the tribe of Dan, with its northern bank.

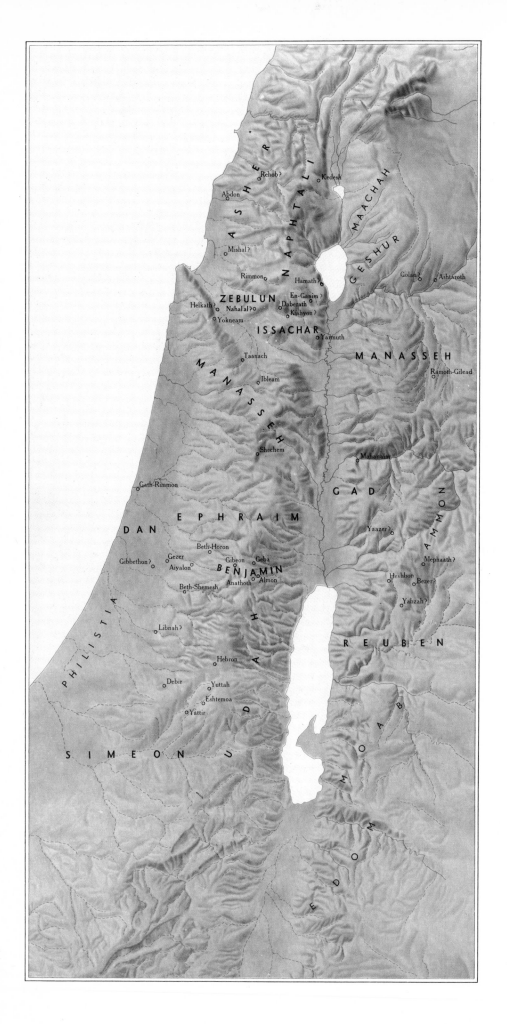

APPOINT the cities of refuge ... that the manslayer who kills any person without intent or unwittingly may flee there ...

The cities of the Levites in the midst of the possession of the people of Israel were in all forty-eight cities with their pasture lands.

(Josh. 20 : 2-3; 21 : 41)

The forty-eight cities allocated to the tribe of Levi were scattered throughout all the tribal territories on both sides of the Jordan. The great majority of these cities possessed no sanctuaries they were set apart for the Levites to live in, since they had no territorial portion in Israel. The "pasture lands" close by the city walls were for the maintenance of their cattle and property. On the other hand, the agricultural lands around these cities were not given to their Levite inhabitants. Hence, even when settled in these forty-eight cities, the Levites remained landless. Some scholars are of the opinion that the list of the Levitical cities presupposes the demographic situation in the reigns of David and Solomon, when families of Levites were appointed in the cities of Israel "for everything pertaining to God and for the affairs of the king" (1 Chron. 26 : 29-32).

Six of the Levitical cities enjoyed a special juridical status as cities of refuge. Three of them were to the west of the Jordan (Kedesh in Galilee, Shechem and Hebron), and the other three east of the river (Bezer, Ramoth in Gilead and Golan in Bashan — see map). It was an immemorial custom that every altar afforded asylum to the fugitive (see p. 203). But in these six cities the right of asylum was not confined to the altar alone — the unintentional murderer fleeing from the avenger of his victim's blood was safe anywhere within the city walls

T HEN Joshua gathered all the tribes of Israel to Shechem . . .　　　　　　　　　　　　(Josh. 24 : 1)

The site of ancient Shechem is at Tell Balata close to modern Nablus (see view). Because of its central geographical position, Shechem was an important Canaanite city as early as the time of the Patriarchs (see Vol. I, p. 90). In the 14th cent. B.C. (just before the Israelite conquest) it was a well-known centre of anti-Egyptian activities. In the Amarna Letters it is recounted that Labaya, the ruler of Shechem, joined forces with the tribes of the *Habiru* (possibly some ethnic group related to the Hebrews) and terrorized the Canaanite kings who were loyal to the Pharaoh. This political situation may have affected the attitude of Shechem to the Israelite conquerors of Canaan in the time of Joshua. Certainly, it is noteworthy that the Bible says nothing at all about any attack on Shechem by the Israelites and that there is no mention of the King of Shechem in the list of the kings defeated by Joshua (c. 12) This silence is interpreted by some scholars as indicating that the city came under Israelite control peacefully.

The environs of Shechem had been steeped in sacred traditions since the days of the Patriarchs. Not far from the city there was a wood of oaks which had been venerated for generations (Gen. 12 : 6; 35 : 4; Deut. 11 : 30; Josh. 24 : 26; Judg. 9 : 6,37).

In Joshua's time there was already "a sanctuary of the Lord" in Shechem itself to which the Bible makes only a passing reference (Josh. 24 : 26). During the period of the Israelite conquest, Shechem was evidently the administrative centre of the tribes and played an important part in the process of welding them together into a stable confederacy. It was here that the dying Joshua commanded the assembled tribes to worship the Lord and to remove strange gods from their midst and made them reaffirm the Covenant between God and His people (Josh. 24 : 1—27).

"PUT away the gods which your fathers served beyond the River, and in Egypt..."
(Josh. 24 : 14)

Joshua's last address is a solemn exhortation to his people to destroy the remnants of the idolatrous cult; to which they had succumbed, as Abraham had spurned the other gods still worshipped by the family of Terah which dwelt beyond the "River" (Euphrates) (Josh. 24: 2 ff.). One of the gods most widely worshipped in that part of the world was Sin, the moon-god, whose cult was centred in Ur and Haran, the two cities in which the family of Terah had sojourned. The lower illustration reproduces a stele (6th cent. B.C.) excavated near Haran, on which there is a pillar surmounted by a crescent moon, the emblem of the god "Sin of Haran".

As a typical example of the idols of Egypt we may take the originally Canaanite goddess Kadesh (cf. the picture above). She is shown standing on a lion with a moon symbol above her head. In her right hand she holds snakes and in her left lotus-flowers. In front of her stands an Egyptian priest who is burning incense in a censer which he is holding, while his wife stands behind him. In the lower portion of the relief the goddess' worshippers are seen kneeling in adoration.

JOSHUA the son of Nun ... died ... And they buried him in his own inheritance at Timnath-Serah, which is in the hill country of Ephraim, north of the mountain of Gaash.

(Josh. 24 : 29-30)

After the Israelites had completed their occupation of Canaan, they gave Joshua Timnath-Serah as his personal inheritance (Josh. 19 : 49—50); and there, Joshua was buried. The Bible states that Timnath-Serah was in the mountains of Ephraim, but the exact position of the grave was never known and several identifications have been in circulation since ancient times. The further topographical reference given by the Bible — "north of the mountain of Gaash" — is of no help, since the location of this mountain has also been forgotten. The original name of the place was Timnath-Heres (Judg. 1 : 9). However, this name, with its apparent reference to the sun-cult practised there (Heb. *heres* — "sun"), was changed by the Israelites into the pejorative form Timnath-Serah (Heb. *serah* — "licentiousness"). Eusebius (4th cent. A.D.) says that in his day the tomb of Joshua was shown in the territory of Dan. This tradition apparently originated in the name of the city Timnah-Timnathah, mentioned in the Samson stories, which lay on the southern border of Dan. Another ancient tradition, which was already known in the time of Eusebius, located the tomb in one of the burial caves near Timnah (Tibna) about 12 miles north-east of Lydda. The view here shows Khirbet Tibna where archaeological remains have been found from the time of the Israelite conquest. This may actually be the site of Timnath-Heres. In the centre of the picture is a tomb traditionally identified with that of Joshua the son of Nun.

JUDGES

AFTER the death of Joshua . . . Judah went up and the LORD gave the Canaanites and the Perizzites into their hand . . . (Judg. 1 : 1, 4)

The Book of Judges relates the vicissitudes of the settlement of the tribes of Israel in Canaan and their fierce and prolonged struggle against both the long-established inhabitants of the country and more recent invaders. The first chapter of the book serves as an introduction to the whole period of the settlement, containing an account of the campaigns and conquests of the different tribes, starting with Judah.

The completeness of the victory of Judah over its enemies is expressed in the words "and the Lord gave the Canaanites and the Perizzites into their hand" — words which faithfully reflect the methods of warfare of those times when the vanquished was utterly at the conqueror's mercy. This expression finds concrete illustration in a relief discovered in the temple at Karnak (see the reproduction) which records the victory of Pharaoh Seti I (end of the fourteenth cent. B.C.) over the peoples of Canaan, not long before the Israelite conquest of the country. At the right is seen the gigantic figure of the Pharaoh striding after his chariot and holding two fettered Canaanites and two further rows of captives drawn after him at the end of a rope.

A<small>ND</small> Adoni-Bezek said, "Seventy kings with their thumbs and their great toes cut off used to pick up scraps under my table . . ." (Judg. 1 : 7).

The brutal treatment of the conquered enemy in the ancient East, such as the mutilation of captives, was the result of the lust for vengeance; it was aimed at the same time at terrorizing the enemy and his allies (cf. p.89). Outstanding in their brutality were the Assyrians who actually gloried in cutting off the limbs of their conquered foes. Hence when the men of Judah cut off the thumbs and toes of Adoni-Bezek (Judg. 1 : 6), they were only following an ancient practice. All the same, the Bible emphasizes that there was also an element of divine justice in this act: it was a fitting requital for the cruelty shown by Adoni-Bezek himself to seventy other kings: "As I have done so God has requited me" (Judg. 1 : 7).

Reproduced here is a section from the bronze panels of a palace gate from the reign of Shalmaneser III (middle of the 9th cent. B.C.), found at Tell Balawat near Nimrud (ancient Calah). Assyrian soldiers are shown dismembering conquered foes from the city of Kulisi (in the region of the headwaters of the Tigris). The Assyrian on the right is cutting off his prisoner's hands and legs.

S HE said to him, "Give me a present; since you have set me in the land of the Negeb..."

(Judg. 1 : 15)

Achsah, the daughter of Caleb and wife of Othniel the son of Kenaz, who conquered Debir, obtained, as a present from her father, the "field and the upper and lower springs" (Judg. 1 : 15). This verse might have been meant to explain how fields and water-sources in the region of Hebron (the territory of Caleb) came into the possession of Othniel the son of Kenaz, whose portion was in the region of Debir in the Negeb. The Hebrew word *berakhah,* which usually means "blessing", is employed here as in other verse, in the sense of "present", a gift of property and land. The transfer of an estate from father to daughter is depicted on a boundary stone which served as a legal document found at Susa (see the picture and cf. Vol. I, p. 274). Meli-Shipak, King of Babylon (c. 12th cent. B.C., i.e. the period of the Judges), is seen presenting his daughter Hunnubat-Nana to the goddess Nana. In front of the goddess there is an incense-stand. Together with other gods whose emblems are shown above the three figures — Ishtar (the star), Sin (the crescent) and Shamash (the sun's orb) — the goddess Nana serves as witness to the deed of transfer of land from the king to his daughter. The text of the agreement is engraved on the reverse side of the stone.

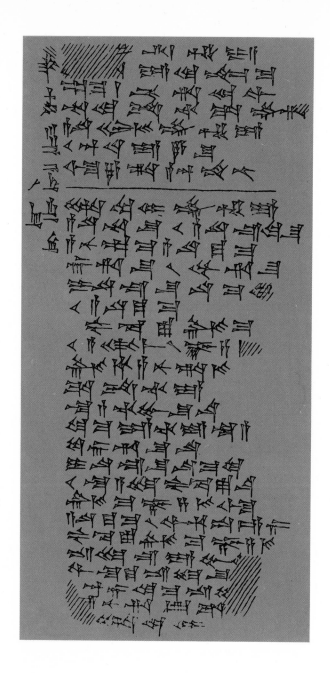

WHEN Israel grew strong, they put the Canaanites to forced labour, but did not utterly drive them out.

(Judg. 1 : 28)

Many of the Canaanite cities in the valleys of the interior and in the coastal plain were able to hold out against the Israelites, because their inhabitants had chariots: "but he could not drive out the inhabitants of the plain, because they had chariots of iron" (Judg. 1 : 19). However, after some time, the Israelites consolidated their position, they brought some of these cities under their control and made them tributary, that is to say, they exacted from them what the Bible sometimes describes as "a forced levy of slaves" (Heb. *mas obed*; Gen. 49 : 15; 1 Kings 9 : 21). Such a corvée was imposed on vanquished foes, prisoners-of-war, aliens (Heb. *gerim*) and occasionally even on Israelites (Deut. 20: 11; 1 Kings 5: 13; 2 Chron. 8: 8). The same term is employed by Scriptures to describe the overseers of the forced labour performed by the Hebrews in Egypt — *sarey missim* (Exod. 1 : 11).

The corvée was common in the ancient East and was well-known in Canaan a long time before the Israelite conquest. In one of the letters (see illustration) found in the el-Amarna archives (14th cent. B.C.), the actual term *mas* occurs. In this letter, Biridiya, the governor of Megiddo, complains to the Pharaoh that he alone of the Canaanite rulers performs his duty to the Egyptian monarch by ensuring that the land in the region of Shunem is worked. He reports that he has transferred a "forced levy" from the city of Japhia for compulsory agricultural labour there. It may be presumed, therefore, that the Israelites took over the corvée system from the Canaanites.

THEY forsook the LORD, and served the Baals and the Ashtaroth. (Judg. 2 : 13)

The period of the Judges, taken as a whole, was one of the low points in the history of Israel. The defeats suffered by the tribes in this period were attributed by the author of the Book of Judges to the backsliding of the Israelites who assimilated themselves to their Canaanite environment and emulated its practices (Judg. 2 : 20—21). Foremost amongst "the other gods, from among the gods of the peoples who were round about them" (Judg. 2 : 12) were Baal and Ashtoreth, the chief gods in the Canaanite pantheon. These two divinities symbolized the forces of nature (Baal — the storm; Ashtoreth — the heavens). Their images have been excavated from the periods of Canaanite settlement that are roughly contemporary with the Israelite conquest. One, from Megiddo, is a bronze statue of a god (see the illustration on the left) overlaid with gold leaf. On his head there is a cone-shaped headdress; his robe reaches to his ankles.

The cylinder-seal of the Late Bronze Age of which an impression is reproduced on the right was discovered at Bethel. Engraved on it are a god (left) and a goddess (right), each of them holding a spear. In his other hand the god is brandishing a scimitar. The goddess is Ashtoreth who is wearing a high Egyptian-style headdress with two streamers attached to the back. In the centre of the seal-impression the name "Ashtart" is inscribed in hieroglyphics.

So the anger of the LORD was kindled against Israel, and he gave them over to plunderers . . .   (Judg. 2 : 14)

The term "plunderers" (Heb. *shosim*) is used in the Bible of enemies who attack suddenly and cause havoc and destruction (1 Sam. 17 : 53; Isa. 17 : 14; Jer. 50 : 11). Here the word refers to all the foes that beset the Israelite tribes at various times during the period of their settlement in Canaan. Sometimes it is used as an appelation for Amalek (1 Sam. 14 : 48) or for kindred desert tribes. *Shosim* also occurs as a Canaanite loan-word in Egyptian records, especially in documents of the Nineteenth and Twentieth Dynasties which correspond to the period of the Israelite settlement. There the word is used to describe nomad tribes, whose attacks disorganized Egyptian rule in Canaan.

Shown here is section from the reliefs of Pharaoh Seti I (end of the 14th cent. B.C.), depicting his campaign against desert raiders (the entire relief has been reproduced in Vol. I, pp. 140—141). This battle took place in the first year of Seti's reign when his army was returning to Egypt through the Sinai desert. The *shosim* are portrayed as typical men of the desert — tall and lean, with long hair and pointed beards. They wear characteristic wrappings round their chests and stomachs. The masses of dead raiders are shown in the relief pierced by the arrows and spears of the Egyptians.

A ND Ehud made for himself a sword with two
edges, a cubit in length . . .   (Judg. 3 : 16)

Planning to assassinate Eglon King of Moab, Ehud the son of
Gera deliberately chose a suitable sword, one of small size
with a blade specially designed for piercing. It may be assumed
that the detailed description of this sword indicates that it was
a special and perhaps even uncommon weapon. The sword in
general use in Ehud's time was still the curved sword with the
cutting edge on its convex side, like that held by the warrior
portrayed on one of the Megiddo ivories (see the reproduction
on the left; and cf. p. 33). Such a sword, which was meant for
slashing, could certainly not have been concealed by Ehud
under his clothes, nor could he have driven it into Eglon's
stomach. Hence we are told that Ehud had recourse to the
straight, two-edged sword which was just coming into use in
his time and was good for stabbing as well as for slashing.
A sword of this type, from the Late Bronze Age, was excavated
at Megiddo (see picture on the right). It is made of bronze and
is 16 in. in length. The lost handle was apparently made of
ivory or wood.

AND they waited till they were utterly at a loss; but when he still did not open the doors of the roof chamber, they took the key and opened them . . .

(Judg. 3 : 25)

The use of bolts to keep doors closed is as old as houses. In the model of a house of the Chalcolithic period found at Hedera (c. 3500 B.C.), there are already signs of the use of bolts on both sides of the door. The system of bolts and keys illustrated here continued in use in the ancient East throughout the whole of the biblical period and even after it. The bolt consisted of a metal bar (bronze or iron) which slid along a groove in the woodwork of the door. When it was closed the end engaged in a corresponding aperture in the door-post, or (where the door was double) in the other panel. Into the bolt itself were bored several holes, to which corresponded movable pins in the door. When the bolt was closed, the pins slipped down into the holes and held it fast. The key was a metal bar with a handle and a number of studs corresponding to the holes in the bolt, so made as to press up the engaging pins and thus release the bolt.

The picture on the left is a reconstruction of a double-door (of Assyrian pattern) with one panel open. The key is in the key-hole and the bolt is in the closed position. In the centre is a drawing of a bolt held fast by the lock-pins, and underneath it a key. This reconstruction is based on a stone door of the Roman period that was discovered at Sur Baḥir near Jerusalem.

AFTER him was Shamgar the son of Anath, who killed six hundred of the Philistines with an oxgoad . . . (Judg. 3 : 31)

The Judges of Israel delivered their people each in his own way. Some of them led large numbers of warriors into battle, while others acted single-handed. In the latter category was Shamgar the son of Anath, whose heroic deed is given only one verse in the Bible. There it is related that he killed six hundred Philistines with an oxgoad. The shape of the oxgoad is known to us from pictorial representations and archaeological finds from the ancient East. It consisted of a wooden stick tipped with a metal point.

Reproduced above is a detail from a relief on the walls of the temple of Pharaoh Seti I at Karnak, showing a Canaanite shepherd driving his oxen with a stick, possibly an oxgoad. The shepherd's haste is due to his fear of his Egyptian pursuers. The picture on the right of p. 78 shows a metal object of the 11th — 10th cent. B.C. found at Megiddo, which appears to be the point of an oxgoad. It was attached to a wooden stick by the aperture at its top.

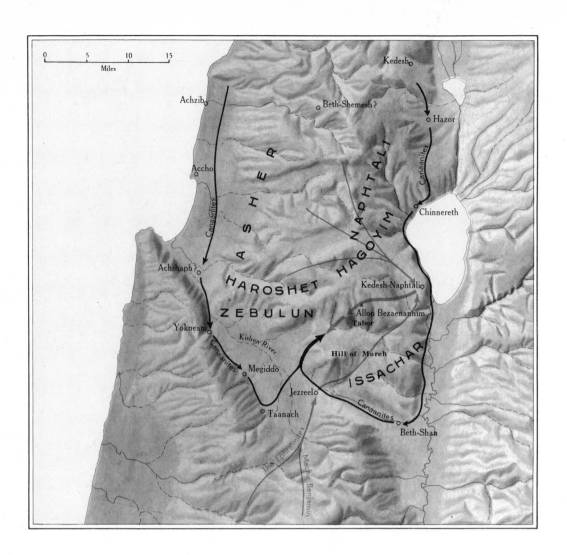

AND the Lord so
them into the hand
Jabin king of Canaa
who reigned in Hazo
the commander of h
army was Sisera, wh
dwelt in Harosheth-H
goyim. Then the peop
of Israel cried to th
LORD for help; for]
had nine hundred ch
riots of iron . . .
(Judg. 4 : 2–

The kings of northern Canaan, against whom Barak and Deborah fought, were led — according to Scripture — by Jabin king of Hazor and the commander of his army Sisera. However, in the actual description of the war, Jabin and Hazor play an insignificant part, and it is Sisera of Harosheth Hagoyim (H. "of the Gentiles") who is the main foe. Harosheth Hagoyim may not be the name of a place, but a general term for the whole wooded area of Galilee. The Hebrew word *harosheth* is cognate with *horesh,* which means "a small wood"; while the term *Hagoyim* ("the nations" or 'Gentiles") is reminiscent of "Galilee of Hagoyim" (Isa. 9 : 1).

Sisera relied principally upon his chariotry which struck terror into the Israelites. The lower figure is a reproduction of one of the sides of an ivory casket from Megiddo (with above it, on p. 81, a reconstruction of its ornament), on which are portrayed Canaanite chariots in action (cf. pp. 40—41 where the Canaanite chariotry is described in detail). Each chariot is drawn by two horses. The horses are advancing at a furious gallop and are overwhelming the enemy. The artist has vividly depicted the crescendo of the charge in the heat of the battle and the tense stance of the charioteers.

WHEN Sisera was told that Barak the son of
Abinoam had gone up to Mount Tabor . . .

(Judg. 4 : 12)

Inspired by Deborah Barak the son of Abinoam mustered his
army at Kedesh Naphtali (which may perhaps be located at
Khirbet Qadish close to the valley of Yabneel). From there he
moved on, for strategic reasons, to Mount Tabor which
dominates the valley stretching to the south and east of it.
When Sisera was informed of the whereabouts of the Israelites,
he led his army out to meet them and drew up his line of
battle beside the river Kishon. Choosing his moment and
assisted by a flood (see p. 83) Barak with ten thousand men
suddenly swept down from Tabor (Judg. 4 : 14) and routed the
Canaanites (see the map on p. 80).
The photograph shows Mount Tabor and the valley to the
southeast of it — the scene of the Israelite onslaught. The
isolated mountain rises to a height of 1000 ft. above the surrounding plain and 1750 ft. above sea-level. Here met the
boundaries of three of the Israelite tribes (see the map on
p. 59). In biblical poetry Tabor is associated with the Hermon
and the Carmel. The prophet Jeremiah gives it pride of place
amongst the mountains of Israel, presumably because it stands
out from afar: "Like Tabor among the mountains, and like
Carmel by the sea, shall one come" (Jer. 46 : 18). To the
Psalmist it is a symbol of God's greatness and might: "Tabor
and Hermon joyously praise Thy name" (Ps. 89 : 12).

shield or spear
to be seen among forty
thousand in Israel?
(Judg. 5 : 8)

The Song of Deborah reveals the plight to which the Israelite tribes had been reduced by Canaanite pressure. Its seriousness can be gauged from the following details: lack of security on the roads ("caravans ceased", Judg. 5 : 6), abandonment of unfortified settlements ("the peasantry ceased in Israel, they ceased", v. 7), and inadequate or inferior military equipment (v.8). The words of this last verse would seem to refer to forty thousand Israelite warriors who did not possess any weapons like the spear and the shield which at that time were standard Canaanite equipment.

The spear (Heb. *romah*) was used for stabbing at close quarters, in contrast to the javelin (Heb. *hanith*) which was thrown from a distance. Both the spear and the shield were among the primary weapons of the foot-soldier in the time of the Judges. The use of other kind of weapons, such as the bow and the sling, required special training and was therefore confined to selected units. Reproduced here is a detail of a Megiddo ivory (for the whole picture see p. 45) showing a Canaanite soldier armed with a long spear and a round shield. About the time of the Judges, this round shield began to replace the square shield that had been in common use till then (see p. 28).

THE torrent Kishon swept them away, the onrushing torrent, the torrent Kishon. (Judg. 5 : 21)

The river Kishon flows through the Valley of Jezreel (see the map on p. 80) in a meandering course. During the greater part of the year only the western part of its course has a permanent flow. This part of the river (photographed here) runs along the foot of Mount Carmel and carries water that comes down from the northern slopes of Mount Ephraim and from Lower Galilee. In the rainy season the waters of the river rise, and in a particularly wet year they rush along in a turbulent current that sweeps away everything in its path. These features of the river are brought out in the Song of Deborah which presumably describes its flooding in the rainy season, to the accompaniment of thunder and lightning. The flood took Sisera by surprise and swept away his chariots. The victory of the Israelites over Sisera's host was thus not entirely due to force of arms, but to the assistance of nature. Deborah saw in this a miracle: "From heaven fought the stars, from their courses they fought against Sisera" (Judg. 5 : 30).

HER wisest ladies make answer . . . "spoil of dyed stuffs for Sisera, spoil of dyed stuffs embroidered, two pieces of dyed work embroidered for my neck as spoil?" (Judg. 5 : 29-30)

Though primarily a poem of war and valour, the Song of Deborah also contains accounts of feelings and impulses that do not belong to the battlefield. Such is the description of the anxiety of Sisera's mother for her son. Her ladies try to calm her fears and she too deludes herself that Sisera is busy dividing up the spoil. In her mind's eye she sees him taking for himself from the booty dyed raiments of the kind that the Canaanites particularly fancied.

Reproduced here are two examples of the rich clothing worn by prosperous Canaanites and their womenfolk at the time of the Judges. The picture on the right shows the figure of a Canaanite on a glazed tile which adorned one of the gates of the temple of Ramses III at Medinet Habu (12th cent. B.C.). The man's long robe, wound around his body, is embroidered in many colours. On the left is an ivory inlay of a woman found at Megiddo (13th—12th cent. B.C.). The pupils of her eyes are made of glass. Her hair falls down over her shoulders and she is wearing an ankle-length robe. The edges of the robe are braided.

F_{OR} they would come up with their cattle and their tents, coming like locusts for number; both they and their camels could not be counted . . . (Judg. 6 : 5)

The decline of Canaanite power and the political weakness of the Israelite tribes provided a favourable opportunity for desert raiders to make inroads into Canaan. In the time of Gideon, the Midianites, followed by Amalek and "the people of the East" (Judg. 6 : 3), invaded the country. They threatened to dislodge the Israelite tribes in the north from their lands and caused havoc to agriculture: "They would encamp against them and destroy the produce of the land . . . and leave no sustenance in Israel, and no sheep or ox or ass" (Judg. 6 : 4).

The Midianites awed the Israelites by their multitudes "like locusts for number" and their possession of camels that "could not be counted". The camel was known to nomad and semi-nomad tribes from the earliest times, (see Vol. I, pp. 71, 96), but its use as a beast of burden or for riding did not become general until the 12th century B.C. In the time of the Judges, however, camels were becoming more and more widely used, even for military purposes. There emerged in the vastness of the Arabian desert tribes and federations of tribes that depended for their existence in peace and war on the camel. Thanks to the camel, the Midianites were able to cover enormous distances from the edge of the Trans-Jordan desert to the western part of Palestine in "the neighbourhood of Gaza" (Judg. 6 : 4) and to develop military tactics with which the Israelites were completely unfamiliar.

The photograph shows a herd of Beduin camel at pasture in the region of Shivtah in the Central Negeb.

THEN Jerubbaal (that is, Gideon) and all the people who were with him rose early and encamped beside the spring of Harod . . .

(Judg. 7 : 1)

In their war against the Midianites, Gideon and his soldiers camped beside the spring of Harod (in modern Arabic Ain Jalud) which lies at the foot of Mount Gilboa to the north-west. This choice of a site for the camp made it possible for Gideon to retreat into the hills, if necessary, unmolested by the camel-riding Midianites. The Bible relates that, at the Lord's command, Gideon took ten thousand men down to the spirng and then chose only a few of all that number to deliver Israel — only the three hundred who had not "knelt down to drink water" but had lapped it up, "putting their hands to their mouths". It has been argued that this mode of drinking was a sign of circumspection and alertness. However that may be, the military operation that Gideon had in mind — a night attack — did not require many men. The real purpose of the sotry is to emphasize that Gideon was fighting the war of the Lord who had the power to deliver His people even with a small band of men and did not need a large host: "Lest Israel vaunt themselves against Me saying, 'My own hand has delivered me'" (Judg. 7 : 2).

The photograph shows a pool which is fed by the waters of the nearby spring of Harod.

AND the camp of Midian was north of them, by the hill of Moreh, in the valley.

(Judg. 7 : 1)

While the Israelites were encamped in the Valley of Jezreel south of the hill of Moreh, the Midianites mustered their forces in the plain that stretches from the other side of the hill as far as Mount Tabor. What is written about the Midianites in Ps. 83 : 10 — i.e. that they "were destroyed at En-Dor" — may provide a clue to the exact location of the Midianite camp. The site of ancient En-Dor is at Khirbet Safsafa close to the modern village of Indur, which lies in the Valley of Jezreel about half a mile from the hill of Moreh. That the Midianites were concentrated in this region may be deduced from the fact that their kings killed the brothers of Gideon at Tabor (Judg. 8 : 18). After their defeat, the Midianites retreated eastwards and southwards to·Beth-Shittah and the Valley of Beth-Shan (Judg. 7 : 22). The hill of Moreh, besides which the Midianites encamped, is not mentioned anywhere else in the Bible. It is the mountain called in Arabic Jebel Dahi which rises to a height of about 900 ft. above the surrounding plain and to 1550 ft. above sea-level. To the south of it lies the level expanse of the Valley of Jezreel and to the north stretches the Valley of Chesulloth (see p. 60). The hill of Moreh, which lay in the territory of Issachar, and the slightly higher Mount Tabor, are the most conspicuous landmarks in the whole area and can be seen for miles around.

The view shows the hill of Moreh from the north-east and at its foot the Valley of Chesulloth.

AND broke the jars, holding in their left hands the torches, and in their right hands the trumpets . . . They stood every man in his place round about the camp, and all the army ran · they cried out and fled.   (Judg. 7 : 20-21)

Falling upon the Midianites in a surprise night attack, Gideon spread panic and confusion through their camp by blasts on the trumpet, the smashing of jars and frenzied shouting (Judg. 7 : 19—21). The use of torches against the Midianites was not merely a psychological stratagem, but had also a practical purpose, since the torch is an extremely useful weapon against dwellers in tents, to set them alight.

Reproduced below is a detail from a relief from the palace of the Assyrian King Assurbanipal at Nineveh (7th cent. B.C.) depicting the Assyrians fighting against nomad tribes. An Assyrian soldier is seen setting a tent on fire with a torch.

Gideon's soldiers presumably took with them jars of the kind commonly found in those times in the homes of peasants. Such a jar from the period of the Judges is reproduced in the picture above; it has one handle and a neck wide enough to take a torch.

ND the officials of Succoth
said, "Are the hands of Zebah
and Zalmunna now in your
hand, that we should give bread
to your army?" (Judg. 8 : 6)

The refusal of the people of Succoth and Penuel in Trans-Jordan to provide food for Gideon's troops in their pursuit of the Midianites (Judg. 8 : 4—10) was presumably the result of their disbelief in Gideon's victory. Their question, "Are the hands of Zebah and Zalmunna now in your hands?" was meant to imply that Gideon still had no real proof that he had vanquished the enemy. In the warfare of the ancient East it was customary to prove the destruction of the enemy by displaying limbs cut off from their dead bodies. In the time of the Judges and the early part of the Israelite Kingdom we find some instances of this practice in the Bible (cf. 1 Sam. 18 : 27; cf. pp. 72, 268).

The picture — which is reproduced from the reliefs of Ramses II at Abydos (13th cent. B.C.) — shows the scribes of the Pharaoh counting the severed hands of their foes which lie piled in heaps in front of them.

AND he caught a young man of Succoth, and questioned him; and he wrote down for him the officials and elders of Succoth, seventy-seven men.   (Judg. 8 : 14)

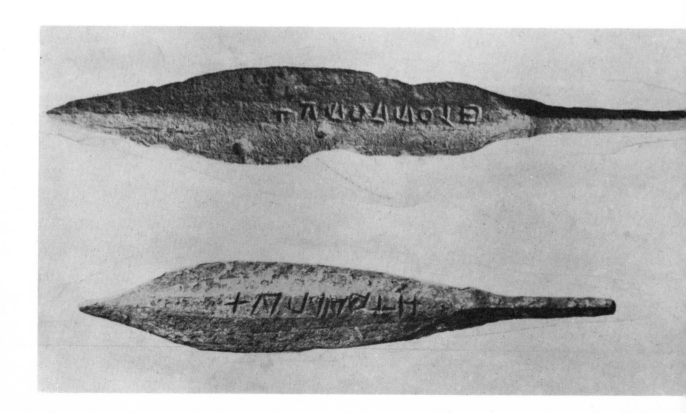

After completing his victory over the Midianites with the capture of their two kings Zebah and Zalmunna, Gideon returned to take vengeance on the people of Succoth (see p. 89). For this purpose he required to know the names of the officials and elders of the city. The fact that a young man — perhaps a city official — of Succoth wrote down for Gideon the names of seventy-seven of the city's dignitaries is noteworthy, as indicating that knowledge of writing was fairly widespread in Israel in those days. The development and diffusion of writing was a lengthy process which started in the fourth millennium B.C. with the cuneiform script of Mesopotamia and the hieroglyphics of Egypt. However, since these two systems of writing were very intricate and could only be mastered after prolonged study, they remained known only to the temple priests and the scribes.

Much later an alphabetic script was developed which was simpler and thus easier to learn. The first tentative attempts at an alphabetic script can be traced in Canaan and the neighbouring countries as early as the first half of the second millennium B.C. (cf. Vol. I, p. 159). But it was not until the end of the second millennium that it attained its perfected form in the Canaanite script, from which the ancient Phoenician-Hebrew script was derived. This script was also adopted by the Aramaeans by whom it was spread through the East. From Phoenicia this alphabet found its way to Greece, where it became the basis of the Greek alphabet, which was the source of the Latin script.

Reproduced here are specimens of the most ancient known inscriptions in the Phoenician-Hebrew script. The upper figure on p. 90 is the reproduction of a bronze blade from the 11th cent. B.C., excavated at Gebal (Byblos). Several of the letters have been damaged and scholars are divided about the correct deciphering of the inscription engraved on the blade. The lower figure shows two bronze arrow-heads of the same period which were found near Bethlehem. Each of them is engraved with the following inscription: hs 'bdlb't "The arrow of Abdlabit." These words may designate the personal name or place of origin of the bowman who carried the arrows.

The table on p. 91 shows the letters of the ancient Hebrew alphabet as they appear in the Gezer calendar (see Vol. I. p. 198) and on the stele of Mesha king of Moab (see below, p. 256).

MESHA	GEZER	
		א
		ב
		ג
		ד
		ה
		ו
		ז
		ח
		ט
		י
		כ
		ל
		מ
		נ
		ס
		ע
		פ
		צ
		ק
		ר
		ש
		ת

WHEN it was told to Jotham, he went and stood on the top of Mount Gerizim, and cried aloud and said to them, "Listen to me, you men of Shechem . . ." (Judg. 9 : 7)

Abimelech the son of Gideon persuaded the leading citizens of Shechem to make him their king, having won their support by stressing that he was bone of their bone and flesh of their flesh, since his mother had been born in Shechem. To ensure himself undisputed sovereignty, he killed all his brothers, the other sons of Gideon, except "Jotham the youngest son of Jerubbaal, for he hid himself" (Judg. 9 : 5). When he heard that Abimelech, the murderer of his brothers, had actually been crowned, Jotham sought to incite the people of Shechem against Abimelech by reciting to them the famous parable. He uttered his words from the top of Mount Gerizim, at the foot of which Shechem lay. Thus he was able to make himself heard far and wide without exposing himself to the wrath of the people of Shechem.

Mount Gerizim (photographed here), to the south of Shechem, is mentioned in the Bible as the mountain of blessing, while Mount Ebal is the mountain of curses (see Vol. I, p. 289). Gerizim, which rises to about 1600 ft. above sea-level, stands at the junction of the highways on the watershed of the Mountains of Ephraim. It owes its special importance to its geographical position and the springs at its foot. The sanctity of the mountain has been kept alive in Samaritan tradition down to the present day.

THEN all the trees said to the bramble, "Come you, and reign over us." And the bramble said to the trees, "If in good faith you are anointing me king over you, then come and take refuge in my shade; but if not, let fire come out of the bramble and devour the cedars of Lebanon."

(Judg. 9 : 14-15)

In Jotham's parable, the fruit trees, renowned for their succulence and sweetness, their good fruit and wine, refused to reign and "go to sway over the trees", because it was too much trouble for them; while the bramble that worthless bush of thorns, agreed. The bramble is the thorny plant known to biologists as *Lycium*. Four kinds are found in Palestine. That mentioned in our verse is apparently the European bramble *(Lycium europaeum L.)* which grows almost everywhere in Palestine. It is a bush with slender prickly branches bent over into the shape of a bow. It has small purple flowers and edible red berries. The thorny branches of the bush overhang and are thus likely to scratch anyone trying "to take refuge in its shade". They were used only for fuel (Ps. 58 : 9); hence Jotham's statement that fire would come forth from the bramble and devour those who took refuge in its shade. The two photographs emphasize the striking natural contrasts between the thorny bramble (above) and the olive-tree with its rich fruit (below) "by which gods and men are honoured" (Judg. 9 : 9).

WHEN all the people of the Tower of Shechem heard of it, they entered the stronghold of the house of El-Berith.

(Judg. 9 : 46)

The excavations carried out on the site of ancient Shechem (see p. 65) brought to light the remains of a massive edifice with walls 15 ft. thick enclosing a hall with an area of 33 by 39 ft. In this hall were found two rows of bases of columns which supported the ceiling and possibly an upper storey. The entrance to the building was to the south-east and was apparently flanked by two turrets. This building — like that excavated at Megiddo in the Late Bronze Age stratum — evidently served both as a shrine and as a fortress, a *migdal* ("tower") in the Hebrew and Canaanite languages. It was built in the Late Bronze Age, or possibly at the end of the Middle Bronze Age, and was still in existence, in the opinion of its excavators, in the Early Iron Age, i.e. the period of the Judges. It may be that this building was "the Tower of Shechem" which was destroyed by Abimelech. Prior to this, Abimelech had laid waste the actual city of Shechem ("and he razed the city and sowed it with salt" Judg. 9 : 45), but had been unable to take the citadel with the means at his disposal. He therefore burnt down the tower with the thousand of the city's inhabitants who had taken refuge inside it (Judg. 9 : 48—49).

The plate shows a reconstruction of the shrine of Shechem on the basis of the archaeological finds made on the site. The strongly built shrine, with its two high towers, stands in the centre of an open space surrounded by a wall, close to one of the city gates.

ND the king of the Ammonites answered the messengers of Jephthah, "Because Israel on coming from Egypt took away my land, from the Arnon to the Jabbok and to the Jordan; now therefore restore it peaceably."

(Judg. 11 : 13)

The territory claimed by both Israel and Ammon, which was the subject of the political negotiations between Jephthah and the King of Ammon, comprised the region between the rivers Arnon and Jabbok. The Ammonite king laid claim to this territory on the ground that it had formerly belonged to Ammon and Moab. Jephthah countered this argument by maintaining that the region had been conquered from Sihon, the Amorite king, and not from Ammon and Moab (Nu. 21 : 26; see Vol. I, p. 224). In support of this contention, he cited the Israelites' right of ownership through prolonged occupation. "While Israel dwelt in Heshbon and its villages, and in Aroer and its villages, and in all the cities that are on the banks of the Arnon, three hundred years" (Judg. 11 : 26).

The river Jabbok formed a natural frontier of the Kingdom of Sihon, the Amorite king, (Nu. 21 : 24); and in its upper reaches it also marked off the country of the Ammonites from the tribal territories of Reuben and Gad (Deut. 3 : 16). It is one of the abundant rivers that flow into the Jordan from the east, being fed by springs that rise to the north of Rabbath Ammon. In the rainy season, it channels off the rainwaters from the central Trans-Jordan plateau. In Arabic it is called Nahr ez-Zerqa, i.e. "the blue river" (for further details and a map see Vol. I, p. 87).

The photograph shows the river Jabbok where it is crossed by the modern road at the approaches to Jerash. At this point the river flows through a rocky gorge, making movement along it difficult.

T<small>HEN</small> Jephthah came to his home at Mizpah;
and behold, his daughter came out to meet him
with timbrels and with dances . . .   (Judg. 11 : 34)

In the biblical period — as to this day in the East — it was
customary for the womenfolk to welcome the victorious hero
on his return from battle with music, song and dance. So the
prophetess Miriam sang her paean of victory to the Lord
while all the women followed her with timbrels and dancing:
"Sing to the Lord for He has triumphed gloriously; the horse
and his rider He has thrown into the sea" (Exod. 15 : 21; see
Vol. I, p. 146). Similarly, the daughters of Israel welcomed the
victorious Saul and David with timbrels, dancing and song:
"Saul has slain his thousands and David his ten thousands"
(1 Sam. 18 : 7; see p. 141). The timbrels (Heb. *tuppim*) mentioned in all these passages were among the most popular
musical instruments (compare the expression "maidens playing
timbrels" in Ps. 68 : 25). In the same way, Jephthah's daughter
went out to meet her father with timbrels and dancing, to the
greater glory of the conquering hero who had wrought
vengeance on the Ammonites.

Reproduced here is the drawing of a restored detail from the
ornament of an ivory casket dating from the 9th cent. B.C.
found in the palace at Calah (the modern Nimrud). The reliefs
are set in panels separated by a stylized frame. Here, next to
the figure of a stag (a very common motif in these ornamenta-
tions), we see a young woman beating a timbrel.

THEY said to him, "Then say Shibboleth," and he said "Sibboleth," for he could not pronounce it right; then they seized him and slew him at the fords of the Jordan.   (Judg. 12 : 6)

The battle between the men of Ephraim and the men of Gilead was fought out on the fords of the Jordan, the natural frontier between their two territories. Jephthah managed to gain control of these fords and thus sealed the escape-route of the Ephraimites. The Gileadites recognized their foes by the latter's pronunciation (*sibboleth*, instead of *shibboleth* meaning a "stream of water"). The story shows that there were differences of pronunciation between the Israelite tribes.

In time of war the ancients tried to gain control of river-fords, with the object of entrenching themselves on the banks and thus barring them to the enemy. The Israelite Judges (Ehud, Gideon and now Jephthah) frequently occupied the fords of the Jordan in order to cut the enemy's lines of retreat.

Decisive battles were often fought on the banks of rivers. Reproduced here is a detail of a relief from the palace of Sennacherib at Nineveh. The bodies of slaughtered enemies of the Assyrians are seen floating on the water, together with the wreckage of their chariots. On the river bank, the survivors are doing obeisance to the victors.

ND the people of Israel again did what was evil in the sight of the LORD; and the LORD gave them into the hand of the Philistines for forty years.

(Judg. 13 : 1)

The Philistines were one of Israel's most formidable foes. Beginning with encroachments upon the territories of Dan and Judah, they eventually threatened the existence of the whole nation. From non-biblical sources (particularly from Egyptian records) it is possible to conjecture their history before their descent upon the shores of Canaan. They probably came from the Aegean islands, being one of the "Sea Peoples", that moved in a succession of waves to the eastern shores of the Mediterranean at the end of the 13th cent. and during the 12th cent. B.C. This invasion of the "Sea Peoples" was a consequence of the great migratory upheaval that came in the wake of the irruption of the Achaean tribes into the Balkans and Greece (see Vol. I, p. 252). At the beginning of the 12th cent. B.C., the "Sea Peoples" overran the Hittite Empire and began moving southwards in the direction of Canaan, to the consternation of the Egyptians. Fierce battles raged, on land and on sea, between these invaders (including the Philistines) and the armies of Ramses III.

Reproduced here is a section of a relief from the temple wall at Medinet Habu, depicting a sea battle between the "Sea Peoples" and the fleet of Ramses III. The Egyptians are shown overwhelming two enemy vessels the crew of which are falling into the water. The armament of the "Sea Peoples" is typical of Aegean warriors as described by Homer and similar to that of the Philistines in the biblical stories (on the feathered helmet and the armour see pp. 118, 120 and cf. pp. 138—139). While the "Sea Peoples" as a whole were defeated in this battle and driven back from the borders of Egypt, the Philistines managed to gain a foothold on the southern coast of Palestine — apparently with Egyptian consent.

AND the Spirit of the LORD began to stir him in Mahaneh-Dan, between Zorah and Eshtaol. (Judg. 13 : 25)

The Israelite tribe that suffered most from Philistine pressure was Dan. Lacking the strength to meet the Philistines in open warfare, the Danites had recourse to guerrilla tactics. In such engagements, great importance attaches to the deeds of single individuals who are distinguished by their courage and cunning. This was the setting for the rise of the popular hero Samson, renowned for his daring exploits, his physical strength and his intrepid spirit, who was successful in his ruses against the enemy and smote them "hip and thigh with great slaughter" (Judg. 15 : 8). Samson's first exploit took place between Zorah and Eshtaol, two adjacent cities in the territory of Dan (Josh. 19:41), the furthest point of Philistine expansion at that time. Zorah is mentioned as early as the 14th cent. B.C., in the el-Amarna Letters, together with Aiyalon, as a city of the king of Gezer. It stood on a high hill north of the Sorek Valley where the mountains of Judah come down to the coastal plain. The name was preserved for a long time in that of the Arab village of Sar'a. Its topographical situation made it a place of great importance in the struggle between the Danites and the Philistines. In later generations its strategic importance was in no way diminished. Rehoboam rebuilt it as a strongpoint in his line of fortresses, which followed the eastern border of the foothills (Shephelah), from Aiyalon to Lachish (2 Chron. 11:5—12). The view shows the undulating landscape around Zorah.

99

SAMSON went down to Timnah . . .   (Judg. 14 : 1)

Although the Israelites and Philistines were almost constantly at war, there was evidently also contact of a peaceful kind between them, even to the extent of intermarriage, as in Samson's case. These peaceful relations were closest in the border region where the expansive pressure of the Philistines met the territory occupied by the Israelites, as for instance in the city of Timnah. The story of Samson indicates that the Philistines were firmly established in Timnah and felt very much at home there. There were two cities with the name Timnah (apart from Timnath-Heres in the Mountains of Ephraim, for which see p. 67): one in the Judaean mountains (Gen. 38 : 12—14; Josh. 15 : 57) and the other in the foot-hills (Josh. 15 : 10). The latter is referred to here. It is sometimes identified with Tell el-Batashi in the Sorek Valley (shown in the plate). This site, by reason of its geographical position, could well have formed a frontier post between the territory of Dan (Josh. 19 : 43) and that of Judah (see the map on p. 51). This Timnah, which was not far from Ekron, was still threatened with Philistine conquest in the period of the Israelite kings. Indeed, in the reign of Ahaz, king of Judah, it was actually occupied by the Philistines, together with other cities of the foot-hills (2 Chron. 28 : 18). Ahaz's son, Hezekiah, recovered it for Judah, only to lose it again to Sennacherib, the Assyrian king, who, according to his own inscription, took the city on his campaign against Jerusalem.

And behold, a young lion roared against him; and the Spirit of the LORD came mightily upon him, and he tore the lion asunder as one tears a kid; and he had nothing in his hand . . .

(Judg. 14 : 5-6)

In biblical times, the lion was found throughout the lands of the East, including Canaan. This mighty beast of prey is mentioned several times in the Bible, both in poetic similes (see Vol. I, p. 229) and in the description of actual events. It is related of three heroes that they overcame lions in single combat: Samson, David (1 Sam. 17 : 35—36), and Benaiah (2 Sam. 23 : 20). Of the three, Samson's courage is the most stressed, for he killed the lion with his bare hands. Similar feats of outstanding valour were attributed to Gilgamesh, the hero of the Mesopotamian epic..

Reproduced here is one of the upright basalt slabs that adorned the royal palace at Gozan (Tell Halaf), from the 10th or 9th cent. B.C. It shows a warrior fighting a lion. As the lion rears up on its hind legs to bite the warrior's left hand, the latter plunges his sword into the beast's body.

So they bound him with two new ropes . . .   (Judg. 15 : 13)

When the Philistines realized that they could not beat Samson in open combat, they sought to get him into their power when his hands were tied. First, they forced the Judahites to hand Samson over to them bound "with two new ropes" (Judg. 15 : 13—14). Next, they prevailed upon Delilah to secure him while he slept, and she did so twice, the first time "with seven fresh cords (Heb. *yetarim*) which have not been dried", and the second "with new ropes that have not been used" (Judg. 16 : 7—12). But each time Samson effortlessly snapped the cords that bound him. The breaking of new ropes or undried cords was evidence of Samson's superhuman strength, since these are much stronger than old ropes that have been weakened by use or than dried cords.

The manufacture of ropes, in its various phases, is vividly portrayed for us in Egyptian frescoes, such as the painting in a tomb at Thebes from the reign of Thutmose III (15th cent. B.C.) reproduced here. It shows three men making ropes on the edge of a river or marsh. The one on the left is twining a single rope out of two cords (possibly these are the *yetarim*), which are kept separate on a device held by his fellow-worker on the right. The third man, who is seated between the other two, is presumably adding threads to the rope as it is twined. Painted above the workmen are instruments used in the making of the ropes and also four coils of finished ropes.

NOW the lords of the Philistines gathered to offer a great sacrifice to Dagon their god . . . And Samson grasped the two middle pillars upon which the house rested, and he leaned his weight upon them, his right hand on the one and his left hand on the other.

(Judg. 16 : 23, 29)

The Philistines thronged into the temple of Dagon at Gaza to celebrate their victory. The god Dagon was particularly venerated by them, and in both Ashdod and Beth-Shan a special temple was built for him (1 Sam. 5 : 2; 1 Chron. 10 : 10). Dagon was probably not originally a Philistine deity; Dagan, the god of the soil and of fertility (Hebrew *dagan*-grain) was worshipped in the region of the Middle Euphrates as early as the third millennium B.C. His cult was widespread in Canaan and was apparently adopted by the Philistines from the Canaanites. In the temple at Ugarit two votive inscriptions from the 14th cent. B.C. have been found which mention sacrifices made to the god *Dgn*. One of them is reproduced below.

In the House of Dagon at Gaza, Samson avenged himself by pulling down the two columns which carried the weight of the building. A pillared building of this kind is illustrated in the upper picture, viz. part of the staircase in the palace of the Cretan kings at Cnossos (15th cent. B.C.). The peculiarity of the Cretan column is that it tapers towards the base. The Philistines, who according to tradition came from Caphtor (i.e. Crete), probably built their temples on the architectural patterns common there; the House of Dagon might accordingly have been supported by columns similar to those in the picture.

HIS mother took two hundred pieces of silver, and gave it to the silversmith, who made it into a graven image and a molten image; and it was in the house of Micah.   (Judg. 17 : 4)

The Law of Moses prohibited the making of idols, even for the worship of the Lord, and this prohibition was still more emphatically reiterated by the Prophets (see Vol. I, p. 153). Nevertheless, the people disregarded this prohibition from ti ne to time, especially during the period of the Judges. Such was the case of Micah who set up a small "house of God" in the mountain of Ephraim and placed in it a graven image (Heb. *pesel)* and a molten image (Heb. *massekhah)* to the Lord. The graven image and the molten image are usually two distinct, if closely related, objects. The one was of metal sections, apparently welded together; whereas the other was cast in a mould in one solid piece. Evidently the two terms are combined in this verse to signify a single object, namely an idol of cast metal. (For such an idol see Vol. I, p. 290).

Reproduced here is a silver idol which, in biblical terms, is a *pesel* and not a *massekhah.* It was found in the excavation of a Canaanite "high place" at Nahariya, and is from the end of the Middle Bronze Age. Such idols, which were common amongst the Canaanites, evidently also found their way into the Israelite cult in the period of the Judges.

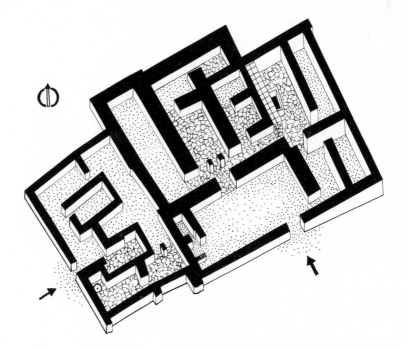

A ND the man Micah had a
shrine . . .   (Judg. 17 : 5)

Micah's shrine, according to the belief of the ancients, had the power to bring his family prosperity (Judg. 17 : 13), especially from the moment that a Levitical youth became its "father and priest" (Judg. 17 : 10). The number of Israelite shrines in the biblical period was probably small in comparison with the high-places and altars under the open sky. Such shrines usually contained holy objects, such as the graven image and the ephod which were in Micah's house of God (see p. 104). The ritual of the shrine was more complex and varied than that of the ordinary altar. Shrines (and likewise altars) were sometimes the property of a private man of means, such as Micah.

The picture above shows the plan of two contiguous dwelling-houses excavated at Megiddo in a stratum dating to the reign of Solomon. In the south-western corner of the large building a chamber was found containing ritual objects. The position of these objects is shown in the enlarged diagram of the chamber at the bottom left of the page. At the bottom right there is a photograph of the objects themselves including altars, incense stands, bowls and goblets for ritual use.

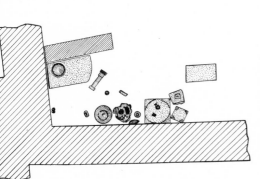

ᴀɴᴅ they named the city Dan, after the name of Dan their ancestor . . . (Judg. 18 : 29)

The pressure of the Amorites (Judg. 1 : 34) and later the inroads of the Philistines (see pp. 63, 98) endangered the position of the Danites in the territory allotted them in the coastal plain. They therefore set out to find for themselves a further portion beyond the areas already occupied by the other Israelite tribes, and conquered Laish at the northern end of the Jordan Valley. The site of Laish is at Tell el-Qadi, at the sources of the Jordan (see the view above). Laish was an ancient Canaanite city which was inhabited already in the Early Bronze Age (third millennium B.C.), as evidenced by potsherds found on the site. It is mentioned in the Egyptian execration texts from the beginning of the second millennium B.C., and then in the list of cities conquered by Thutmose III. After the Israelite conquest, its name was changed to Dan. The city stood on the highroad connecting the Lebanon and Damascus with the Jordan Valley and dominated well-watered and fertile lands. The Bible gives a vivid description of the city and its surroundings and of the inhabitants' confidence in their security: "When you go, you will come to an unsuspecting people. The land is broad . . . a place where there is no lack of anything that is in the earth" (Judg. 18 : 10). The natural advantages of Laish made it an administrative and religious centre also in the Israelite period. From the time of the Israelite conquest there was a shrine there; and it was in Dan that Jeroboam the son of Nebat set up one of the two golden calves that he had made (1 Kings 12 : 29). Dan was the northernmost settlement of importance in the area occupied by the Israelites. Hence the Bible frequently defines the extent of this area on the west side of the Jordan by the words "from Dan to Beersheba".

AND they turned aside here, to go in and spend he night at Gibeah. And he went there and sat down in the open square of the city . . .

(Judg. 19 : 15)

The Hebrew expression *rehob*, or *rehob ha-ir*, is sometimes used in the Bible to indicate the open space either inside or outside the city gateway, as in Neh. 8 : 1: "the square before the Water Gate". Hence the word *rehob* is used parallel with *shaar* (= gate), as in Job 29 : 7: "When I went out to the gate of the city, when I prepared my seat in the square". On account of the small size of most of the cities of ancient Israel, the density of their populations and the narrowness of the alleys, the gateways and squares were the focus of the city's public life (see p. 262; and also Vol. I, p. 96). As the city gates were always closed at night (see Josh. 2 : 5), strangers coming to the city after dusk were obliged to spend the night in the open space outside the gateway. The Levite, his concubine and his servant, who had turned aside to Gibeah in Benjamin for a night's lodging, thus had to sit in "the open square of the city" until the old man took them in.

Squares in front of the city gates have been excavated in various parts of Palestine, such as Megiddo and Tell en-Nasbe (possibly the site of Mizpah). To this day the walled cities of the East have squares in front of their gates which serve functions similar to those of biblical times.

Photographed here is the Damascus gate of the Old City of Jerusalem, showing a part of the paved square in front of it.

A<small>ND</small> when he entered his house, he took a knife, and laying hold of his concubine he divided her, limb by limb, into twelve pieces, and sent her throughout all the territory of Israel.

(Judg. 19 : 29)

In times of emergency, the Israelites were occasionally mustered for war by means of some tangible summons to arms, such as pieces of the body of a man or animal that were sent "throughout all the territory of Israel" (see 1 Sam. 11 : 5—8). So, when the Levite's concubine was murdered at Gibeah, he cut up her dead body in order to rouse the people to a punitive expedition against the Benjaminites who had killed her. General levies by such horrific means had been customary among the western Semitic tribes from olden times. In a letter from Mari — the western Semitic kingdom on the banks of the Middle Euphrates in the days of the Patriarchs — we read that, when the men of the tribe of Hana failed to report for military service five days after the appointed time, an official of the King of Mari advised his master to cut off the head of an imprisoned criminal and to send it through all their cities as a warning. (The letter is reproduced above).

The instrument with which the Levite cut up his concubine is called in Hebrew *maakheleth,* the same word as is used in the story of the sacrifice of Isaac (Gen. 22 : 10). This was apparently a special kind of knife used for the dismembering of sacrificial animals. From Canaanite representations it can be seen that such a knife was like the curved sword, with a single cutting edge on its convex side, that was used for smiting the enemy (see p. 33), the only difference being that the blade of the knife was a little straighter than of the sword. The lower illustration is a drawing of a cylinder seal impression from the Late Bronze Age discovered at Gezer, portraying the offering of a sacrifice. The man on the far left is holding a chopper which is apparently a *maakheleth.*

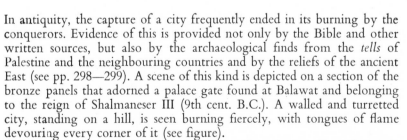

B<small>UT</small> when the signal began to rise out of the city in a column of smoke, the Benjaminites looked behind them; and behold, the whole of the city went up in smoke to heaven.

(Judg. 20 : 40)

In antiquity, the capture of a city frequently ended in its burning by the conquerors. Evidence of this is provided not only by the Bible and other written sources, but also by the archaeological finds from the *tells* of Palestine and the neighbouring countries and by the reliefs of the ancient East (see pp. 298—299). A scene of this kind is depicted on a section of the bronze panels that adorned a palace gate found at Balawat and belonging to the reign of Shalmaneser III (9th cent. B.C.). A walled and turretted city, standing on a hill, is seen burning fiercely, with tongues of flame devouring every corner of it (see figure).

Such was the fate of Gibeah in Benjamin when the Israelite tribes took retaliatory action against it for the murder of the Levite's concubine. As at the time of the conquest of Canaan under Joshua, so now the Israelites preferred a pitched battle in the open field to conquest by siege. By a feint retreat they drew the defenders of Gibeah outside the walls and away from the city. The Israelite forces lying hidden took the city by assault and set it on fire. When the pall of smoke that rose from the burning city showed the Israelites that it had been taken, the pursued turned and became the pursuers.

"AND watch; if the daughters of Shiloh come out
to dance in the dances . . ." (Judg. 21 : 21)

In biblical times, popular festivals were connected with the agricultural seasons, especially with the harvest and
grapegathering (Judg. 9 : 27; Isa. 16 : 9—10), and were celebrated with religious ceremony and boisterous
merrymaking. The dance of the daughters of Shiloh at the yearly festival of the Lord was also a popular celeb-
ration of this kind, even though it was performed at the central shrine of the tribe (see p. 113). Dancing is a
characteristic feature of ancient festivals; indeed, some scholars trace the original meaning of the Hebrew word
for "festival" *(hag)* to the root *hog* meaning "to go round in a circle", "to dance". In Israel, the dance was part
of popular celebrations and the priests took no part in it. Hence the dance of the daughters of Shiloh took place
in the vineyards outside the city. There the Benjaminites were able to carry off "wives according to their number"
(Judg. 21 : 23).
The picture is a reproduction of a wall-painting from the tomb of Antefoker of the Middle Kingdom in Egypt.
In it pairs of female dancers, dressed in short skirts and wearing ornaments round their necks, are performing
a dance. Three other women are clapping out the rhythm with their hands.

SAMUEL

NOW this man used to go up year by year from his city to worship and to sacrifice to the LORD of hosts at Shiloh . . .   (1 Sam. 1 : 3)

The Book of Joshua (18 : 1) relates that, after the conquest of Canaan, the Israelites set up the tent of meeting at Shiloh. Shortly before the establishment of the Israelite Kingdom, the sanctuary of Shiloh became the most important religious centre in Israel. The priests that officiated there were of the family of Eli. The tribes that occupied the centre of the country used to make the pilgrimage to Shiloh to offer up their sacrifices and celebrate their religious festivals there (Judg. 21 : 19). So did Elkanah of Ramathaim who went up to Shiloh every year accompanied by the members of his family "to offer to the Lord the yearly sacrifice and to pay his vow" (1 Sam. 1 : 21). Shiloh was presumably destroyed by the Philistines in the middle of the 11th cent. B.C., as a result of the Israelite defeat at the battle of Eben-Ezer (see p. 117). The destruction of the city at this time is also attested by archaeological evidence. However, some sort of settlement on the site must have survived into the period of the Kingdom, since the prophet Ahijah is called "the Shilonite" (1 Kings 11 : 29).

Shiloh stood in a fertile plain, 2000 ft. above sea level, near the main thoroughfare running along the central mountains "north of Bethel, on the east of the highway that goes up from Bethel to Shechem and south of Lebonah" (Judg. 21 : 19; see the map on p. 116). The remains of ancient Shiloh can be seen on the hill at the right of the photograph. The valley in the lower part of the picture is the Wadi Seilun which runs into the Yarkon close to Migdal Aphek.

Hannah came to the sanctuary at Shiloh to redeem her vow and, in a transport of joy at the granting of her prayer, poured out her heartfelt gratitude to the Lord. Her prayer is a hymn, or an individual song of thanksgiving. From the earliest times, it was customary in the House of the Lord for the offering of sacrifices to be accompanied by prayer (Deut. 26 : 1—11), especially when vows were being redeemed (Jonah 2 : 9). Hannah was thus following an established practice when she added her prayer to the sacrifice. She brought her son to Shiloh "along with a three-year-old bull, an ephah of flour, and a skin of wine" (1 Sam. 1 : 24), and together with this sacrifice she offered up a song of thanksgiving (1 Sam. 2 : 1—11).

Reproduced here is a stone statue in the Egyptian style of a woman on her knees presenting an offering with uplifted gaze. Her whole expression is one of reverent entreaty, while her lips seem to move in prayer. The statue was found in the obelisk temple at Gebal (Byblos) and is dated to the Late Bronze Age.

H ANNAH also prayed . . .
(1 Sam. 2 : 1)

THE custom of the priests with the people was that when any man offered sacrifice . . . the priest's servant would come and say to the man who was sacrificing, "Give meat for the priest to roast . . ."

(1 Sam. 2 : 13, 15)

The Law of Moses ordained that everyone who made a "peace-offering" (Heb. *zebah shelamim*) should put aside the breast and the right thigh of the animal sacrifice for the priest (see Vol. I , p. 185). The priests of Shiloh insolently extorted much more than this customary portion from those who came to sacrifice at their shrine. They would send their servants to carry off pieces of the sacrifice from "the pan, or kettle, or cauldron, or pot; all that the fork brought up". Moreover, what was still worse, the servants, in open defiance of the Law, would take the flesh while it was still raw, before the fat had been burnt, thus "treating the offering of the Lord with contempt". The situation described in this story is one of corruption and sin: "Thus the sin of the young men was very great in the sight of the Lord" (1 Sam. 2 : 17). In normal circumstances, the priests were content to receive their legal portion. Sacrificial laws of this kind were not confined to Israel, but were common throughout the ancient East. The illustration reproduces a relief from the temple of Ramses III at Medinet Habu (12th cent. B.C.— the period of the Judges), which portrays the slaughtering of animals and the setting aside of the portions reserved for the priests. As usual in Egyptian artistic representations, the sequence of events runs from the bottom to the top. In the bottom register, the animals, with wreaths round their necks, are being led to the slaughter; in the middle, they are being slaughtered to the accompaniment of burnt incense and the pouring of libations; while at the top, birds and animal limbs, including the thigh, are being presented to the priest in charge.

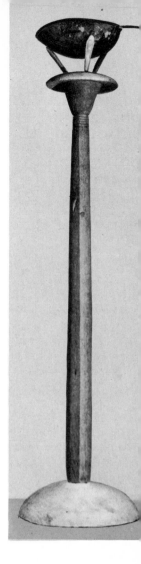

THE lamp of God had not yet gone out . . .

(1 Sam. 3 : 3)

The lamp (Heb. *ner*) mentioned here as one of the appurtenances of the House of God at Shiloh was apparently the popular name for the *menorah*, the tall stand on which lights were lit (Ex. 27 : 20; Lev. 24 : 2). The lighting of the *menorah*, first in the tabernacle in the wilderness and at Shiloh, and later in the Temple at Jerusalem, was considered a most significant act of worship (1 Kings 7 : 49; Jer. 52 : 19). It came to be associated with other similar acts, such as the offering up of incense and the laying out of the shew-bread.

The liturgical use of lamps was very common in antiquity, both in the Orient and elsewhere. The illustration at the top right shows a lampstand from the time of the Eighteenth Dynasty in Egypt. It consists of a bronze fire-bowl resting on a wooden stand in the form of a lotus-flower, with a stone base. On the left is a section from a wall-painting in the tomb of Amenemonet (Nineteenth Dynasty), at Deir el-Medineh in Egypt, showing fire in a fire-bowl.

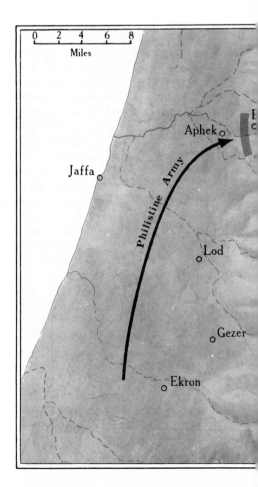

Now Israel went out to battle against the Philistines; they encamped at Eben-Ezer and the Philistines encamped at Aphek. (1 Sam. 4 : 1)

The battle of Eben-Ezer (approximately in the middle of the 11th cent. B.C.) was fought by the Israelite tribes in an attempt to check the expansion of the Philistines into the central mountains of Palestine. The enemy had successfully forced their way along the coastal plain and into the mountains of Judah, and had gained the approaches to the mountains of Ephraim. The Philistine army was drawn up for battle at Aphek, which was situated on the north-eastern edge of the area controlled by them. The site of Aphek is to be found in the large mound of Rosh ha-Ayin (in Arabic Ras el-Ein), at the source of the Yarkon. The Israelites, for their part, encamped by Eben-Ezer, the exact site of which has not been located. It must have been opposite Aphek in the foothills of Ephraim, near the modern Migdal Aphek (see the map). The battle resulted in a decisive victory for the Philistines who captured the ark of the Covenant from the Israelites (1 Sam. 4 : 11). This victory gave the Philistines free access to the mountains of Ephraim, so that they were able to conquer the key-places of the region, among them, apparently, Shiloh itself (see p. 113). Their control of this region lasted till the time of Saul.

Seen in the photograph here is the site of Migdal Aphek (Arabic Majdal Yaba) standing on a hill dominating the Shiloh Valley (Wadi Deir Ballut), which runs to the south of it. In the foreground is the level expanse of the Aphek gap, assumed to have been the scene of the battle against the Philistines.

117

So they sent and gathered together all the lords of the Philistines...
(1 Sam. 5 : 8)

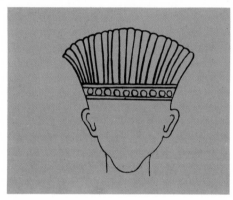

The Philistine title *seren* (here translated "lord") may be related to the Greek *tyrannos*, since it is known that the Philistines came from the Aegean islands. The five Philistine lords of Gaza, Ashkelon, Ashdod, Ekron and Gath were essentially military leaders (cf. 1 Sam. 29 : 2). The appearance of such Philistine warriors is known from Egyptian reliefs, and also from anthropoid coffins discovered at Lachish, Tell el-Farah and Beth-Shan.

One such coffin from Beth-Shan is reproduced on the left. It is a pottery cylinder into which the body was inserted through an opening at the top. The opening was then closed by a cover. The head adornments of these covers are of special interest. They consist of horizontal bands embellished with a row of circular bosses (see the top row), occasionally with additional vertical bands (see the first two heads from the right) recalling the characteristic Philistine feathered head-dress. The drawings in the bottom row follow representations of the Sea Peoples in the reliefs of Ramses III (see pp. 120—121) and the coffin-covers described above. Differences in ornamentation might indicate military ranks or kin affiliations.

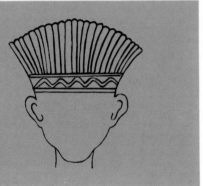

"So you must make images of your tumours images of your mice that ravage the land ..."

(1 Sam. 6 : 5)

Scripture relates that the Philistines intended to send a guilt-offering to the God of Israel (1 Sam. 6 : 3—4, 8, 17) to atone for the desecration of the ark, for which God had brought a plague upon them. The guilt-offering was in the form of gold images of *apholim* — a Hebrew word which seems to mean running sores — and of mice, the gold being a substitute for a sacrifice. According to the Law of Moses, the guilt-offering in Israel was usually the sacrifice of an animal — a ram or a sheep. Yet, for all that, in the reign of Joash also "money from the guilt-offerings and money from the sin-offerings" is mentioned (2 Kings 12 : 16). It would appear that the Philistines intended to work magic by casting the gold of the "guilt-offering" in the form of tumours and mice. By sending these images beyond their frontiers they presumably sought to prevail upon the forces responsible for the plagues to leave their land also.

Images of mice from various periods, some of which may have been made for use in ritual magic, have been found in excavations in the Middle East. Reproduced here is an alabaster image of a mouse from the Middle Bronze Age. It was found in the obelisk temple at Gebal (Byblos) and apparently had some ritual significance.

"NOW then, take and prepare a new cart and two milch cows upon which there has never come a yoke, and yoke the cows to the cart..." (1 Sam. 6 : 7)

Seven months after the Philistines had captured the ark of the Lord, their rulers decided to return it to its rightful place in a new, unused cart (cf. 2 Sam. 6 : 3). This cart was to be drawn by two cows "upon which there has never come a yoke", such animals being particularly suitable for use in sacred rites.

The upper figure is reproduced from a relief portraying the war of Ramses III against the Sea Peoples (see p. 98). In it are seen the types of carts characteristic of these peoples which included the Philistines. The tops of the carts are made of crossed wooden bars, primarily designed for the transport of agricultural produce. The wheels are all of the solid wooden type found to this day in Asia Minor and among the Circassians of Trans-Jordan. In place of the two cows mentioned in our verse, each of the carts in the relief is drawn by four animals.

So the Philistines were subdued...
(1 Sam. 7 : 13)

In the long-drawn struggle waged in Samuel's lifetime between the Israelites and the Philistines, the latter usually had the upper hand. But at the battle of Mizpah the Philistines were for once routed and subdued by the Israelites. The Bible glorifies this victory over the Philistines, who were renowned warriors and feared even by the Egyptians.

The records of Ramses III (12th cent. B.C.) frequently refer to his wars against the Sea Peoples (i.e. the Philistines and kindred nations). His victory over them is depicted on the reliefs of his temple at Medinet Habu. The detail of one of these reliefs reproduced below shows eight Philistine captives wearing their feathered headdress (see p. 118, and also Vol I, p. 38). Their short garment with points and tassels is typical of the peoples of Syria, the Sea Peoples and other northerners. The first three captives are bound neck to neck by a rope. The rest have their hands tied in various ways: across the chest (the fourth and eighth from the left), over the head (the sixth), and behind the back (the fifth and seventh).

SAMUEL judged Israel all the days of his life. And he went on a circuit year by year to Bethel, Gilgal, and Mizpah . . . Then he would come back to Ramah . . . (1 Sam. 7 : 15-17)

The prophet Samuel embodies in his own person the transition in Israel from one form of national leadership to another. He is both the last of the judges and the anointer of the first king to rule over Israel. Like Moses during the wandering in the wilderness, Samuel's pre-eminence expresses itself in various ways: he is the prophet of his generation, the judge of his people, and its leader and saviour in time of war. His residence was at Ramah (the modern er-Ram) in the centre of the territory of Benjamin. As God's emissary he made the circuit of the country, holding court in the holy cities in its central parts: Bethel (the modern Beitin), Gilgal (east of Jericho), and Mizpah (apparently Tell en-Nasbeh to the north of Jerusalem). The sanctity of Bethel goes back to Patriarchal tradition (Gen. 28 : 10—22; 35 : 1—15). At a later time it was "the king's sanctuary . . . and temple of the kingdom" of Ephraim (Amos 7 : 13). Gilgal, which was hallowed in the time of Joshua, is mentioned together with Bethel as a famous holy place (Amos 4 : 4). The sanctity of Mizpah is first referred to in the period of the Judges (Judg. 20 : 1—11); it was there that the Israelite tribes assembled before their war against Benjamin.
The view above shows part of the area of Samuel's jurisdiction in the vicinity of the Arab village of Beit Iksa which is close to the ancient border of Benjamin. On the horizon is seen Nebi Samwil, the traditional burial-place of the prophet.

HE said, "These will be the ways of the king who will reign over you: he will take your sons and appoint them to his chariots . . . and to make his implements of war and the equipment of his chariots. He will take your daughters to be perfumers and cooks and bakers."

(1 Sam. 8 : 11–13)

Finding that a loose confederacy of tribes could not withstand the united Philistine forces, the Israelites resolved to set a king over themselves. Their elders demanded of Samuel that he anoint a ruler to govern them "like all the nations" (1 Sam. 8 : 5, 20). In an attempt to deter them, the prophet drew a vivid picture of four of the exactions that such a king would enforce: the drafting of his subjects for military service and the manufacture of arms; the employment of men and women as forced labour in the fields and in the palace; the tithing of agricultural produce and of cattle; and the expropriation of private property for the benefit of those in authority. This description of royal rule reflects the practices that had been followed in the Canaanite kingdoms for centuries, as for example in a document from Ugarit (p. 123 below) from the reign of Ammistamru II (13th cent. B.C.). It states that the king could raise any one of his slaves to the rank of *maryannu*, i.e. the chariot-owning aristocracy; could levy taxes, including a tithe on the produce of the soil and a tax on flocks; could put men to work in his fields; could transfer landed property, and even property in an entire city, from one owner to another.

The exactions demanded by the king can be illustrated from the art of the ancient East. A wall-painting from the tomb of Hapu at Thebes from the end of the Eighteenth Dynasty (top of p. 122) shows the construction of a chariot and its appurtenances. At the right of the upper register a workman is stretching a piece of leather over a wooden block. In front of him lie shields already covered with leather. In the centre a workman is finishing a chariot-wheel. Behind him yet another is busy cutting strips of leather while a third covers a quiver with them. At the left of the bottom register a chariot-frame stands ready, with parts of the harness hanging from its shafts and a quiver fastened to its side. The manufacture of bows and arrows is depicted too in a painting from Thebes on the wall of the tomb of Menkheperreseneb from the reign of Thutmose III (see the middle of p. 122). Second from the left a workman is bending a wooden stick over his knee into the form of a bow. Behind him another man is working on the bow-shaped stick. At the right a workman examines the straightness of a finished arrow, while opposite him another is drawing a finished bow to test its elasticity.

The work of the perfumers is illustrated by a Late Egyptian stele (reproduced in part below, pp. 122—123). It shows women gathering lotus-flowers and bringing them in baskets to a press where two other women are squeezing out the juices of the flowers into a large jar.

THEY met young maidens coming out to draw water . . .　　　　(1 Sam. 9 : 11)

In antiquity, most of the settlements in Palestine were situated near to a source of water, but were built for security reasons on a hill or eminence. Such a well or spring was normally outside the wall of the city at the foot of the hill (see p. 202), and was sometimes connected with it by steps cut in the rock (see p. 291). Such steps are perhaps referred to in the story of Saul and his servants who climbed "up the hill to the city" of Ramah to seek the seer's counsel (1 Sam. 9: 11). On their way, they met maidens going down to the spring to draw water, as was customary for women in the Orient. In just the same way, Eliezer, the servant of Abraham, met Rebecca at the well (Gen. 24 : 11 ff.); Jacob, too, saw Rachel first beside the well (Gen. 29: 9—12). As a focal point of the life of every village, the well became associated with various customs and traditions to which reference is made in the Bible (see Vol. I, p. 222). It served as a meeting place for women, shepherds and travellers. To this day, the women of the Palestinian villages go out to fetch water from the well, carrying it home on their heads in large clay jars (see the picture).

So the cook took up the leg and the upper portion and set them before Saul . . .

(1 Sam. 9 : 24)

It so happened that, on the day when Saul came to see Samuel at Ramah, a public sacrifice was being offered on the high place (1 Sam. 9 : 12). There were present a small number of special guests, "about thirty persons" (1 Sam. 9 : 22), who had gathered in the hall next to the high place. This gathering of the leaders of the people apparently served as a preliminary to the anointing of Saul at Mizpah (1 Sam. 10 : 17—25). Similarly, when Absalom (2 Sam. 15 : 11—12) and Adonijah the son of Haggith (1 Kings 1 : 9, 25, 41, 49) sought to usurp the throne, they held sacrificial feasts for this purpose: they invited only a small group of guests chosen from the notables and princes of the people. As a sign of honour, Samuel placed Saul and his servant at the head of those present. For the same reason, he also ordered the cook to put before Saul "the leg and the upper portion" or "the tail", according to an emendation of the Hebrew text which is alluded to already in the Babylonian Talmud (Abodah Zarah 25a). The leg was considered to be the choicest part of the animal's flesh; hence the right leg and the "tail" were put aside for the priest (Ex. 29 : 22; see above p. 115, and Vol. I, p. 185).

The leg of an animal often features prominently in Egyptian representations of sacrificial feasts and banquets. Reproduced here is a section of a burial stele from the Middle Kingdom, showing the deceased's attendants serving their master and his wife with various delicacies, including the leg of an animal.

THEN Samuel took a vial of oil . . .   (1 Sam. 10 : 1)

Before Saul was presented to the people who acclaimed him as their ruler
at Mizpah (1 Sam. 10 : 17—26), Samuel, at God's command, privately
anointed him king over Israel. In Israel, as in other ancient nations, it was
customary to dedicate persons or objects to sacred use by anointing them
with oil. Thus, Jacob poured oil over the stone at Bethel, thereby sanctifying
it as the foundation of the house of God (Gen. 28 : 18—22). Moses hallowed
both the appurtenances of the tabernacle and Aaron the high priest with
the anointing oil (Lev. 8 : 10—12; cf. Ex. 30 : 25—30). The Canaanites
and Egyptians, as well as the Israelites, used to anoint their kings. In Israel,
by virtue of this anointing, the king was called "the Lord's anointed"
(1 Sam. 24 : 6; 2 Sam. 19 : 21, and elsewhere).

In contrast to the usual practice of anointing by pouring the oil from a horn
(see p. 135), Samuel anointed Saul from "a vial of oil". In the same way,
Jehu was anointed by the prophet Elisha's emissary from "a vial of oil"
(2 Kings 9 : 1). The picture shows a small oil-jug of the type common in
the Iron Age.

THREE men going up to God at Bethel will meet you there, one carrying three kids, another carrying three loaves of bread, and another carrying a skin of wine. (1 Sam. 10 : 3)

In Israel, an offering usually comprised three items: an animal for sacrifice, fine flour for a meal-offering and wine for a drink-offering (Nu. 15 : 1—12). Thus, when Hannah had weaned Samuel, she took him up to the house of the Lord at Shiloh "along with a three-year old bull" (for the sacrifice or burnt-offering) "an ephah of flour" (for the meal-offering) "and a skin of wine" (for the drink-offering; 1 Sam. 1 : 24). Similarly, the three men "going up to God at Bethel", who were to meet Saul on his way, also carried a comprehensive offering of this kind. These three items — meat, cereal (wheat or barley) and wine — also formed the components of the sacrifice that was offered up "on the table" of God.

In antiquity, sacrifice was generally regarded as a feast of honour before the god. A ritually prepared meal of this kind is portrayed on the two long sides of the sarcophagus of Ahiram King of Gebal (Byblos; apparently from the 10th cent. B.C.). These show a line of men and women presenting gifts to a figure seated on a royal throne, who may be king Ahiram (cf. p. 143) or possibly a god. Reproduced here is the rear side of the sarcophagus, showing the presentation of the offering, in the following sequence: first come two women carrying on their heads baskets containing what may be loaves of bread; they are followed by two men carrying on their shoulders jars or skins which presumably contain wine; after them comes another man leading a ram which is the animal-sacrifice; and the line ends with three men who have their hands raised in prayer. The whole picture thus illustrates the three typical components of a complete sacrifice and festive meal.

THEN Nahash the Ammonite went up and besieged Yabesh-Gilead . . .   (1 Sam. 11 : 1)

When Nahash the Ammonite king attacked Yabesh-Gilead east of the Jordan, the inhabitants of the city appealed for help to their fellow-Israelites on the western side of the river. Saul hastened to their aid, took the Ammonites by surprise and routed them (1 Sam. 11 : 1—11). The people of Yabesh remembered their debt to Saul and showed their gratitude to him when, after his death, they took down his body and the bodies of his sons, under the cover of night, from the walls of Beth-Shan, where they had been impaled by the Philistines (see pp. 158—159). It is very likely that the people of Yabesh were closely related to the tribe of Benjamin to which Saul belonged. They alone took no part in the punitive attack of the other tribes on Benjamin after the affair of the concubine at Gibeah; and it was their daughters who were given as wives to the surviving Benjaminites (Judg. 21). The story of Saul's attack on the Ammonites suggests that Yabesh-Gilead was about one night's march from Bezek in the mountains of western Palestine, where Saul mustered his army (1 Sam. 11 :8—12). It was also near enough to Beth-Shan for its inhabitants to travel there and back again in a single night (1 Sam. 31 : 11—13). Presumably, therefore, it was near Wadi Yabis in Gilead. It may have been at Tell el-Maqlub, or on the double mound close to it, Tell el-Meqbereh — Tell Abu Kharaz, which rises to the north of the point where Wadi Yabis runs into the Jordan depression.

The illustration shows a view of the landscape south of Wadi Yabis.

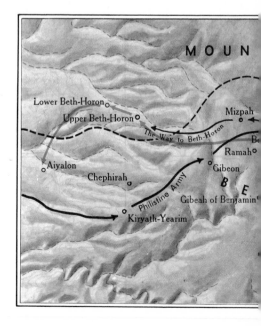

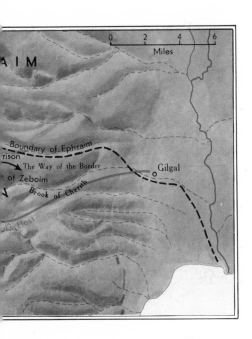

Aₙᴅ Saul, and Jonathan his son, and the people
who were present with them, stayed in Gibeah of
Benjamin; but the Philistines encamped in Michmash. And raiders came out of the camp of the
Philistines in three companies . . .

(1 Sam. 13 : 16-17)

The primary task for which Saul was chosen king was to fight
the Philistines. After the battle of Eben-Ezer (see p. 117) and
the destruction of Shiloh, the Philistines had penetrated deeply
into the heart of the Israelite territory up to the main centres
of Judah, Benjamin, and Ephraim. To check their advance, Saul
disposed his forces at three key-points in the mountains: at
Bethel and Michmash under his own command, and at Gibeah
of Benjamin under the command of Jonathan, his son (1 Sam.
13 : 2). Jonathan attacked first and succeeded in routing the
Philistine garrison at Gibeah. The Philistines reacted by sending
out a punitive expedition ("the raiders") against the centre
of the Israelite battle-line at Michmash, while Saul with six
hundred of his men entrenched himself at Gibeah of Benjamin
(1 Sam. 13 : 15). The Philistines split their forces into three
columns which advanced north, west, and east. Now was the
moment for Saul to act. After Jonathan's daring sally (see p.
132), he suddenly fell upon and defeated the main body of the
Philistines which was still at Michmash and consisted partly of
Hebrew mercenaries. After Saul's victory, many of these
mercenaries came over to his side (1 Sam. 14 : 21) and joined
his troops in the pursuit of the Philistines who fled westwards
past Aiyalon (1 Sam. 14 : 31). The course of the battle is
marked on the map.
The view above is of Tell Michmash, near modern Mukhmas,
about seven miles north-east of Jerusalem.

NOW there was no smith to be found throughout all the land of Israel; for the Philistines said, "Lest the Hebrews make themselves swords or spears"; but every one of the Israelites went down to the Philistines to sharpen his ploughshare, his mattock, his axe . . . and the charge was a pim for the ploughshares and for the mattocks . . .   (1 Sam. 13 : 19-21)

Wrought iron, its malleability, and various methods of working it, were known in the ancient East as early as the second half of the second millennium B.C. and probably before it. The Iron Age proper in the ancient East and in Canaan began, however, with the spread of a harder kind of iron obtained by the carbonisation of wrought iron. There are grounds for supposing that it was the Philistines who introduced the use of this hardened iron. There is archaeological evidence of the manufacture of such iron implements in Philistia and the Shephelah. The verses quoted above indicate that, in the time of Saul, iron implements were already used by Israelite farmers. The Philistines supplied the Israelites with finished iron implements, but jealously guarded the secrets of the working of the metal and the methods by which the implements were made and sharpened. The Israelite peasant. who had purchased his implements ready-made from the Philistines, was thus always dependent on the Philistine smiths whenever their implements needed sharpening or repairing. The Scripture describes how the Philistines charged the Israelite peasant one *pim* for the sharpening of each of his agricultural implements. The *pim* was a weight of approximately 7.5 grm. with a monetary value of about two thirds of a *shekel*.

On p. 131 below is the reproduction of a weight from Lachish with its standard written on it in the ancient Hebrew script. At the top of this page is shown an iron implement for agricultural use (possibly a ploughshare) from Tell Jemmeh, belonging to the period of the United Israelite Kingdom. On p. 130 are shown from left to right : an iron sickle, from Tell Jemmeh, an axe, and a spearhead.

ONE day Jonathan the son of Saul said to the young man who bore his armour, "Come let us go over to the Philistine garrison..." (1 Sam. 14 : 1)

Saul's son Jonathan, on his own initiative, made a sortie into the camp of the Philistines at Michmash, supported by his armour-bearer who "killed them after him" (1 Sam. 14 : 13—14). The function of the armour-bearer depended on the nature of ancient warfare. The limitations of the weapons of antiquity, each with its different range, obliged the individual warrior to equip himself with all the weapons that he was likely to need in the varying phases of the combat: the bow — for long-range fighting; the javelin — for medium range; and the spear and sword for hand-to-hand combat. Hence, warriors of the upper class took with them men who carried these weapons and handed them to their master, according to the requirements of the battle. The armour-bearer accompanied the warrior in assaults on the enemy, served him loyally and obeyed his orders in battle. In the words of Jonathan's servant: "Do all that your mind inclines to; behold, I am with you, as is your mind so is mine" (1 Sam. 14 : 7). The armour-bearer did not desert his master in time of peril; and sometimes even death did not separate them, as was the case with Saul's armour-bearer who fell on his own sword after his master's death "and died with him" (1 Sam. 31 : 5).

Shown here is a relief of the armour-bearer of the king of Carchemish on one of the panels which adorned the royal palace (9th or 8th cent. B.C.). In his right hand he holds a javelin and in his left a club, while a sword is buckled to his waist.

Saul's war against the Amalekites provides us with a glimpse of Israel's struggle with the tribes of desert raiders in the south of the country in the early days of the monarchy. This victory of Saul's may be hinted at in the prophecy of Balaam: "His king shall be higher than Agag, and his kingdom shall be exalted" (Nu. 24 : 7). Samuel's demand that the Amelekites be destroyed utterly emphasizes the religious character of the war and its connection with the Amalekite attacks on the Israelites during their wandering in the wilderness (1 Sam. 15 : 2—3; Deut. 25 : 17—19; Vol. I, p. 150). Samuel himself, therefore, completed what Saul had left undone and with his own hands hewed Agag, the Amalekite king, in pieces in the presence of the elders of the people and the whole congregation, "before the Lord, in Gilgal".

This ceremonial hewing in pieces of a conquered enemy as a symbol of his utter defeat was a common practice with ancient kings. Such a scene is depicted on the magnificent ceremonial axe of the Pharaoh Ahmose (16th cent. B.C.), which was found at Thebes. The axe-blade (reproduced above) is made of bronze and gold. Under the name of the Pharaoh, there is a representation of his victory over one of his enemies. Ahmose is seen grasping his enemy by the hair with his left hand, while he hews him in pieces with the sword in his right. The axe, with its narrow, elongated blade, is typical of the axes of this period. The blade was designed to hack its way through the coat of mail and metal helmet which were already worn by the soldiers of the ancient East in the second millennium B.C.

A**ND** Saul went up to his house in Gibeah
of Saul.   (1 Sam. 15 : 34)

Gibeah of Saul, also called Gibeah of Benjamin or simply Gibeah, was the chief city of the tribe of Benjamin
and the capital of the Israelite kingdom in the time of Saul. Its site is the modern Tell el-Ful, almost three miles
north of Jerusalem on the road to Ramallah. It lay in the heart of the territory of Benjamin on a height (Heb.
gibe'ah) 2500 ft. above sea-level at the meeting-place of four main highways running to the four points of the
compass: northwards to Bethel and Shechem; southwards to Jerusalem and Hebron; westwards, to Gibeon,
Beth-Horon and the coastal plain; and eastwards, along Wadi Kuzeibeh, to Jericho, Rabbath-Ammon and
Gilead. The excavations carried out at Tell el-Ful have revealed that the site was first occupied about 1200
B.C. (the early part of the period of the Judges) and that the city was destroyed a few generations later, presumably in the Israelites' punitive attack on Benjamin (Judg. ch. 20; cf. p. 109). The new city built on the ruins
of the old was more developed and better fortified than its predecessor. The citadel built on the top of the height
was occupied by a Philistine garrison in Saul's day (see p. 129) and, after its capture by the Israelites, became
the king's residence. After the division of the kingdom, Gibeah was in the territory of Judah. King Asa fortified
the town as a strong-point to defend the northern approaches of Jerusalem (1 Kings 15 : 22), where "Geba"
is apparently an alternative form of "Gibeah".
The picture shows the remains of the citadel at Gibeah of Saul, which goes back to the early days of the monarchy.
At the bottom right there is a plan of the citadel reconstructed from the remains of a tower and wall discovered
in the excavation (indicated by full black lines). The citadel had a double casemate wall with towers at its corners.

T HEN Samuel took the horn of oil,
and anointed him . . .   (1 Sam. 16 : 13)

There are two references in the Bible to anointing from a horn (Heb. *qeren*) of oil, and two others to anointing from a vial (Heb. *pakh*) of oil. Samuel anointed David and Zadok anointed Solomon (1 Kings 1 : 39) from a horn of oil, while Saul and Jehu were anointed from a vial (see also p. 126). It seems probable that these two types of vessel were used in much the same way and differed only in the material of which they were made. The vial was a clay vessel, whereas the horn was usually made of a ram's horn. Particularly valuable and exquisite horns were made of ivory, like the ivory tusks listed amongst the imports of Tyre (Ez. 27 : 15). The anointing horn was filled with oil (1 Sam. 15 : 1) at its wide end which was closed with a cover. For anointing, the horn was held with its pointed end downwards; the oil dripped through a hole pierced in this end on to the head of the person being anointed.

The picture on the right is of an ornamented ivory oil-horn, from the Late Bronze Age, which was found at Megiddo. The hole for the oil to drip through is specially adorned. In the picture on the left a man is holding a horn of the same shape as the one on the left. He is a Canaanite notable, walking in a procession of people who are presenting offerings to the king of Egypt. (Part of a wall-painting which is reproduced in its entirety in Vol. I, p. 110.)

A MAN who is skilful in playing the lyre . . . (1 Sam. 16 : 16)

David the shepherd was brought to calm Saul's troubled spirit by playing the lyre to him. In the opinion of the ancients, music had a healing effect on the soul of man. The playing of musical instruments, especially the lyre, was a common accomplishment among the shepherds of Palestine, as it was throughout the East. A Philistine jar from the 11th cent. B.C., which was found in fragments at Megiddo, has a red and black decoration which depicts a man walking among animals and playing on a stringed instrument (see the figure below).

The ancient lyre, which was a plucked instrument, consisted of a flat sounding-box with two curved arms of unequal length joined by a slanting cross-piece. The strings, usually four in number, were stretched from the sounding-box to the cross-piece (see the illustration). Being of different thicknesses, they could be made to produce a variety of notes. They were adjusted by means of special knots tied round the cross-piece. It is almost certain that their tuning was pentatonic, i.e. based on a scale of five tones.

NOW the Philistines gathered their armies for battle . . . and encamped between Socoh and Azekah, in Ephes-Dammim. And Saul and the men of Israel were gathered, and encamped in the valley of Elah . . .   (1 Sam. 17 : 1-2)

Saul's first campaign against the Philistines had been fought mainly in the territory of Ephraim and ended in the liberation of the mountains of Ephraim (see p. 129). Now the Philistines mustered their hosts to attack the mountains of Judah. To this end, they advanced as far as the Valley of Elah and camped between Socoh and Azekah. The Valley of Elah was of great strategic importance, since through it access could be gained to Hebron, Bethlehem, and the whole hilly region of Judah. The two armies were drawn up for battle facing each other on either side of the valley (1 Sam. 17 : 3).

The view shows the Valley of Elah near the modern settlement of Netiv ha-Lamed-He. Its name commemorates perhaps the numerous terebinth trees (Heb. *elah*) which once grew there. Socoh (to-day Khirbet Abbad), one of the cities of the Judaean Shephelah, lay to the south of the Valley of Elah. Its ancient name is preserved in Khirbet esh-Shuweikeh, close to Khirbet Abbad. Azekah (Tell Zakariyeh) is also situated south of the valley, west-north-west of Socoh. The site of the Philistine camp — Ephes-Dammim (Pas-Dammim in 1 Chron. 11 :13)— is unknown.

AND there came out from the camp of the
Philistines a champion . . . .   (1 Sam. 17 : 4)

The story of David's fight with Goliath extols the heroism
of the son of Jesse who slew a gigantic Philistine warrior whose
stature and arms (see p. 139) had struck terror into the poorly
equipped Israelites. The Bible mentions other single combats,
such as that fought by the men of Joab and Abner (see p. 165)
and that of David's heroes (2 Sam. 21 : 16—22; 23 : 21). This
form of duel was a particularly common feature of the wars
of the Aegean peoples, including the Philistines. In such combats, the two sides agreed in advance that the war should be
decided by the outcome of a single duel between their champions.
Reproduced above is a Rhodian painting on the inside of a
plate (end of the 6th cent. B.C.) portraying a Greek warrior
whose armament is very similar to that of Goliath.

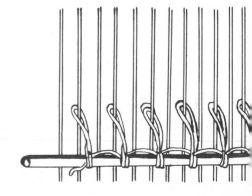

AND he was armed with a coat of mail... And he had greaves of bronze upon his legs, and a javelin of bronze slung between his shoulders. And the shaft of his spear was like a weaver's beam...

(1 Sam. 17 : 5-7)

Goliath's armament was that of a typical Aegean warrior: spear and javelin, bronze helmet, a coat of mail, and bronze greaves to protect the legs. The manufacture of the coat called for great technical skill, for it had to satisfy three requirements: a) proper protection; b) light weight; c) freedom of movement (see p. 249). The upper plate shows part of the coat of mail of Pharaoh Shishak (middle of tenth cent. B.C.).

The Bible gives a particularly detailed description of Goliath's spear, the like of which had never been seen before in Israel; the iron head of the spear was a completely new departure in in weapons. The Bible compares the spear to a weaver's "beam" (leash rod). This was a piece of wood separating the threads of the warp so that the threads of the woof could be passed between them (see the bottom figure). A characteristic feature of the rod were the loops of cord which were tied to it (see the diagram at the bottom of p. 138). The typical Aegean javelin (see middle figure, p. 139) likewise had on it a loop by means of which it could be thrown to a great distance. The warrior on p. 138 has his whole body tensed for throwing the javelin, with his fingers inserted in the loop. This type of a javelin was called by the Greeks: "loop"

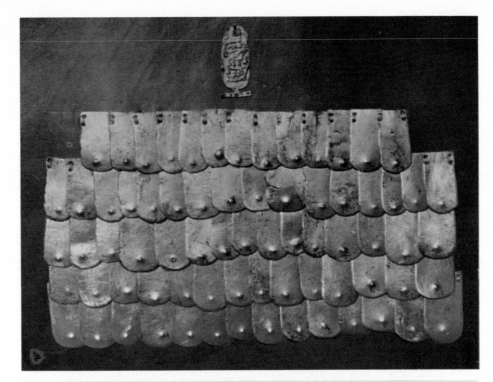

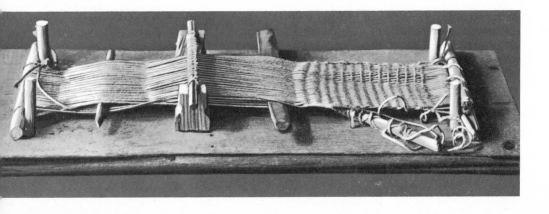

The youthful David stood his ground fearlessly as the Philistine giant advanced upon him (1 Sam. 17 : 41), even though his whole equipment consisted only of a staff, a sling and five smooth stones (1 Sam. 17 : 40). For a long time the sling had been a weapon used by individual warriors, and also by shepherds and hunters. In the 8th cent. B.C., the slingsmen of the Assyrian army (especially in the reign of Sennacherib) were organized in regular units that fought alongside the bowmen (see pp. 286—287).

The sling was composed of three parts: the sling-strap, made of leather or cloth; two thongs to impart momentum to the strap; and the sling-stones. One of the orthostats in the royal palace at Gozan (Tell Halaf), from the 10th or 9th cent. B.C. (i.e. the time of David or Solomon) gives a very good idea of how the sling was used (see the reproduction). After placing the stone in the strap, the soldier holds it firm in his left hand, while with his right he stretches the free ends of the thongs above his head. Then he whirls the sling in his right hand with the ends of the thongs forming the pivot of the movement. When the required momentum has been attained, he releases the end of one of the thongs, thus freeing the sling-stone from the strap.

AND David put his hand in his bag and took out a stone, and slung it . . .

(1 Sam. 17 : 49)

THE women came out of all the cities of Israel, singing and dancing, to meet King Saul, with timbrels, with songs of joy, and with instruments of music. (1 Sam. 18 : 6)

From the earliest times it was customary for women to welcome the commanders of the army on their victorious homecoming from the field of battle, as Jephthah's daughter welcomed her father after his victory over the Ammonites (see p. 96; cf. Ex. 15 : 20—21). This custom is also implied in David's lament over the death of Saul and Jonathan in the battle of Gilboa: "Lest the daughters of the Philistines rejoice, lest the daughters of the uncircumcised exult" (2 Sam. 1 : 20). Hence, after Saul's victory over the Philistines, the women of Israel went out to meet Saul and David with joyous dances and paeans of praise: "Saul has slain his thousands, And David his ten thousands" (1 Sam. 18 : 7).

A picture of women greeting a distinguished dignitary was found in the grave of Neferhotep at Thebes from the time of the Nineteenth Dynasty (see the reproduction). There Neferhotep, "chief scribe of the god Amon, superintendent of the oxen and heifers of Amon", is seen seated in all his glory in his chariot which is drawn by two horses and driven by a charioteer. A negro (or a member of some other southern dark-skinned race) runs before the chariot to clear the way. Behind the chariot there are two young men who are holding in their hands long staves to keep back passers-by. Women and children are advancing towards the scribe singing, dancing and beating the timbrel. The women's legs can be seen moving in dance through their transparent garments. Two of them are beating on round timbrels and two others on square ones.

"AND I will shoot three arrows to the side of it, as though I shot at a mark." (1 Sam. 20 : 20)

Jonathan was able to communicate with David without arousing suspicion by means of target-practice with arrows and according to a previously agreed system of signs. If Jonathan shouted to his servant, "Look, the arrows are on this side of you," that was a sign to David that he should come, since he was in no danger. But if Jonathan shouted, "Look, the arrows are beyond you," then David was to flee for his life (1 Sam. 20 : 20—24, 35—40).

Marksmanship was a popular sport throughout the ancient world, and apparently in Israel too, especially with kings and notables. Since shooting with the composite bow (see Vol. I, p. 64) called for intensive training, special practice ranges were established. Egyptian paintings and Assyrian reliefs show that sometimes each bow-man on the range shot three successive arrows, exactly as Jonathan did. The target was set up on a post specially made for the purpose and was either oblong (see p. 161), or round, as in the relief discovered at Dur-Sharruken (Khorsabad) in the palace of the Assyrian king Sargon II (721—705 B.C.; see the reproduction). The relief shows an Assyrian youth shooting at a target. Behind him stands his groom. The target has been set up in a forest of conifers which serves as the range. It is amazingly similar to modern targets, with its concentric circles divided into segments by lines radiating outwards from the bull.

THE king sat upon his seat, as at other times . . .   (1 Sam. 20 : 25)

Saul's rule naturally gave rise to the beginnings of a royal etiquette, even though there was not yet any proper royal court and the unsophisticated simplicity of the period of the Judges still lingered on. On festive days, when the king dined in the company of his courtiers and attendants, he would sit on a special seat reserved for him. In those days, the usual custom was to sit on the floor or recline on cushions. It was rare for anyone to sit either on a seat with both back and arms, or on a chair with only a back, or even on a stool which had no back. Such a privilege was reserved for lords and nobles; and only those who sat on chairs ate from a table. Hence, in most of the passages in the Bible where a table is mentioned for other than ritual purposes, it is intended for a king or notable (Judg. 1 : 7; 2 Sam. 9 : 7—13; 1 Kings 10 : 5; and see p. 259).
The detail of a relief reproduced above is from the sarcophagus of Ahiram, king of Gebal (Byblos; probably from the 10th cent. B.C., roughly contemporary with Saul). It shows the king (or a god) seated on his chair, with a stool beneath his feet and a table laden with food before him. The side of the chair is in the form of a winged cherub with the body of a lion and the head of a woman. The king is holding a lotus-flower in his left hand and a cup in his right. Opposite him stands his servant who is keeping the flies off the food of his royal master.

THEN came David to Nob to Ahimelech the priest . . .　　(1 Sam. 21 : 1)

From various indications in these verses it is clear that there was a shrine in the small city of Nob, to which David came in his flight from Saul. Mention is made here of two of the ritual objects to be found in a shrine: holy bread, i.e. the shewbread (1 Sam. 21 : 5, 7). and an ephod (ibid. 9). The service of the shrine was performed by a family of priests, headed by Ahimelech the son of Ahitub, one of the descendants of Eli (cf. 1 Sam. 14 : 3). They had apparently found their way to Nob after the destruction of Shiloh at the end of the period of the Judges (see p. 113). The number of priests at Nob was considerable — "eighty-five persons who wore the linen ephod" (1 Sam. 22 : 18) — so that the place was called "the city of the priests" (ibid. 19). In a list of settlements from the time of the return from the Babylonian exile (Neh. 11 : 32) Nob is mentioned between Anathoth and Ananiah in the territory of Benjamin. It may thus have been near to Saul's capital, Gibeah. Nob was Sennacherib's last halt in his advance on Jerusalem: "This very day he will halt at Nob, he will shake his fist at the mount of the daughter of Zion, the hill of Jerusalem" (Isa. 10 : 32). On the basis of this evidence it has been proposed to identify Nob with modern Shafat close to Gibeah of Saul. Other scholars would locate it at et-Tur on the slopes of the Mount of Olives, or in the region of Anathoth, where the photograph above was taken.

NOW a certain man of the servants of Saul . . . his name was Doeg the Edomite, the chief of Saul's herdsmen. (1 Sam. 21 : 7)

As a result of the growth of royal property under the monarchy, the king was obliged to appoint ministers and trained officials to administer his extensive possessions. The first kings of Israel necessarily employed foreign officials with a wide and varied experience of administrative matters. Several such officials and distinguished commanders are known to us from the courts of Saul and David, such as Doeg the Edomite, Itai the Hittite, Uriah the Hittite; and David's stewards, Obil the Ishmaelite and Jaziz the Hagrite (1 Chron. 27 : 30—31). These officials helped to consolidate the monarchy not only by their expert knowledge and their initiative, but also by their loyalty to their royal masters. Thus Doeg the Edomite, who was "the chief of Saul's herdsmen", demonstrated his loyalty by informing the king of what David had done at Nob, the city of the priests (1 Sam. 22 : 9—10), and by exterminating the family of Ahimelech at Saul's command (ibid. 18—19). "Chiefs of herdsmen" are known to us from other countries of the East; they are apparently what is meant by those "in charge of cattle" in Egypt that are mentioned in the Book of Genesis (47 : 6; see Vol. I, p. 117). Reproduced here is a relief from the tomb of the Egyptian Khaemhet at Sheikh Abd el-Gurnah (14th cent. B.C.). In every one of the three registers "chiefs of herdsmen" are seen displaying choice specimens of their flocks to their master. In their hands they hold papyrus scrolls containing a detailed inventory of the flocks.

DAVID departed from there and escaped to the cave of Adullam . . .   (1 Sam. 22 : 1)

After the fugitive David had failed to find refuge in the country of the Philistines (1 Sam. 21 : 14—15), he made a hide-out for himself at Adullam in the border country between Philistia and Judah. There he gathered around him a band of four hundred men (1 Sam. 22 : 2) who made audacious sorties from this base into the surrounding district (2 Sam. 23 : 13 ff.). Adullam, close to which lay David's cave, is located by most scholars at Tell esh-Sheikh Madkur in the Shephelah between the hills that dominate the Valley of Elah, at a height of 1150 ft. above sea-level. The ancient name of the place is preserved in the nearby Khirbet Id el-Ma. Adullam is mentioned as one of the thirty-one royal cities conquered by Joshua (Josh. 12 : 15) and was incorporated in the territory of Judah together with Socoh and Azekah (Josh. 15 : 35). Adullam had several natural advantages. Its position in the hills made it difficult of access and therefore a good place of refuge. Together with the neighbouring settlements, it controlled the Valley of Elah which served as the gateway to the mountains of Judah. At the same time, the district contained rich agricultural soil, with fields for crop-growing in the valley and expanses of pasture on the lower slopes of the hills. Finally, the rocky terrain of Adullam was naturally suited to the digging of cisterns and the sinking of wells.
The region of Adullam is rich in mounds and ruins which show that it was densely populated in ancient times. The city itself was fortified in the reign of Rehoboam, King of Judah, to protect the road to Beth-Zur. Part of the rugged and broken region, with its hills and caves, is shown in the view above.

"GO, make yet more sure; know and see the place where his haunt is, and who has seen him there ... See therefore, and take note of all the lurking places where he hides ..."

(1 Sam. 23 : 22-23)

Leaving the Shephelah (see p. 146), David withdrew to the desert of Judah, the age-old asylum of refugees and rebels, and also of hermits in search of God. The desert of Judah — i.e. the eastern slopes of the Judaean mountains— is geologically different from the rest of the hill-country. The mountains are mainly built-up from soft whiteish chalk and the contours of the hills and their slopes are therefore smooth and rounded. They are transversed by a great number of valleys, which often form gorges with precipitous craggy sides. In the slopes of these valleys and in the sheer escarpments facing the Dead Sea there exist numerous caves, which afford exellent hiding places (see p. 149). Rainfall in this region is scanty, and hence the surface of the desert is all but denuded of vegetation (see view) except for a few weeks in the rainy season. The water stored in natural cisterns is sufficient to quench the thirst of occasional nomads, but quite inadequate to support a large population. For this reason, the region is virtually inaccessible to regular military units. Another obstacle is the lack of roads. There are only a few paths,nearly all of them tracks made by sheep or goats or mountain gazelles. Movement in the desert therefore calls for thorough knowledge of the terrain and great mobility. Hence the advantage that David's small, hunted band had over the royal army of Saul. Saul knew that in the desert David held the upper hand, since he could outwit his pursuers by moving from one hiding-place to another: "for it is told me that he is very cunning" (1 Sam. 23 : 22).

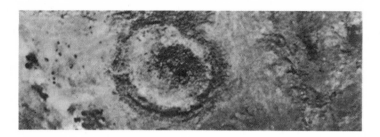

AND David went up from there, and dwelt in the strongholds of En-Gedi.   (1 Sam. 23 : 29)

David retreated still deeper into the desert and established his base in "the strongholds of En-Gedi", beside the most important oasis on the western shore of the Dead Sea. In this oasis, palms and balsam-trees were grown in antiquity. The strongholds of En-Gedi were of particular importance, on account of their being near three large springs: En-David to the north, En-Gedi proper in the centre, and En-Arugoth to the south. The term "strongholds" (Heb. *meṣadoth*) well describes the cliffs towering over the Dead Sea, nearly all of which are like natural fortresses. The Israelites who lived in the place made full use of its natural advantages and even improved on them. Three fortresses from the period of the kings of Judah, built at three important topographical points, have been discovered at En-Gedi. One is at Tell el-Jurn not far from the shore of the sea. The second lies beside the spring of En-Gedi, half way up the ascent to it. The third is on the top of the cliff called Sakhrat en-Najjar, which dominates the road from En-Gedi to Hebron. Possibly this is the district referred to in the Bible as "the Wildgoats' Rocks" (1 Sam. 24 : 2).

The upper view is an aerial photograph of a fortress of the Middle Iron Age (perhaps from the reign of Uzziah king of Judah), built on the top of the cliff. In design it is a central rectangular structure girt with a polygonal wall. The view below shows the rocky, fortress-like landscape of En-Gedi.

AND he came to the sheepfolds by the way, where there was a cave ... Now David and his men were sitting in the innermost parts of the cave.

(1 Sam. 24 : 3)

The region of En-Gedi, where David went into hiding, has the natural conditions required for sheep-rearing: pasture-land, a perennial water-supply (see p. 148) and open spaces suitable for sheepfolds. Grass, the sheep's Main food, grows on the limestone of the eastern slopes of the desert of Judah, especially in the shaded gorges. The sheepfolds have to be close to the pasture and water. Sometimes the shepherds construct them in the open field, sometimes at the entrances of caves. In the latter case, the cave serves the sheep as a shelter from the withering summer heat, from the bitter winter storms and from predatory beasts at night. The region around En-Gedi is honeycombed with caves, in "the Wildgoats' Rocks", at the top of the cliffs, in the gorges dividing them, and on the rock-terraces that rise above the oasis (see the upper photograph). These caves, which to this day are used as sheepfolds by the beduin, were formed, for the most part, through the erosion of the limestone by percolating rainwater and subterranean springs which have in some cases also washed away the paths that led to them.

The illustration below shows part of a cave in one of the cliffs of the strongholds of En-Gedi, with a drinking-trough built into it. The path leading to it has been destroyed, and its opening is high above the ground. It was such a cave as this that served David and his band as their secret hiding place.

H E was shearing his sheep in Carmel.   (1 Sam. 25 : 2)

From the earliest times sheep and goats were the principal possessions of the villagers in the mountains of Judah and on the edge of the Judaean desert. A man's wealth was measured by the size of his flocks. The importance of Nabal the Carmelite can therefore be judged from the biblical statement that he had "three thousand sheep and a thousand goats" (1 Sam. 25 : 2). Everything connected with the rearing and care of the flocks was done with much ado in these regions. The most joyous occasion of all was the shearing-festival which was celebrated with a public feast, like the harvest-festival, the grapegathering and the bringing home of the corn in the agricultural districts. Sheep-shearing and the shearing-festival are mentioned many times in the Bible. Jacob's son, Judah, went to Timnah to shear his flock (Gen. 38 : 12). Absalom gave a great banquet at Baal-Hazor, on the edge of the desert of Ephraim, to the king's sons and attendants to celebrate the completion of the shearing of his sheep (2 Sam. 13 : 23—27). In the same way, Nabal the Carmelite entertained his shearers to a banquet at the end of the shearing of his flocks in the desert of Carmel, south-east of Hebron (1 Sam. 25 : 36).

At the annual sheep-shearing the sheep were first dipped in a pool of water to clean their fleeces of dust; hence the poetic simile "like a flock of ewes, that have come up from the washing" (Song of Sol. 6 : 6). Next, the flock was hobbled to prevent it from interfering with the work of the shearers. The sheep to be sheared was stretched out on the ground or on a mat. The methods of shearing employed by the inhabitants of the desert and the customs connected with the shearing have changed but little from ancient times to the present day (see the illustration, taken at an Arab village of to-day).

THEN Abigail made haste, and took two hundred loaves, and two skins of wine, and five sheep ready dressed, and five measures of parched grain, and a hundred clusters of raisins, and two hundred cakes of figs, and laid them on asses. (1 Sam. 25 : 18)

While in the desert, David and his band lived off the presents and levies paid them, either willingly or out of fear, by the local land-owners in return for protection of their property (1 Sam. 25 : 16). When Nabal the Carmelite refused to pay the customary dues, only Abigail's presence of mind and tact prevented David from taking by force what had not been given to him readily. The list of the various kinds of food in v.18 seems not a chance compilation, but an indication of the diet on which the members of the band subsisted. Even the quantities may represent a kind of ration-scale of provisions for one company. An instructive parallel to this list is contained in the Papyrus Anastasi I (13th cent. B.C.; see p. 55), which includes a sort of arithmetical quiz on the allocation of food to the Egyptian troops on their campaign in Canaan. Here too the food to be distributed is characteristic of Canaan: wine, sheep and various kinds of pastries.

Reproduced above is a section from the paintings in the tomb of Haremheb (second half of the 14th cent. B.C.) portraying a distribution of rations. At the bottom, an officer is regulating the entry of the soldiers into the building in which the food is to be distributed. In the middle, packs are filled with rations that have already been made up and placed in baskets. At the top, elderly men (pensioned officers?) are seated before baskets filled with delicacies and being waited on by a servant.

"BUT take now the spear that is at his head, and the jar of water, and let us go."   (1 Sam. 26 : 11)

When David the hunted had the hunter, Saul, at his mercy, Saul's life was still precious in his sight (1 Sam. 26 : 24). David was thus prevented from doing any violence to the sleeping king: he merely took Saul's spear and water flask to show that he had had Saul in his power, but had not touched him. The water flask is an essential part of the equipment of any traveller in the desert. It is natural that it should have been beside Saul's head at his resting-place in the wilderness of Ziph. The water flask was a clay vessel with a flattened body and two small pierced handles through which a cord could be passed. It could thus easily be slung over the shoulder and carried at the side. The flask shown on the left above was found at Gezer. A peculiar feature of it is the widening of the neck into a saucer-shaped mouthpiece to facilitate drinking.

On the right there is a reproduction of a spear-head from the Early Iron Age (roughly contemporary with Saul). Preserved together with the spear-head is a spiral of metal ribbon wound around its base by which it was apparently attached to the wooden shaft of the spear.

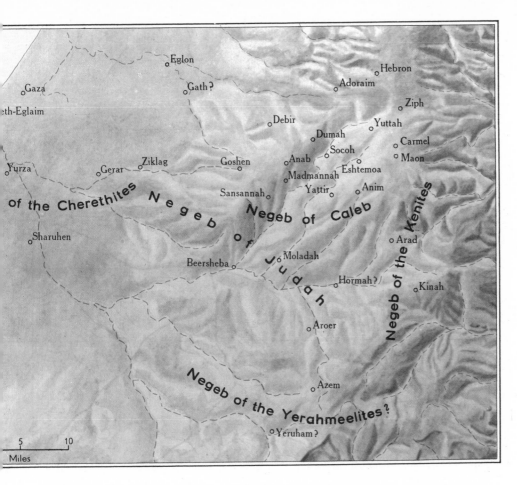

WHEN Achish asked, "Against whom have you made a raid today?" David would say, "Against the Negeb of Judah," or "Against the Negeb of the Yerahmeelites," or, "Against the Negeb of the Kenites." (1 Sam. 27 : 10)

While David remained in the country of the Philistines, Achish the king of Gath appointed him a special place of residence — Ziklag (1 Sam. 27: 5—6). This was a fortified city on the border of the district of Gath, dominating the approaches to the Negeb (recently identified tentatively with Tell esh-Shari'a in the Gerar Valley). From this base, David made sorties into the Negeb and harassed the Amalekite nomads who were constantly giving trouble to the Israelite settlers. However, as a refugee in Philistia, David was compelled to mislead Achish by telling him that the object of his sorties were parts of the Judaean Negeb. These regions are defined by the names of the clans and tribes that lived in them at the time of the Israelite conquest of Canaan. This seems to indicate that in David's days there was not much Israelite settlement in the Negeb. The archaeological survey has indeed revealed that there was, in this period, no settled population of any density in this region and that most of the settlements were founded only in the Middle Iron Age (9th—7th cent. B.C.). The Negeb districts belonging to Judah were the Negeb of Caleb, the Negeb of the Yerahmeelites, the Negeb of the Kenites and the Negeb of Judah (see map). To the west of the Negeb of Judah lay the Negeb of the Cherethites, i.e. the Philistine area of the Negeb (including Gerar), which was attacked by the Amalekites while the Philistines were fighting against Saul (1 Sam. 30 : 14).

The figure on the faience plaque (picture on the right) from the temple of Ramses III at Medinet Habu is a northerner whose Philistine origin is indicated by his headdress (see p. 118). It probably gives us a fair idea of the appearance of a Philistine notable such as Achish, king of Gath.

T HE Philistines assembled, and came and encamped at
Shunem; and Saul gathered all Israel, and they encamped at
Gilboa.   (1 Sam. 28 : 4)

The biblical Shunem, which is usually identified with the modern village
called Sulem, lay south-west of the Hill of Moreh, on the watershed between the Kishon River and the Valley of Jezreel to the west and the Brook
Harod and the Valley of Beth-Shan to the east (see map). Shunem was the
starting-point of a main highway which led to the "Way of the Sea"
running along the shores of the Mediterranean. Another road connecting
the district of Samaria with Mount Tabor and Galilee also passed through
Shunem. The town was already well-known in the Canaanite period, as it
is mentioned in the list of cities taken by Thutmose III (15th cent. B.C.).
At the time of the el-Amarna Letters (14th cent. B.C.) it was sacked by
the king of Shechem and its territory divided among the neighbouring
Canaanite cities, such as Megiddo. After the Israelite conquest, Shunem was
included in the territory of Issachar together with two other important
cities, Jezreel and Chesulloth (Josh. 19: 18), which control the main cross-
roads in the Valley of Jezreel. Hence the Philistines mustered their
forces at Shunem for the attack on the Israelites, their intention being to
cut off Judah and Samaria from the Valley of Jezreel and Galilee. The
Philistines pitched their camp to the north of the valley, while Saul drew
up his battle-line on its south side, close by the spring at the foot of Mount
Gilboa (see p. 155). The two mountains, Gilboa on the one side and the
Hill of Moreh on the other, served as strongholds, and if necessary as
places of refuge, for the two armies.
The photograph shows the village of Shunem at the foot of the Hill of
Moreh, with the fertile fields of the Valley of Jezreel. The Gilboa range can
be seen in the background.

N OW the Philistines gathered all their forces at Aphek; and the Israelites were encamped by the fountain which is in Jezreel.   (1 Sam. 29 : 1)

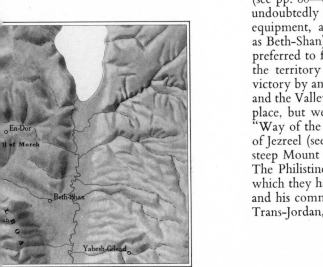

The battle against the Philistines, in which Saul and his sons met their death, was fought in the Valley of Jezreel (see p. 154), whither the Philistine army had advanced from its forward base at Aphek, the modern Rosh ha-Ayin (see p. 117). The Valley of Jezreel was the scene of frequent fighting in antiquity, from the campaign of Thutmose III down to Deborah's battle against Jabin, King of Hazor and Gideon's assault on the Midianites (see pp. 80—81, 86—87). Like the Canaanites before them, the Philistines undoubtedly chose this terrain because it allowed full use of their heavy equipment, and also because there they had strongly fortified cities (such as Beth-Shan) to serve as bases. The lightly armed Israelites, for their part, preferred to fight in the hills. By this battle, the Philistines tried to cut off the territory of the Joseph tribes from Galilee and to follow up their victory by an assault on the Mountains of Ephraim by way of Beth-Hagan and the Valley of Dothan. They were not fighting to capture any particular place, but were intent on conquering the whole region traversed by the "Way of the Sea". Saul's troops encamped at the spring north of the city of Jezreel (see the view above) with their back towards this town and the steep Mount Gilboa. The battle ended in the utter defeat of the Israelites. The Philistines thereby regained control of considerable areas of Canaan which they had lost during Saul's reign. Saul's son Ishbaal (or Ishbosheth) and his commander-in-chief, Abner the son of Ner, fled to Mahanaim in Trans-Jordan, which they made their new capital.

SO David set out, and the six hundred men who were with him, and they came to the Brook Besor, where those stayed who were left behind.

(1 Sam. 30 : 9)

The Brook Besor of the Bible (in Arabic Wadi Shellaleh) is the southern of the two tributaries of the Wadi Ghazzah, the northern being the Gerar. The source of the Besor is in the heart of the Negeb near the Maktesh ha-Gaddol. Near the point at which it runs into the Wadi Ghazzah its channel widens and its banks, which consist of loess, become precipitous (see the aerial photograph below). The Besor divides the sown area to the north from the desert region to the south. The plentiful flood waters that it carries in the winter and the many cisterns dug in its bed provide suitable conditions for the establishment of permanent settlements along its course. Many mounds, the most important of which are Tell Sharuhen (Tell Farah: see p. 58) and Tell Jemmeh, bear witness to the large settlements which existed on its banks in antiquity. On the other hand, southwards from the water-course there were only temporary encampments of nomads or semi-nomads. In his pursuit of the Amalekites who had sacked his city of residence, Ziklag, and carried off his two wives, David reached the Besor with his six hundred men. "and two hundred stayed behind, who were too exhausted to cross the Brook Besor" (1 Sam. 30 : 10). It appears that David left part of his force as a kind of garrison on the banks of the water-course, and continued his pursuit with a striking force of only four hundred men.

A_{ND} David smote them
from twilight until the evening
of the next day; and not a man
of them escaped, except four
hundred young men who
mounted camels and fled.

(1 Sam. 30 : 17)

After crossing the Besor (see p. 156), David fell suddenly upon the Amalekites who "were spread abroad over all the land, eating and drinking and dancing, because of all the great spoil they had taken" (1 Sam. 30 : 16) and defeated them. Only by exploiting the moment of surprise could the Israelite foot-soldiers get the better of the camel-riding Amalekites, whose swift incursions had carried them deep into Philistia and Judah. These tent-dwelling nomads relied on the speed of their camels in their raids upon the settled areas, robbing, plundering and making off before the farmers could rally to the defence. The camel, with its stamina and ability to move quickly and easily, is by nature suited to mobile warfare. Assyrian reliefs from the reign of Tiglath-Pileser III and Assurbanipal (8th and 7th cent. B.C.) show how the peoples of the desert used camels for military purposes. Sometimes, as in the reliefs of Assurbanipal, two fighters ride on one camel. One of them holds the reins, while the other uses his weapons (see Vol. I, p. 56). Or again, as in a relief from the palace of Tiglath-Pileser III at Calah (Nimrud), reproduced above, the camel is ridden by a single warrior. The rider in this relief is fleeing from his pursuers, just as the four hundred young men fled on their camels from David and his men. The word trans-lated "young men" (ne'arim) has here, as in some other places in the Bible, the meaning of "picked warriors".

THEY put his armour in
the temple of Ashtaroth;
and they fastened his body
to the wall of Beth-Shan.
(1 Sam. 31 : 10)

On account of its strategic importance, its plentiful water supplies and the fertile land around it, Beth-Shan has been a centre of population almost without a break from the Chalcolithic period (the fourth millennium B.C.) right down to the present day. The city lies at a junction of two roads, one running from the Valley of Jezreel and the Mountains of Ephraim eastwards to Trans-Jordan and the other northwards to Galilee. It controls the north-eastern approaches to western Palestine. Because of these natural advantages, Beth-Shan served foreign rulers of Canaan as one of their most important strongholds. In the time of Thutmose III (15th cent. B.C.) it was in Egyptian hands, and in the time of Saul it was under Philistine control. It may well be that the Philistines originally came to Beth-Shan as mercenaries in the Egyptian army and made themselves masters of the city after the decline of Egyptian rule in Canaan. It was not until the reign of David that the Israelites were able to drive out the inhabitants of the city (Judg. 1 : 27). In the reign of Solomon, the city was included, together with Taanach and Megiddo, in the fifth administrative district (1 Kings 4 : 12; see map on pp. 208—209).

The photograph at the left is a view of Tell el-Husn, the site of ancient Beth-Shan, to the north-east of the modern town. The excavations carried out on the mound have brought to light several temples. The northern temple was dedicated to a Canaanite goddess. This temple was discovered in a stratum contemporary with the reign of Ramses III (12 th cent. B. C.; see reconstruction below) and continued in use with some changes until the time of David. Possibly this was the temple of Ashtaroth to which Saul's weapons were brought to be dedicated to the gods. The bodies of Saul and his sons, who had fallen in the battle of Gilboa, were impaled by the Philistines on the walls of Beth-Shan. Such public impalement of fallen enemies (cf. p. 194) was widely practised in antiquity, as can be inferred, for example, from the fate of the inhabitants of Kulisi. When the Assyrian king, Shalmaneser III, conquered this city in 852 B.C. in the course of his advance on the headwaters of the Tigris, he had the heads of its slaughtered inhabitants stuck on the city wall (see the plate at the bottom of p. 158 which is reproduced from the bronze gates found at Balawat).

IT should be taught to the people of Judah to use the bow ...   (2 Sam. 1 : 18)

David's lament over Saul and Jonathan is in martial strain. It describes the king and his son as skilled and intrepid warriors: "From the blood of the slain, from the fat of the mighty, the bow of Jonathan turned not back, and the sword of Saul returned not empty" (2 Sam. 1 : 22). Some scholars are of the opinion that the opening words of the lament—"to teach the people of Judah the bow" — show that it was intended to be sung as an accompaniment to the training of the Israelite army in marksmanship and the use of the composite bow (see Vol. I, p. 64), which was then the principal long-range weapon. The method of instruction is vividly illustrated in an Egyptian wall-painting at Thebes from the time of the New Kingdom (see the illustration). Bowmen were taught marksmanship on special training ranges. Behind the pupils stood instructors who corrected their movements and tested their ability to shoot straight. Usually the bowman held the bow in his left hand and not as in the picture reproduced here. With his right hand he held the arrow and stretched the bow-string. The reliefs and paintings from the ancient East show that the main emphasis in this training was laid on the correct way of holding the arrow with the fingers of the right hand.

"YE mountains of Gilboa, let there be no
dew or rain upon you . . ."

(2 Sam. 1 : 21)

In Saul's last battle against the Philistines, the king and his army retreated to their base on Mount Gilboa (see
pp. 154—155). There Saul met his death, together with his three sons. In his lament over Saul and Jonathan,
David calls down a curse of perpetual barrenness upon Gilboa, the scene of the battle, where fell the mighty
warriors whose heroic deeds had brought Israel so many victories. A similar curse is apparently also found in
the Ugaritic text: *bl ṭl bl rbb bl šrʻthmṭm* ("let there be no dew, nor rain, nor upsurging of waters under the
ground").
The etymology of the name Gilboa is obscure. The word is preserved in the name of the Arab village Jelbun,
which is called Gelbus by Eusebius, one of the Church Fathers who lived in the 3rd—4th cent. A.D. Mount
Gilboa is a spur of the Mountains of Samaria, projecting north-westwards between the Valley of Beth-Shan and
the Valley of Jezreel; it is thus bounded on all sides by fertile level ground. The fields around it are watered by
the many springs that rise from three sides at the foot of the mountain, especially on the north (see view).
Hence the Church Father Jerome (5th cent.A.D.) thought the name could appropriately be explained as *gal nobeʻa*—
"a heap of stones from which water flows." The mountain itself, with its bare and barren slopes, looks just as
described in David's curse.

D AVID said, "To which shall I go up?" And he said, "To Hebron." (2 Sam. 2 : 1)

There were several reasons why David chose Hebron as his first capital. The principal city of Judah, Hebron was situated in the centre of the tribal territory (see map on p. 64) at the point where side-roads to the coastal plain, Edom and the desert of Judah branch off from the main north-south highway from Jerusalem to Beersheba. In addition, the region around it had good soil for crops and fruit orchards. Finally, the city was steeped in sacred traditions going back to patriarchal times (see Vol. I, p. 70). It is also possible that David's connections with the clans of Caleb (1 Chron. 2 : 50—54), who had been established in Hebron since the time of the Israelite conquest (Josh. 15 : 13; Judg. 1 : 20; 1 Chron. 2 : 43), were a further inducement to him to settle with his followers "in the towns of Hebron" (2 Sam. 2 : 3). At Hebron, David was anointed king of the tribe of Judah and there he began to forge those connections with the other Israelite tribes which resulted in his being anointed there king of all Israel (2 Sam. 5 : 3). Hebron remained a city of note, even after the capital had been transferred to Jerusalem (2 Sam. 15 : 7—10). Rehoboam re-fortified it (2 Chron. 11 : 10) and, even after his time, it continued to be an economic and administrative centre, as witnessed by the stamped jar-handles bearing the legend "To the King — Hebron" which have been found in various places in Judah.
The illustration is a view of modern Hebron, called by the Arabs el-Khalil, i.e. "(the City) of the Friend (of God)", after Abraham the Hebrew who dwelt at the oaks of Mamre by Hebron. Some scholars think that the site of the citadel, which was David's capital, is south-west of the modern town, at Jebel er-Rumeideh, a mound in which remnants of ancient fortifications and potsherds from the Iron Age have been found.

AND Joab the son of Zeruiah, and the servants of David, went out and met them at the pool of Gibeon; and they sat down, the one on the one side of the pool, and the other on the other side of the pool. (2 Sam. 2 : 13)

There was a long and bloody struggle between the houses of Saul and David: "and David grew stronger and stronger, while the house of Saul became weaker and weaker" (2 Sam. 3 : 1). The Bible describes in detail only one encounter between the men of Abner, the captain of the Israelite army, and those of Joab, David's captain beside the pool of Gibeon. Now Gibeon, as we know from the Book of Joshua (see p. 37), lay in the territory of Benjamin which was in the domain of Ishbaal (or Ishbosheth, 2 Sam. 2 : 9) the son of Saul. Presumably, therefore, David's men had penetrated as far as this point into the territory ruled by Ishbaal. The two opposing forces met at the pool of Gibeon, which appears to have been well known. Some scholars think it is mentioned again four hundred years later as "the great pool which is in Gibeon" in Jer. 41 : 12.
The illustration shows the pool of Gibeon which has recently been excavated. It is cut out of the rock in cylindrica shape (diameter 36 ft., depth 35 ft.). 42 steps lead down to the bottom of the pool, from which a tunnel, with another spiral stairway, descends a further 45 ft. to the water-level. (The uppermost steps are seen on left.) In the pool itself fragments of jars of the 7th cent. B.C. were discovered with inscriptions mentioning Gibeon and the names of local vineyard-owners.

AND Abner said to Joab, "Let the young men arise and play before us . . ."

(2 Sam. 2 : 14)

The contest described in this chapter exemplifies one of the forms of warfare customary in the ancient East. Each of the two armies chose a number of champions who then fought each other in single combat (see p. 138). In the verse above they are called "young men" (Heb. *ne'arim*), a term which, in the Bible as in Canaanite, denotes youthful, well-trained warriors. In many cases, such single combats replaced the general engagement of the two opposing armies and the issue of the battle was decided by their result (1 Sam. 17 : 9, 51, see page 138). The intention of this procedure was to reduce the number of casualties. However, the hand-to-hand combats at the pool of Gibeon ended indecisively — "they fell down together" — so that Joab and Abner had to engage their entire forces; "And the battle was very fierce that day" (2 Sam. 2 : 17). David's troops had twenty casualties, while Abner's losses were three hundred and sixty killed (2 Sam. 2 : 30—31). The description of the "play" of the young men — "each caught his opponent by the head and thrust his sword in his opponent's side" — give an exact and vivid picture of a duel to the death customary in the ancient East. This can be seen in the relief of the 10th or 9th cent. B.C. (roughly contemporary with David) found at Tell Halaf (Gozan), which is reproduced here.

A BNER smote him in the belly with the butt of his spear, so that the spear came out at his back; and he fell there, and died where he was . . .

(2 Sam. 2 : 23)

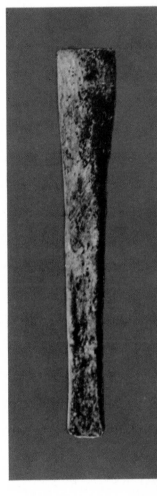

After Ishbaal's soldiers had been defeated by David's forces, they fled through the wilderness of Gibeon towards their base at Mahanaim in Trans-Jordan (2 Sam. 2 : 24, 29). In hot pursuit of the retreating enemy, Asahel, Joab's brother, "swift of foot as a wild gazelle" (ibid. 22), made after Abner, Ishbaal's commander-in-chief. Without pausing in his flight, Abner killed Asahel by thrusting him through with the butt-end of his spear. The spear consisted of a wooden shaft with two metal ends: one the spear-head, and the other a sharp point on the butt. This butt served various purposes, such as fixing the spear upright in the ground when in camp (cf. 1 Sam. 26 : 7), or spurring on the horse when riding. Large numbers of spear-butts have been found in excavations, though they have not always been correctly identified.

The plate on the right is a reproduction of a spear-butt from the Iron Age. On the left is a detail of a wall-painting from the beginning of the 8th cent. B.C., discovered at Til Barsip in Assyria. Here the spear of an Assyrian soldier, with its head and butt, is clearly seen.

"AND may the house of Joab never be without one who has a discharge, or who is leprous, or who holds a spindle . . ."

(2 Sam. 3 : 29)

The murderers of Abner were too powerful for David, the young king, to dare bring them to justice. "And I am this day weak, though anointed king; these men the sons of Zeruiah are too hard for me" (2 Sam. 3 : 39). He therefore called down on Joab and his house a curse of wasting their strength through sickness (leprosy), war ("who is slain by the sword") and poverty ("who lacks bread"). The expression "one who holds a spindle" might denote a cripple or invalid who can walk only with the support of a crutch or spindle-like staff.

A sick man, holding such a staff, is portrayed on a votive stele from the Eighteenth Dynasty of Egypt, which was found at Memphis (reproduced above). "The door-keeper Ram", accompanied by his wife and son, is seen bringing an offering to the Canaanite goddess Ishtar (Ashtoreth), known also as the goddess of healing, and beseeching her to cure his diseased leg. The portraiture shows that Ram was suffering from the results of poliomyelitis. He is unable to walk without support, but, as both his hands are occupied with the offering, he is holding the staff under his left arm.

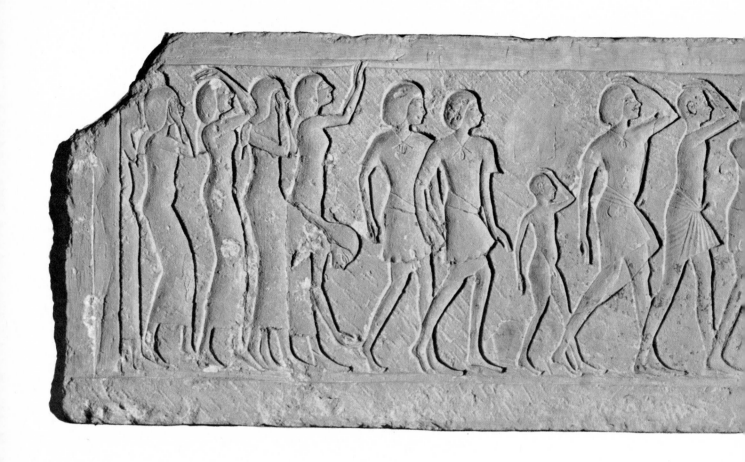

AND all the people wept.   (2 Sam. 3 : 32)

In his desire to prove to "all the people and all Israel . . . that it had not been the king's will to slay Abner the son of Ner" (2 Sam. 3 : 37), David commanded the people to mourn Abner as befitted so great a captain: "Rend your clothes, and gird on sackcloth, and mourn before Abner" (ibid. 31). These words describe the forms of mourning customary at that time both in Israel and among other peoples. It is true that some of the mourning rites practised in the ancient East were forbidden by the Law of Moses (see Vol. I, p. 195), as being an integral part of idol-worship (for instance: "You shall not cut yourselves or make any baldness on your foreheads for the dead" — Deut. 14 : 1). But the Israelites adopted many other funerary customs, such as rending garments, wearing sackcloth, sitting on the ground, walking barefoot, sprinkling ashes on the head and covering the head with the hands. David himself walked behind Abner's bier to pay homage to a great man.
A similar scene of public mourning is depicted on an Egyptian relief from the Twenty-Sixth Dynasty (7th and 6th cent. B.C.) which was excavated at Abydos (see reproduction). The procession is headed by a shrine, followed by members of the family, three of whom are making typical gestures of grief with their hands. They are followed by the professional mourning-women with their hands on their heads, or over their temples. One of them is actually bending down and picking up earth from the ground, in order to sprinkle it on her head (see p. 181). An unusual feature in this funeral procession is the presence of children who are seen imitating the actions of their elders.

From this brief and sketchy description it is impossible to ascertain the tactics David employed in the conquest of Jerusalem. Perhaps Scripture has combined cultic and military matters. Possibly, it was for cultic reasons that the Jebusites lined up the blind and the lame on the walls (see view), perhaps to the accompaniment of a solemn execratory rite which threatened anyone who attempted to scale the walls with lameness and blindness. Such a rite was customary amongst the Hittites. The verse contains a reference to the *ṣinor* (translated above "watershaft"). According to this explanation, the *ṣinor* was the "watershaft" by which, in time of siege, the Jebusites used to reach the spring outside the city-wall. Such a tunnel has been excavated in Jerusalem, near the Gihon spring. It dates from the end of the Late Bronze Age or the beginning of the Early Iron period. By means of this tunnel the inhabitants of Jerusalem could reach the spot to which the water of the spring was channelled towards the city by means of a slightly sloping conduit. From here the water was drawn up in buckets through a vertical shaft (see the cross-section below).

Other scholars consider the *ṣinor* to have been a weapon, like a three-pronged fork.

Nevertheless David took the stronghold of Zion, that is, the city of David. And David said on that day, "Whoever would smite the Jebusites, let him get up the water shaft to attack the lame and the blind, who are hated by David's soul" ... (2 Sam. 5 : 7-8)

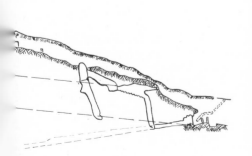

NOW the Philistines had come and spread out in
the valley of Rephaim. (2 Sam. 5 : 18)

After David had been anointed king of all Israel and had established his capital at Jerusalem, the Philistines advanced into the valley of Rephaim in order to prevent his kingdom from becoming any stronger. They intended
to drive a wedge into the heart of Israelite territory, cutting off the capital from its lines of communication
with the hill country and the coastal plain; but they were defeated and driven back by David's army. The valley
of Rephaim runs to the west of the watershed, from south-west of Jerusalem, as far as the upper reaches of the
Sorek Valley. Through the valley and beside it ran two of the main highways passing through Jerusalem: one
from the mountains of Ephraim to Bethlehem and Hebron, and the other from the coast to the Sorek Valley
and thence to Jerusalem and on to Jericho. The northern part of the valley formed the boundary between the
tribes of Judah and Benjamin (Josh. 15 : 8; 18 : 16); but for most of its length it was inside Judah.
As the only large expanse of level ground in the environs of Jerusalem suitable for crop-growing and pasture,
the valley of Rephaim has had a considerable population from pre-historic times. The view shows part of the
valley, looking to the south-west.

When David had finally put an end to the Philistine threat, he turned his attention to a triumphal conveying of the ark of the covenant from the house of Abinadab on the hill *(gibe'ah)* of Kiryath-Yearim (2 Sam. 6 : 3—4; cf. 1 Sam. 7 : 1). After a temporary halt in the house of Obed-Edom the Gittite (2 Sam. 6 : 11) the ark was brought to Jerusalem which thus became the spiritual capital and religious centre of Israel. From now on, the city of David took the place of Shiloh, as the Psalmist sang: "He forsook his dwelling at Shiloh, the tent where he dwelt among men ... But he chose the tribe of Judah, Mount Zion, which he loves" (Ps. 78 :60, 68). Great crowds accompanied the ark on its way with joyful music and songs, as described in the parallel passage in 1 Chron. 13 : 8: "And David and all Israel were making merry before God with all their might, with song ..."

The lyre (see p. 136), the harp, the tambourine, the castanet and the cymbal were common musical instruments in the ancient world. A quartet composed of such instruments is seen in a relief (reproduced here) from the reign of Assurbanipal (7th cent. B.C.). The player at the front left is beating a tambourine; the one to the right in the rear is clashing hand-cymbals together, while next to him a harpist is plucking an eight-stringed harp with both hands. The fourth player in the ensemble (in the rear on the left) is playing an oblong, five-stringed harp.

AND David and all the house of Israel were making merry before the LORD with all their might, with songs and lyres and harps and tambourines and castanets and cymbals.

(2 Sam. 6 : 5)

MICHAL the daughter of Saul looked out of the window . . .   (2 Sam. 6 : 16)

David's wife, Michal, stood at the window to welcome home her husband who was bringing the ark of the covenant to Jerusalem in a joyful procession. This welcoming of guests and dignitaries "out of the window" was a common practice at the Egyptian court from the very earliest times down to the days of the Ptolemies, as also amongst the ruling classes of other countries of the East. The mother of Sisera looked out of the window, when she was anxiously waiting for her son's return (Judg. 5 : 28), and Jezebel did the same when she was to meet Jehu after he had usurped the throne of Israel (2 Kings 9 : 30; cf. p. 267).

Artistic representations of a woman looking out of a window — in ivory and bronze reliefs — have been found in Cyprus (from the 13th and 12th cent. B.C.), and in Mesopotamia (from the 9th and 8th cent. B.C.). The ivory plaque from Calah in Assyria (the modern Nimrud), which is reproduced here, is a typical specimen of Phoenician art of the 9th and 8th cent. B.C. It is made in the shape of an oblong window-frame. The lower part of the window is closed in by a parapet resting on four pillars over which peers the face of a woman who apparently symbolizes the goddess Ashtoreth.

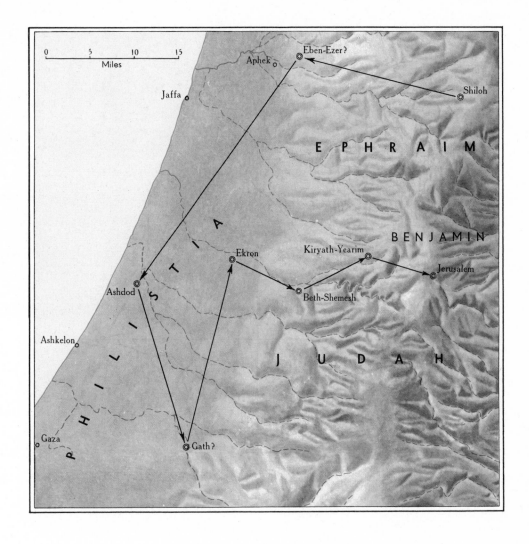

"I HAVE not dwelt in a house since the day I brought up the people of Israel from Egypt to this day, but I have been moving about in a tent for my dwelling."

(2 Sam. 7 : 6)

The ark was regarded as one of the most ancient and venerable of Israelite sacred objects. It was made in the period of the wanderings in the desert and, until finally installed in the Temple at Jerusalem, it was always housed in accord with the same nomadic conditions of life: in a tent or tabernacle. These two types of temporary shrine were relics from the period preceding the Israelite settlement in Canaan. Throughout David's reign the ark stood in a tent which the king had pitched for it (2 Sam. 6 : 17); this very same tent is mentioned also at the beginning of Solomon's reign (1 Kings 1 : 39; 2 : 28). The tabernacle, though somewhat more permanent than the tent, was also typical of a nomadic or semi-nomadic society. According to Mosaic tradition, the ark was carried in the tabernacle throughout the wanderings in the desert and was still inside it when it reached Shiloh (Josh. 18 : 1). It seems that the House of God at Shiloh was also constructed in the form of a tabernacle as a religious tradition from a bygone age.

The journey of the ark from Shiloh to Jerusalem was long and devious (1 Sam. chap. 4—6; and see map): through Eben-Ezer (for the location see p. 117), Ashdod, Gath, Ekron, Beth-Shemesh, the Hill (gibe'ah) of Kiryath-Yearim and the house of Obed-Edom the Gittite. From this last place David brought the ark up to Jerusalem which became its permanent resting place, as described by the Psalmist: "This is my resting place for ever; here I will dwell, for I have desired it" (Ps. 132 : 14).

TOI sent his son Joram to King David, to greet him . . .
And Joram brought with him articles of silver, of gold, and
of bronze . . .   (2 Sam. 8 : 10)

The wars which David fought with the Aramaeans in Syria (see p. 175) paved the way for the establishment
of political relations with the central Syrian kingdom of Hamath which was also at war with Aram. It was
therefore natural for David and Toi the king of Hamath, to join forces against their common enemy, Hadadezer
the king of Aram-Zobah. As a sign of his friendship, Toi sent to Israel a diplomatic mission, headed by his son
Joram, thus perhaps conceding David's superior status. The members of the mission brought with them gifts of
great value — articles of silver, gold and bronze.
The upper plate is a section of the bronze gates discovered near Balawat. It depicts delegations bringing gifts to
the Assyrian king Shalmaneser III, in the year 857 B.C. In the upper register are tribute-bearers from Unqi,
a country near Hamath. In the lower register, a Syrian prince is seen presenting his daughter (the figure at
the extreme left) to Shalmaneser. In the lower plate are reproduced the fragments of an engraved silver dish —
apparently from the 8th cent. B.C. — which was found near the city of Hamath. Between the braided borders pairs
of griffins face each other.

THE Ammonites sent and hired the Aramaeans of Beth-Rehob, and the Aramaeans of Zobah, twenty thousand foot soldiers, and the king of Maachah with a thousand men, and the men of Tob, twelve thousand men.   (2 Sam. 10 : 6)

In the 12th and 11th centuries B.C., Aramaean tribes surged out of the Arabian desert into the region of the Middle Euphrates and onwards towards Syria and northern Trans-Jordan. By the time of David, they were already organized in political federations, one of which was the kingdom of Aram-Zobah to the north of Damascus. The king of Zobah — Hadadezer, David's foe — imposed his rule upon other Aramaean states: Aram-Damascus, Aram Beth-Rehob (in the Anti-Lebanon), Aram-Maachah (in the region of Abel Beth-Maachah in the northern Golan), and the land of Tob (in the region north of the Yarmuk; see map). To the north-east, Zobah's sphere of influence stretched as far as the Euphrates and even beyond it (2 Sam. 8 : 3; 10 : 16). David's steadily increasing strength was a threat to these Aramaean kingdoms which consequently hastened to the aid of the Ammonites when the latter were attacked by the Israelites. In this, and in two further battles, the Aramaeans were so utterly defeated that their kingdoms became tributary to Israel (2 Sam. 8 : 3—8; 10 : 15—19). But Israel's control of these regions did not last long. In Solomon's reign Aram-Damascus regained its independence and became a strong and dangerous rival of the kingdom of Israel.

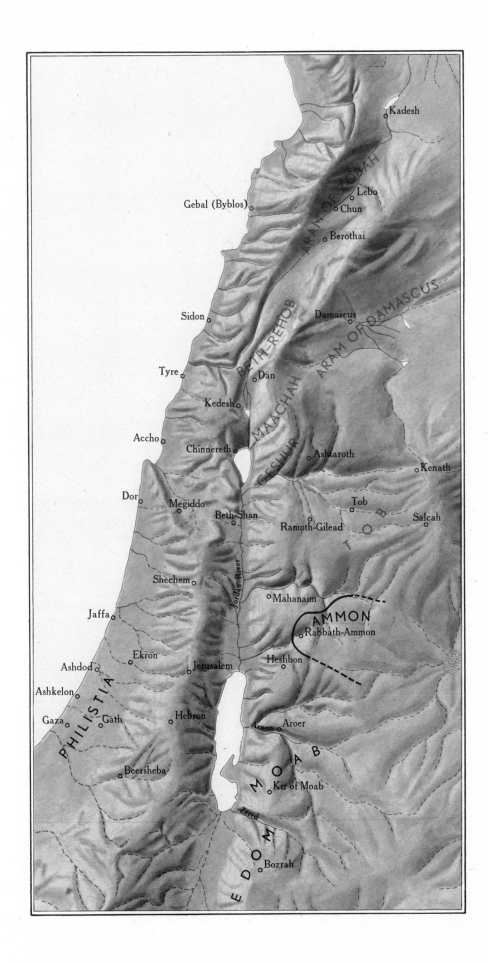

ND the Aramaeans fled before Israel; and David slew of the Aramaeans the men of seven hundred chariots . . .

(2 Sam. 10 : 18)

After their defeat by the Israelites, the Aramaean allies of the Ammonites (see p. 175) mustered a reserve force from the Euphrates region for a second engagement at Helam (aapprently a place in northern Trans-Jordan: 2 Sam. 10 : 16). In this battle the enemy made full use of the chariotry wherein lay their chief military advantage over the Israelites. But even these chariots did not avail to save them from defeat by David's army: "They made peace with Israel, and became subject to them" (2 Sam. 10 : 19).

The picture shows a limestone relief from the kingdom of Gozan (Tell Halaf), from the 10th cent. or early part of the 9th cent. B.C.; it illustrates the type of chariot used by the Aramaeans in David's time. Though crudely executed, the relief shows the structural essentials of the chariot which is similar to the Assyrian chariots of the first part of the 9th cent. B.C. It has two wheels and is drawn by two horses (only one of which is visible on the relief). Each wheel has six spokes and the axle is somewhat to the back of the chariot. The shaft is attached to the bottom of the chariot and passes between the two horses. The twined cord which can be seen in the relief running over the backs of the horses and under the reins is a characteristic feature of the chariots of the time. It performed a two-fold function: a) by connecting the upper part of the chariot with the yoke, it lessened the danger of the chariot's being severed from the shaft; b) it prevented the reins from becoming entangled when held loosely. In the chariot stand two men: the charioteer, who is holding a whip, and the warrior. A quiver can be seen at the side of the chariot (cf. the similar chariot on p. 263).

IT happened, late one afternoon, when David arose from his couch and was walking upon the roof of the king's house, that he saw from the roof a woman bathing . . . (2 Sam. 11 : 2)

When David walked on the roof of his lofty palace he could look down into the courtyards of the neighbouring nobles. It was in this way that he saw Bathsheba, the wife of Uriah the Hittite, bathing herself. Apparently Bathsheba took her bath not, after the manner of kings, in a room specially set aside for the purpose, but, like the majority of the people, in an ordinary bowl that was filled with water from the well. The ancients made a great point of washing, especially after a journey along dusty highways (Gen. 18 : 4; 19 : 2; Song of Sol. 5 : 3 etc.). In places where there were rivers and water-channels it was customary to bathe in them; even the daughters of kings would go down to the river to bathe (see Vol. I, p. 132).

The reproduction is of a statuette of a woman (3⅓ in. high) from the period of the Israelite Monarchy, which was found at Achzib. The woman is sitting in an oval, flat bowl and washing herself. Her hair is let down over her shoulders.

AND Joab sent messengers to David, and said, "I have fought against Rabbah; moreover, I have taken the city of waters."

(2 Sam. 12 : 27)

When Hanun the son of Nahash ascended the throne of Ammon, open war broke out between him and David (2 Sam. 10 : 4). In this war the Ammonites summoned the Aramaean kingdoms to their aid (see p. 175). Though the Aramaeans were defeated, the struggle with the Ammonites still remained undecided (2 Sam. 10: 14). Hence David again sent out his army to defeat the Ammonites in battle and to take their capital, Rabbah of the Ammonites (2 Sam. 11 : 1). The siege was protracted, but eventually Joab managed to take "the city of waters". He thereupon sent a message to David to come and capture the rest of the city, so that it should be called by his name (2 Sam. 12 : 27—28). Presumably Rabbath-Ammon was divided into two parts: "the city of waters" which lay beside the Jabbok river, and the main part of the city containing the citadel and the royal palace.
The photograph shows part of Amman, the capital of the Kingdom of Jordan, which is built on the site of Rabbah of the Ammonites in a mountain gorge, about 2250 ft. above sea-level. The remains of the Roman theatre are seen on the left. The city has been a place of special importance from the Bronze Age right down to the present day. It stands astride a network of highways connecting Syria with the Red Sea and the Arabian desert with the cities of Palestine on both sides of the Jordan.

AND he took the crown of their king from his head; the weight of it was a talent of gold, and in it was a precious stone; and it was placed on David's head . . .

(2 Sam. 12 : 30)

To symbolize his sovereignty over the land of the Ammonites, David took possession of the crown worn by their king (Heb. *malkam*) which weighed "a talent of gold" (i.e. more than 36 kg.). As it can hardly be supposed that such a heavy crown was made for any mortal king, the reference in this verse may be to *Milkom*, the god of the Ammonites (cf. 1 Kings 11 : 5). Presumably, then, David took the crown off the head of the idol of the god and set the jewel which it contained in his own crown.

The illustration shows a limestone head, 11 in. high, found at Rabbath-Ammon. The figure portrayed in it has a moustache and is wearing the Atef crown (a white headdress or crown with a feather at either side) as worn by the god Osiris and also by the king of Egypt. As the face is typically Semite, the figure presumably represents an Ammonite god or king. The head is from the beginning of the Early Iron Age — the time of the Judges and the early Israelite Monarchy.

So Tamar went to her brother Amnon's house, where he was lying down. And she took dough, and kneaded it, and made cakes in his sight, and baked the cakes.

(2 Sam. 13 : 8)

Unlike the preparation of ordinary meals, a sick man's repast (Heb. *biryah*) had to be prepared for him by specially trained women. Hence David acceded to the request of his son Amnon, who was feigning illness, that Tamar, his sister, be sent to his house to make cakes in his presence and feed him with them (2 Sam. 13 : 6). Some scholars hold that such cakes (Heb. *lebiboth*) were shaped like a heart (Heb. *leb*); while others explain the term as meaning that they melted the heart with their succulence, and compare them with the sweetmeat called in Akkadian *'akal libbu*. To make the cakes, Tamar first kneaded the dough and shaped the cakes in Amnon's sight; she then baked them, apparently outside the room in the open air.

Reproduced above is a wooden model of the house of an Egyptian farm-steward from the Twelfth Dynasty (20th and 19th cent. B.C.). The left-hand room on the ground-floor of the house has apparently been set aside for the preparation of food. In it a woman is seen kneading dough on a kind of bench. The rest of the ground floor appears to have been used as a store-room. In the upper chamber sits the steward, keeping a watchful eye on all that happens in his house or sunning himself at ease.

AND Tamar put ashes on her head, and rent the long-sleeved robe which she wore; and she laid her hand on her head, and went away, crying aloud as she went.

(2 Sam. 13 : 19)

The conventional expressions of grief customary in antiquity were employed not only in mourning for the dead, but in every misfortune, whether private or public. Thus, for example, King Jehoram went into mourning during the famine in Samaria, when he saw the women cooking the flesh of their own sons (2 Kings 6 : 30); David and his supporters mourned and covered their heads when Absalom usurped the throne (2 Sam. 15 : 30); and Mordecai and the Jews put on sackcloth and ashes and fasted, to demonstrate their grief at the decree of Ahasuerus (Esther 4 : 1).

Tamar performed thus the rites of mourning for the shame that her brother Amnon had brought upon her, sprinkling ashes on her head, tearing the robe she was wearing, placing her hand on her head and crying loudly and bitterly like a mourning-woman (cf. p. 168).

The illustration shows a reproduction of a painting from the tomb of Ipuki and Nebamon at Thebes (14th cent. B.C.). The widow of Nebamon, weeping and with her hair in disarray, is seen crouching at the feet of her embalmed husband (right-hand edge of the picture). She is wearing greenish mourning garb. With one hand she is sprinkling ashes on her head, while with the other she is touching the feet of the mummy.

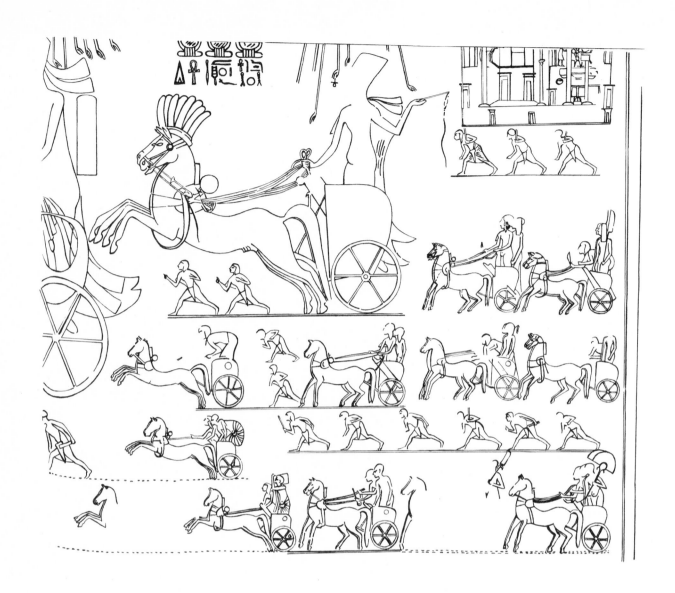

A<small>BSALOM</small> got himself a chariot and horses, and
fifty men to run before him.   (2 Sam. 15 : 1)

Puffed up by his ambition to be king, Absalom arrogated to himself the prerogatives of royalty. Like the rulers
of those days and their families, he too set men to run before his chariot. The runners' main function was to
display the exalted rank of the man who rode in the chariot (see p. 123), as well as to clear a way for the chariot
through the narrow, crowded streets of an oriental city. The higher the rank of the owner of the chariot, the
greater the number of the runners who preceded it. The verse above implies that the largest single body of such
runners in David's reign numbered fifty.
The detail of a painting from Tell el-Amarna, reproduced here, shows the chariots of the Queen of Egypt,
Nefertiti, the wife of Amenhotep IV (14th cent. B.C.) and of the king's daughters, with their retinues. These are
the typical Egyptian chariots of the 14th cent., having wheels with six spokes. The runners can be seen in front
of the chariots with their bodies bent forward in a characteristic running posture.

AND the king crossed the Brook Kidron . . .
(2 Sam. 15 : 23)

The Kidron Valley passes between the Temple Mount and the Mount of Olives (1 Kings 2: 37). Starting to the north-west of the Temple Mount it runs into the Dead Sea south of Ain el-Feskhah and Khirbet Qumran. From its bed rises the spring of Gihon (Shiloah), the original source of Jerusalem's water-supply. Concealed at the bottom of one of the precipitous gorges of the Judaean desert, the Kidron, in its lower course, provided numerous hiding places, and was a natural refuge for fugitives. When David abandoned Jerusalem to Absalom, he and his loyal supporters crossed the Kidron and made their escape into the Judaean desert. In the days of the First Temple, the Kidron Valley served as a burial-ground for the inhabitants of Jerusalem (2 Kings 23 : 6) who shrank from interring their dead in the city. In the time of the Second Temple, this cemetery stretched for over three miles along the Kidron Valley, from the so-called "Tombs of the Judges" at its northern end to south of the Mount of Olives. The most famous of the tombs were "Absalom's Tomb" (see p. 189), the Tomb of the priests of the Hezir family (1 Chron. 24 : 15), and the Mausoleum of the Adiabene royal family (the "Tombs of the Kings"). The view shows the lower part of the Kidron. From this point the valley runs in front of the southern spur of the Mount of Olives which can be seen in the background.

ZIBA the servant of Mephibosheth met him, with
a couple of asses saddled . . .   (2 Sam. 16 : 1)

In the time of Absalom's uprising, David and those who remained loyal to him fled from Jerusalem. As they were making their way up the Mount of Olives in the direction of the desert to the east (2 Sam. 15 : 30), they were met by Ziba, a servant of the house of Saul, who brought them food, "Two hundred loaves of bread, a hundred bunches of raisins, a hundred of summer fruits, and a skin of wine" (ibid. 16 : 1). Like Abigail, the wife of Nabal, Ziba transported his produce on the backs of asses (see p. 151). The ass was the normal beast of burden in the ancient East (see Vol. I, p. 169). It was customary to yoke together a pair of asses, since the combined carrying capacity of two yoked animals was greater than that of two asses separately.
Reproduced above is a section of a relief from the tomb of Neferartenef excavated at Sakkarah (middle of the third millennium B.C.). It shows an ass loaded with a sack of corn. The sack appears to be made of cords or reeds and is fastened by ropes to the animal's back, which is covered with a cloth to protect it from chafing. The ass is being driven by a man who is brandishing a stick.

ᴀɴᴅ when Hushai the Archiet, David's friend, came . . .

(2 Sam. 16 : 16)

Hushai the Archite is called in the Bible "the friend of the king" or "David's friend"— a title given to a court functionary (cf. Gen. 26 : 26 and 1 Kings 4 : 5). This appellation may originally have been used quite literally to denote the king's close friend and have become through long usage the regular title of a royal minister. The precise duties of "the king's friend" are not known. One theory is that he was the king's "best man" and his advisor in matrimonial matters (see 2 Sam. 13 : 3—4). Since it was customary for oriental monarchs to take many wives, and since their marriages very often had a political significance, the office of "friend" was, in this view, a permanent appointment of a political nature. Officers of this kind are known from Mesopotamia in the code of Lipit-Ishtar and in the code of Hammurabi. According to another conjecture, the title originated in Egypt where it was given to the highest ranking officials in the royal court.

The illustration shows a reproduction of a funerary stele from the period of the Eighth Dynasty (end of the third millennium B.C.), from the tomb of Neferyu who bore the title of "chancellor" or "sole companion" of the king". At the top of the stele Neferyu is seen sitting in the palace: he is also seen at the right and left of the palace gate with his wife.

"AND we shall light upon him as the dew falls on the ground..."
(2 Sam. 17 : 12)

Ahithophel advised Absalom to lose no time in pursuing the weary David with a force of picked troops and swooping down upon his followers in a surprise attack, thereby scattering them and taking the king captive (2 Sam. 17: 1). As against this, Hushai the Archite "the friend of David", who was playing to gain time for David to escape into safe hiding, dwelt on the great danger involved in any armed encounter with David and his followers. He therefore suggested mustering all the Israelite men-at-arms and then attacking the king's forces with an army as numerous as the sand by the sea (2 Sam 17 : 11). He compared the large force required for the campaign against David to the dew from heaven, which descends in such abundance that it covers the whole land. The photograph shows leaves of a plant covered with morning dewdrops. Dew often falls in Palestine in the summer nights. It is especially heavy in the western Negeb, the coastal plain, on the western slopes of Mount Carmel and in the Valley of Jezreel.

Now Jonathan and Ahimaaz were waiting at En-Rogel . . .   (2 Sam. 17 : 17)

En-Rogel, which lies to the south of the Temple Mount near the junction of the Valley of Hinnom and the Kidron (see p. 183), is near the point at which one of the roads from Jerusalem to the Judaean desert and the Jordan Valley leaves the city. There Jonathan and Ahimaaz, who were of a priestly family and had remained loyal to David, waited to obtain for the king news of what was happening in Jerusalem. They subsequently made their way to David's refuge in the Judaean desert, not far from the Jordan (2 Sam. 17 : 21—22). Some scholars hold that En-Rogel was the site of the "Dragon's Well" which, according to the book of Nehemiah (2 : 13), was situated near to the Gate of the Valley (of Hinnom?). The place marked the boundary between the tribe of Judah to the south and the tribe of Benjamin to the north (Josh. 15 : 7; 18 : 16). Today En-Rogel, called in Arabic Bir Eiyub ("the Well of Job"), is no longer a flowing spring but a well. The inhabitants of Jerusalem used formerly to water their gardens from it, while water for drinking and washing was provided by the spring of Gihon in the Kidron Valley, the only perennial spring in and about Jerusalem (cf. p. 202).

It is conjectured that in ancient times, En-Rogel too was a flowing spring as is implied by the use of the word *en* (spring in Hebrew) in its name. It may have been blocked in the great earthquake in the reign of Uzziah (Amos 1 : 1).

Shown in the illustration is the stone building erected over the well At the top right can be seen some houses of the village of Silwan.

T HE battle spread over the face of all the country; and the forest devoured more people that day than the sword.

(2 Sam. 18 : 8)

The decisive battle between the forces of David and Absalom was fought in wooded terrain, apparently not far from Mahanaim in Trans-Jordan (2 Sam. 17 : 24). The Hebrew word *ya'ar* (here translated "forest") has two meanings in the Bible: (a) a wood; (b) rocky terrain dotted with undergrowth. Fighting in either of these was extremely difficult. In the first it was easy to surprise the enemy at close quarters; in the second the soldiers were likely to lose their footing on the boulders or in the bushes while running in the heat of the battle.

The relief from the palace of Sennacherib at Nineveh, reproduced above, gives a vivid illustration of warfare in wooded terrain. The Assyrian troops are seen trying to ascend a hill with the help of sticks. Very laboriously they force their way through the trees which separate them from each other; as a result, the battle becomes a hand-to-hand mêlée. The description of Absalom's plight is in keeping with fighting of this kind in thick woodland: "His head caught fast in the oak, and he was left hanging between heaven and earth" (2 Sam. 18 : 9).

NOW Absalom in his lifetime had taken and set up for himself the pillar which is in the King's Valley . . . and it is called Absalom's monument to this day.   (2 Sam. 18 : 18)

It was customary in the ancient world for those who had no children to erect a memorial to themselves in their own lifetime. It is true that it is elsewhere related of Absalom that "three sons and one daughter" were born to him. But apparently these children died in their childhood, and hence he set up a memorial to himself in "the King's Valley". Another possibility is that it was a kind of commemorative monument, like that erected by Saul at Carmel in Judah after his victory over the Amalekites (1 Sam. 15 : 12), or the "name" made by David to commemorate his victory over the Aramaeans (2 Sam. 8 : 13; cf. also Isa. 56 : 5). The location of "the King's Valley" is uncertain. The only clear fact that emerges from this verse is that, besides the cairn of stones raised over the grave of Absalom in the forest of Ephraim (2 Sam. 18 : 17), there was also another well-known monument which Absalom had erected near Jerusalem in his own lifetime.

The edifice, partly hewn out of the rock and partly built of ashlar, which is today called "Absalom's Tomb" (see the illustration) was given this name by popular tradition. It was the most magnificent of the tombs in the Kidron Valley, identified by the same tradition with "the King's Valley". This monument dates back only to the beginning of the first century B.C. The lower part of the edifice is the actual grave, while the upper part is a "memorial" (Heb. *nefesh*). It stands at the entrance to a large burial cave popularly known as "the cave of Jehoshaphat"

"CAN I still listen to the voice of singing men and singing women?..." (2 Sam. 19 : 35)

Barzillai the Gileadite declined David's invitation to accompany him to Jerusalem and reside in his court, on account of his extreme old age which made it impossible for him to enjoy royal pleasures (cf. Eccl. 2 : 8). Singers played an important part in the entertainments of the court. Sometimes they sang to the accompaniment of a pipe or dancing; hence the combination of singers and dancers in Ps. 87 : 7. In other countries of the ancient East, too, there were male and female singers in the royal courts and in the houses of the nobility.

The two works of Egyptian art reproduced here portray both kinds of singers and their accompanists. The upper picture is a detail of a relief from the tomb of Nikauher, a judge at Sakkarah, from the time of the Fifth Dynasty (middle of the third millennium B.C.). It shows a flute-player and singer performing together. The singer is accompanying his song with gestures that mark the rhythm and tone. The lower plate is a section of a relief from the tomb of Neferu, from the time of the Eleventh Dynasty (the Middle Kingdom). It shows women singing and clapping their hands.

AND he passed through all the tribes of Israel to Abel-Beth-Maachah...
(2 Sam. 20 : 14)

Abel-Beth-Maachah occupied a position of strategic importance, for it dominated the valley of Iyon (Ayun) to the north, and the Hulah Valley to the south. It was also the junction of the highroads running from Tyre on the west to Damascus on the east, and from the valley of the Lebanon on the north to Hazor on the south. The name Abel-Beth-Maachah seems to imply that the city had once been part of the Aramaean kingdom of Beth-Maachah, which existed in the early part of David's reign (1 Chron. 19 : 6, see p. 175). Sometimes it is called Abel for short (2 Sam. 20 : 18). The potsherds discovered on the site testify that the city was inhabited as early as the Bronze Age, and it seems to appear in the list of cities taken by Thutmose III (14th cent. B.C.). In the latter part of David's reign it was already "a city which is a mother in Israel" (2 Sam. 20:19). When Sheba the son of Bichri raised the standard of revolt against David, he ensconced himself within the city's walls, no doubt with the intention of establishing his authority over the whole region. In the reign of Baasha, king of Israel, the Aramaean king Ben-Hadad attacked Abel (- Maim) and captured it (2 Chron. 16 : 4). In 733/2 B.C. it fell to Tiglath-Pileser III, king of Assyria. It is apparently mentioned in an inscription of Tiglath-Pileser in the form Abilakka (see pp. 280—281). The mound of Abel-Beth-Maachah (Tell Abil) is seen in the rear and centre of the picture, with the Hulah Valley beyond it.

AND they came and besieged him in Abel-Beth-Maachah; they cast up a mound against the city, and it stood against the rampart; and all the men who were with Joab were battering the wall, to throw it down.

(2 Sam. 20 : 15)

With the intention of striking at the centre of Sheba's revolt, Joab laid siege to the walled city of Abel-Beth-Maachah (see p. 191). In ancient times there were three ways of destroying a wall: (a) shattering it with siege-engines or battering-rams; (b) breaking it down with picks and axes; and (c) undermining it. These three methods are clearly illustrated in a relief from the reign of Assurnasirpal II (first half of the 9th cent. B. C.) discovered at Calah (see plate below). The battering-ram, with an axe-shaped blade attached to its end, is propelled forwards and backwards by a team from inside a wooden turret which is surrounded by a protective screen of soldiers. The ram was aimed at the joint between the courses of the stones and bricks of the wall, while at the same time arrows were shot at the troops defending the wall. There was also a movable siege-tower usually operated in co-ordination with the battering-ram. The soldiers in this tower harrassed the defenders on the walls with their bows in order to prevent any attempt to ward off the blows of the ram. Against this attack the besieged troops are seen trying to pull up the ram with chains, only to be frustrated by two Assyrian soldiers who are hanging on to the ram by hooks. Another much practised method was for the besieged to fling lighted torches at the ram-turret, which was made of wood and leather, so that its operators were compelled to pour water on the flames (see the relief; and cf the representation of the siege of Lachish on pp. 286—287). The two soldiers on the left, who are engaged in breaking down the outer wall, are protected by heavy coats of mail in place of the usual shield which they are unable to hold. In the bottom-centre of the relief Assyrian soldiers are seen trying to undermine the city wall.

NOW Joab was in command of all the army of Israel; and Benaiah the son of Jehoiada was in command of the Cherethites and the Pelethites...
(2 Sam. 20 : 23)

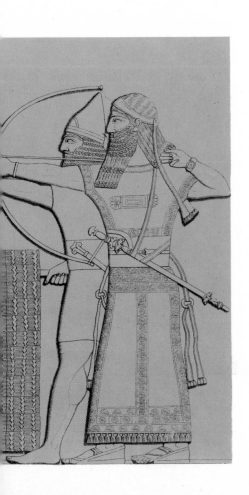

In the early days of the Monarchy, the Israelite kings employed at their court administrative officers and military commanders from the neighbouring nations (see p. 207), because of their superior professional qualifications. But what above all recommended these foreigners to their royal masters was the fact that their loyalty was not qualified by any local tribal patriotism and that they themselves took no side in internal disputes. For this reason, David went so far as to form a special fighting unit from the descendants of the Sea Peoples who still remained in Palestine. These Cherethites and Pelethites were apparently of the same racial stock as the Philistines. The Cherethites gave their name to the Negeb of the Cherethites in southern Palestine (see p. 153). The Sea Peoples provided most of the mercenary troops that served in the armies of the Mediterranean countries in the time of David and during the preceding two or three centuries. They frequently had to fight against their own kinsmen who were serving in the enemy's ranks.

The picture above is a pictorial reconstruction of a relief from the reign of Ramses III (12th cent. B.C.) which was found at Medinet Habu. It shows Sea People mercenaries in the royal bodyguard. The soldiers in the upper register armed with shield and spear are Egyptians. The first three soldiers in the lower register, following the trumpeter, are Sherden (one of the Sea Peoples from whom, apparently, the island of Sardinia derives its name) with their distinctive round shield, long sword and horned helmet.

A<small>ND</small> he gave them into the hands of the Gibeonites, and they hanged them on the mountain before the L<small>ORD</small>, and the seven of them perished together . . .   (2 Sam. 21 : 9)

Saul had put to death many of the Gibeonites "in his zeal for the people of Israel and Judah" (2 Sam. 21 : 2), apparently because he wished to reduce the number of non-Israelites living in the heart of his kingdom. In so doing, he broke the covenant made between the Gibeonites and the Israelites in the time of Joshua (Joshua chap. 9) and provoked God's wrath against Israel. At the Gibeonites' demand, David expiated the wrong done by the "house of blood" by handing over to them seven members of Saul's family to be executed before the Lord that His wrath might be stayed. A similar procedure is found in the affair of Baal-Peor: "Take all the chiefs of the people, and hang them in the sun before the Lord, that the fierce anger of the Lord may turn away from Israel" (Num. 25 : 4).

The actual form of execution is not described in the Bible, but can be inferred from the reliefs of the Assyrians who were in the habit of putting to death a number of their vanquished foes. Reproduced above is a section from a relief on the bronze gates found at Balawat portraying the campaign of Shalmaneser III (9th cent. B.C.) into northern Syria. Having captured the city of Dabigu in Syria, the Assyrians execute six of its inhabitants. The bodies of the dead men are impaled on stakes prominently erected on an embankment outside the city wall.

T HEN Rizpah the daughter of Aiah took sackcloth, and spread it for herself on the rock, from the beginning of harvest until rain fell upon them from the heavens; and she did not allow the birds of the air to come upon them by day, or the beasts of the field by night.

(2 Sam. 21 : 10)

After putting to death seven members of Saul's family, the Gibeonites left their bodies unburied as carrion for wild beasts, the fate of those slain in battle in ancient times. This was an outrage to the dead, the more so as they were scions of royalty (cf. 2 Kings 9 : 34—36; Isa. 14 : 18—20, and elsewhere), and also a departure from normal Israelite tradition (Deut. 21 : 23; Josh. 10 : 26—27). Rizpah the daughter of Aiah, the mother of two of the executed men, could not bear to see her sons thus dishonoured. She therefore took off the sack that she was wearing in her mourning, stretched it as a tent over the rock on which her sons were impaled and sat there day and night to keep bird and beast away from their dead bodies. When David was told of this, he was moved to pity and ordered the bones of the impaled men to be gathered together and buried with the remains of Saul and Jonathan in the territory of Benjamin.

Reproduced above is a fragment of the base of an obelisk from Susa, from the end of the third millennium B.C., depicting a captured citadel. The dead bodies of its defenders are strewn about the rocks, with birds of prey pecking at them.

THEY fell under my feet.
(2 Sam. 22 : 39)

David's song (2 Sam. 22), like all ancient Hebrew poetry, contains forms of expression and turns of phrase similar to those found in Canaanite literature. This is confirmed by the remains of literary works discovered at Ugarit in northern Syria, which include epics about the wars and adventures of the gods. For instance, the Ugaritic poet describes the battle between the goddess Anath and the robbers who attacked her temple in the following lurid terms: battling, smiting, vanquishing, Anath lays low her foes till their heads roll at her feet and their severed hands lie piled up before her (Epic of Baal, II, col. 2 end — 3 beginning; see the reproduction of the text with the translation beside it). The throwing down of the defeated foe, or of his head, at the victor's feet was thus a common figure in the martial-minded literature of the East.

The reproduction above is of an ivory tablet of the 14th cent. B.C. from the royal palace of Ugarit. The king of Ugarit is shown seizing a cowering foe by his hairlock. The arms of the vanquished man are raised in entreaty, but the victor is drawing his sword to despatch him.

THESE are the names of the mighty men whom David had . . . (2 Sam. 23 : 8)

on of the Ugaritic text:

ng came bands of robbers
e two gates of the House of Anath,
servants huddled in the recesses of a cave.
nath smote them through,
did she hew the sons of the two towns;
ote the nation of the sea-coast,
ly destoyed the people from the rising of the sun.
h her feet heads were like balls,
r body hands were like the locust
erless as the grasshopper the hands of the swift.
g heads upon her back
dangled from her girdle,
ed her knees in the blood of the fleet-footed,
ighs in the life-blood of the swift.
e off her would-be captors with her staffs,
es with the back of her bow.
th has reached her house,
oddess has come to her temple.
eart's desire she smites within it
y does she hack at the sons of the two towns.
s chairs at the swift,
urls tables at the warriors
ls at the mighty men.

While David was still at Ziklag, there rallied to him a group of intrepid warriors, the "mighty men" of Scripture (1 Chron. 12 : 1—7), who subsequently were instrumental in enthroning him at Hebron (ibid. 11 : 10). In the course of time, this band developed into a kind of permanent military body, known as "the thirty mighty men", which played an important part in David's army. Preserved in the Bible are two lists of the names of these heroes, together with their genealogies or places of origin which were mostly in Judah. In 2 Sam. 23 : 8—38 the list contains thirty-seven heroes (see v. 39); while in 1 Chron. 11 : 11—47 there are an additional sixteen who came from the districts conquered by David. Both the lists are interspersed with descriptions of the heroic feats performed by the warriors, fighting either singly or in groups.

Fighting-men who had gained renown by their heroic deeds were sometimes portrayed in the artistic representations of the ancient East (see p. 101; cf. 2 Sam. 23 : 20). Reproduced above is a fragment of pottery from Megiddo (apparently from the end of the second millennium B C.) on which is painted a procession of armed soldiers wearing coats of mail. In their left hand they hold a round shield and in their right a battle-axe.

A<small>ND</small> Gad came that day to David, and said to him, "Go up, rear an altar to the L<small>ORD</small> on the threshing floor of Araunah the Jebusite." (2 Sam. 24 : 18)

At the prophet's bidding, David bought the threshing-floor of Araunah the Jebusite for the purpose of building there an altar to the Lord, that the plague might be stayed from Israel. Presumably, the reference here is not to a private threshing-floor, but a public one, the latter being usually a large open space near to the city which also served for the performance of public ceremonies (Gen. 50 : 11; 1 Kings 22 : 10; Hos. 9 : 1, and elsewhere). There is an ancient tradition that the Temple of Jerusalem was built on the site of the threshing-floor of Araunah (or Ornan) the Jebusite (2 Chron. 3 : 1). A later tradition makes the threshing-floor of Araunah the location of the long venerated foundation-stone on which the ark was believed to have rested.

Photographed above is the rock which today occupies the centre of the Dome of the Rock on the Temple Mount. It is 45 ft. long and 36 ft. wide. The stone is sacred to the Moslems who give numerous legendary interpretations to every detail and mark on it.

KINGS

" AND he shall come and sit upon my throne; for he shall be king in my stead . . ."
(1 Kings 1 : 35)

The first chapter of the Book of Kings describes the story of an intrigue at David's court, concerning the succession to the throne. Until it became an established law in Israel for the eldest son to succeed his father, the heir was apparently chosen by the reigning king. Hence, at Bathsheba's instigation, David designates Solomon as his successor. Similar instances of the queen-mother having the final word in the choice of the heir to the throne were not unknown in other countries of the ancient East. Thus, it was through his mother's influence that Esarhaddon, the younger son of Sennacherib, came to the throne; and Esarhaddon's own younger son, Ashurbanipal, displaced his first-born brother with his grandmother's support.

From the moment of Solomon's anointment, at which David himself presided, until his own death, David shared the throne with his son (cf. 1 Chron. 23 : 1; 28 : 1—11; 29 : 20—25). Such a co-regency of father and son was not unusual in the ancient East, and seems also to have been known in the kingdoms of Judah and Israel after the division of the monarchy.

Reproduced above is a relief from Carchemish, from the first half of the 8th cent. B.C. On it the king Araras is seen with the royal sceptre in his left hand, while with his right he holds the arm of his son Kamanas. The son has a staff in his hand and a long sword hanging from his shoulder, as befits a princely heir-apparent.

AND caused Solomon to ride on king David's
mule, and brought him to Gihon. (1 Kings 1 : 38)

When Adonijah made an attempt to seize the throne, Solomon was taken down to the spring Gihon on the back of the king's mule at David's command. This was done both to mark the honour conferred upon him (cf. Gen. 41 : 43; Esther 6 : 9—11) and to symbolize the transfer of the royal power. At the spring, Solomon was anointed by Zadok the priest and Nathan the prophet, just as the first kings of Israel, Saul and David, had been anointed by the prophet Samuel.

The Gihon, here mentioned in the Bible for the first time (cf. 2 Chron. 32 : 30; 33 : 14), is the spring now called Ain Umm ed-Daraj, hard by the Kidron, David's City and the Ophel. Its waters flow out of a cleft in the rock at the rate of 250,000 gallons a day. This spring provided water for the inhabitants of Jerusalem as early as the third millennium B.C. At first, its waters were left to pour out into a natural pool. Later, in the patriarchal period, the inhabitants of the city cut a tunnel through the rock to give them access to the spring itself. Then, in the reign of Hezekiah, the mouth of the Gihon was blocked and its waters diverted along a rock-cut tunnel to the pool of Siloam (see p. 291). Presumably, the Gihon was chosen as the site of public ceremonies, such as the anointing of Solomon, on account of the important part it played in the life of the city. The view shows the Temple Mount and the City of David from the south. In the distance the steep course of the Kidron Valley can be seen to the right of the city wall. The spring of Gihon is in the part of it that lies in shadow. The Mount of Olives is seen on the horizon.

ᴀɴᴅ Adonijah feared Solomon; and he arose, and went, and caught hold of the horns of the altar.

(1 Kings 1 : 50)

An altar is never mentioned in the Bible without reference being made to its horns. From this it may safely be inferred that every altar — whether intended for animal sacrifices or for the burning of incense — had horns at its corners, like the altar ex-excavated at Megiddo (reproduced in the upper figure). This altar is made of limestone and stands a foot and a half high. Its form is typical of the altars found in Palestine, and is to be dated to the time of David and Solomon, or a little later. The original significance of the horns of the altar is still un-certain. Some scholars hold that they are the relics of ritual pillars; others that they were meant to symbolize the horns of sacrificial animals; still others that they were used as pegs for the various ritual implements. How-ever that may be, it is certain that the horns were regarded as the most sacred part of the altar not only in Israel, but also by other Semitic nations, as well as by the Minoans and the Greeks. In Israel it was customary to sprinkle some of the blood of the sin-offering on them (Lev. 4 : 7, 18, 25 and else-where). Fugitives clung to them for asylum, as did Adonijah in our verse here and Joab the son of Zeruiah (1 Kings 2 : 28), when they were fleeing from Solomon. The horns of the altar saved Adonijah, but not Joab.

The lower figure is a detail of a temple from the Late Bronze Age (middle of the second millennium B.C.) excavated at Beyçe-Sultan in south-western Anatolia. In the temple was discovered a pair of terra-cotta horns, about a yard high, standing on a low platform. This platform projects some distance in front of them, forming a hearth. Clay bins and benches behind the low wall indicate the sacrificial purpose of the struc-ture.

THEN David slept with his fathers, and was buried in the city of David.   (1 Kings 2 : 10)

According to the Bible, most of the kings of Judah were buried in the City of David. These graves are probably "the tombs of David" mentioned in Nehemiah (3 : 16) as being near "the pool that was made", perhaps the Pool of Siloam. The tomb of David is also mentioned in Josephus (Antiq. vii. 15.3 : xvi.7.1) and in the New Testament (Acts 2 : 29); but none of these passages gives any precise indication of the original site.

The photograph shows three rock-cut tombs which were excavated within the confines of the City of David and are set apart from other graves by their size and shape. Since tombs of such unusually large dimensions, situated moreover inside the city, must have been intended for the burial of princes, they are sometimes identified with the tombs of the kings of Judah. One of the graves, better preserved than the others, is in the form of a double vaulted tunnel (50 ft. long and 8 ft. wide). At the far end of the floor of the upper branch of the tunnel there is a niche hewn out of the rock (a sign of Phoenician influence) which was apparently designed to receive a sarcophagus. Since the tombs were first plundered and then used as a quarry in the Roman period, no archaeological remains have been found in them and their identity is still a matter of pure conjecture.

So Bathsheba went to king Solomon, to speak to him on behalf of Adonijah. And the king rose to meet her, and bowed down to her; then he sat on his throne, and had a seat brought for the king's mother; and she sat on his right.

(1 Kings 2 : 19)

In the ancient world, the queen-mother's position was one of prestige and honour; the court of the king of Judah was no exception to this rule. There, too, the queen mother had great authority and sometimes even ruled herself (2 Kings 11 : 1; Jer. 13 : 18). She also occasionally influenced the religious life of the country (1 Kings 15 : 13), especially when she was a foreigner (ibid. 16 : 31; 18 : 4). Solomon, too, shows his mother the respect owing to her high rank: he rises from his throne to greet her, bows low before her, waits upon her and seats her at his right hand. This is exactly the relationship depicted between Amenhotep I of Egypt and his mother Nefertari on a wall-painting from the "Tomb of the Two Sculptors" belonging to the 16th cent. B.C. (see the reproduction). The accompanying inscription accords to the queen-mother, who is seen seated at her son's right hand, the blessing "may she live (for ever)".

SOLOMON made a marriage alliance with Pharaoh king of Egypt; he took Pharaoh's daughter . . .

(1 Kings 3 : 1)

Solomon's marriage with the daughter of Pharaoh is given special emphasis in the Bible. It was unusual for the kings of Egypt to give their daughters in marriage to foreign potentates, even though they themselves were in the habit of taking the daughters of such rulers as wives. It is known from the el-Amarna letters that, when the king of Babylon sought the hand of the daughter of Amenhotep III, the Egyptian monarch rejected his suit on the grounds that "from of old, a daughter of the king of Egypt has not been given to anyone" (i.e. to a foreigner). Herodotus, too, (Book III, chap. 1) implies that the king of Egypt refused to wed his daughter to Cambyses, king of Persia. It is, therefore, most likely that the biblical reference to Solomon's marriage with the daughter of Pharaoh is meant to stress the power and the high esteem in which the kingdom of Israel was held by the Egyptians who, after a period of decline, were once more beginning to cast covetous glances in the direction of Palestine.

Only one other foreign ruler, besides Solomon, is known to have taken an Egyptian princess as his wife, and he is Niqmad, King of Ugarit (14th cent. B.C.). This follows from the fragment of a jar from Ugarit (reproduced above) portraying the king's wedding to an Egyptian princess, perhaps even a daughter of the King of Egypt. The identification of Solomon's father-in-law presents a difficult problem. Possibly he was the Pharaoh Siamon, one of the last monarchs of the Twenty-first Dynasty. In one of the reliefs excavated at Tanis in Lower Egypt (see the lower plate) this Pharaoh is shown smiting an enemy belonging to the Sea Peoples. The relief may have commemorated an expedition against the Philistines, as a consequence of which Siamon perhaps conquered from the Canaanites the city of Gezer, the city which Solomon's father-in-law gave to his daughter as a dowry (1 Kings 9 : 16).

A ND these were his high officials: Azariah the son of Zadok was the priest; Elihoreph and Ahijah the sons of Shisha were secretaries . . .   (1 Kings 4 : 2-3)

David's organization of a unified Israelite kingdom gave rise to certain forms of political administration which were, in part, modelled on the practice of the neighbouring nations. "The scribe" (Heb. *sofer*) is mentioned in the Bible as one of David's chief ministers. According to his name in its various forms (in our verse: Shisha), he seems to have been of foreign origin. The first Israelite kings, having no experience in the management of state affairs on a large scale, had recourse to foreign experts. The scribe was one of the most important officials in the Israelite monarchy. He sometimes took part in political negotiations (2 Kings 18 : 18 ff.), together with the minister "who was over the household" and "the secretary". In addition to his other functions, it was his task to record the important events that occurred at the royal court. These records may have been collected into an official chronicle, as was customary in other states of the ancient East (Esther 6 : 1). Presumably it was Solomon's scribes that recorded the history of his reign in "the book of the acts of Solomon" (1 Kings 11 : 41).

In a relief from the 8th cent. B.C. found at Zinjirli — the site of the capital of the Aramaean Kingdom of Yaadi (or Shamal) in northern Syria — a royal scribe is seen holding his writing implements in his left hand and a clay tablet under his arm. He is standing before the throne of his king and master Bar-Rakab.

SOLOMON had twelve officers over all Israel . . . Solomon ruled over all the kingdoms from the Euphrates to the land of the Philistines and to the border of Egypt . . . For he had dominion over all the region west of the Euphrates from Tiphsah to Gaza, over all the kings west of the Euphrates . . . (1 Kings 4 : 7, 21, 24)

Preserved in the fourth chapter of the First Book of Kings is one of the most important of the royal documents found in the Bible, dealing with the administrative division of Israel in the time of the United Monarchy. The list contains twelve administrative districts (see the map on p. 209). Judah is omitted, as are the conquered areas which lay outside the limits of the territory occupied by the Israelites. Of the twelve districts, six are given the names of tribes: Ephraim (1), Naphtali (8), Asher (9), Issachar (10), Benjamin (11) and Gad (according to the Septuagint translation, 12). The rest are referred to by the names of cities within their confines. This reflects the different historical origin of these two classes of district. The former (1 Kings 4 : 8, 15—19) are virtually identical with the original territorial portions allotted to the Israelite tribes, with the addition of the district of Mahanaim (7) in Trans-Jordan (ibid. 14) which had a population composed of different tribes. The latter (ibid. 9—13, numbered 2—6 on the map), on the other hand, are former Canaanite areas which were only conquered in the reign of David.

By his victories, David left Solomon an empire which included conquests far beyond the borders of Judah and Israel (see the map on p. 208). Solomon thus originally ruled over a wider extent of territory than any other Israelite ruler after him. This control of the international trade-routes connecting the Fertile Crescent with Egypt was one of the reasons for the political power and economic prosperity of the "Israelite empire".

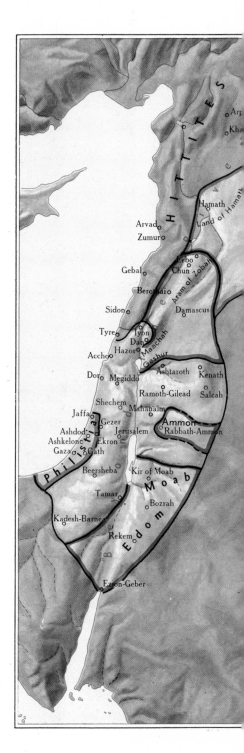

Cities fortified or built by Solomon

○ Hazor

Boundary of Israel

Miles
0 5 10 15 20

Iyon

Tyre

Kanah

Dan

Hammon

Kedesh

Accho

Ramah

Hazor

MAACHAH

Chinnereth

GESHUR

Karnaim

Bezer

Boundary

Hannathon

Aphek

Ashtaroth

ARGOB

Kenath

LAND OF CABUL at the End of Solomon's Reign

NAPHTALI

ZEBULUN

Yabneel

Tabor

Shimron

Anaharath

HAVOTH JAIR

Edrei

Dor

Yokneam

ISSACHAR

Ramoth

Camon

Tob

Salcah

Megiddo

10

Jezreel

Ham

Ramoth-Gilead

6

Taanach

5

Beth-Shan

Dothan

Ibleam

Yabesh-Gilead

Hepher

Abel-Meholah

Socoh

3

Tirzah

Zaphon

Shechem

Mahanaim

1

Zarethan

Tappuah

Adam

Gath-Rimmon

Aphek

Betonim

Yogbehah

Jaffa

Yehud

Yaazer?

Rabbath-Ammon

PHILISTIA

2

Bethel

Beth-Nimrah

AMMON

Beth-Horon

Mizpah

Shaalbim

Jericho

Gezer

Gibeon

Aiyalon

BENJAMIN

Beth-Haram

Ekron

Jerusalem

Heshbon

Ashdod

Beth-Shemesh

Beth-Yeshimoth

Bethlehem

Medeba

Ashkelon

GAD

12

Lachish

Hebron

Gaza

Gath?

JUDAH

Dibon

Aroer

MOAB

MOUNT EPHRAIM

4

209

A ND fatted fowl.   (1 Kings 4 : 23)

The twelve district officers appointed by Solomon to ensure the proper supply of provisions for the court devoted themselves to the levying of taxes and the orderly administration of the royal income. In Solomons' reign, the royal household grew in size and complexity and its requirements increased accordingly. To judge by the quantity of food listed in the Bible as "Solomon's provision for one day", 4000—5000 people must have eaten daily at the king's table (cf. Neh. 5 : 17—18). In Mesopotamia and Egypt too, the rulers used to appoint special officials to take charge of the royal economy and to be responsible for the levying of taxes. In the painting from the tomb of Rekhmire (reproduced above) officers of various districts in Upper Egypt are seen presenting their taxes in the form of agricultural produce, cattle, goats, and also gold and silver rings. This procedure resembles that customary in Solomon's court. There the officers first collected together all the taxes and then "brought them to the place where they were required, each according to his charge "(1 Kings 4 : 28).

Amongst the fare brought to Solomon's court, the Bible singles out "fatted fowl" (Heb. *barbur*) which were no doubt a delicacy like the harts, gazelles and roebucks mentioned in the same verse. Modern scholars incline to the view that the bird referred to is the goose, which was fattened for food in the ancient East. Evidence of this is provided by an ivory from Megiddo, dating from the 13th or 12th cent. B.C. (see the lower plate), on which the artist has engraved a scene showing the presentation of geese, possibly as taxes.

The wisdom of Solomon was of the kind widespread in ancient times, especially in Egypt and Mesopotamia. Hence, the Bible praises Solomon's wisdom as surpassing that "of all the people of the east, and all the wisdom of Egypt". The subjects of Solomon's proverbs were "the trees... beasts and birds, and reptiles, and fish". Presumably, then, Solomon was credited with a compilation of parables taken from the world of nature and animal life, like the "onomastica" (word lists) that were current among scholars and priests in Mesopotamia and Egypt.

Photographed above is a fragment of an Egyptian compilation of this kind on a papyrus found in the Ramesseum at Thebes and dating from the Middle Kingdom. It lists twenty kinds of cattle, the names of birds, fishes, and other animals, plants, crops, fruits, pastries, cereals, liquids, minerals, the various parts of an ox (possibly for sacrificial use), together with the names of towns and fortifications.

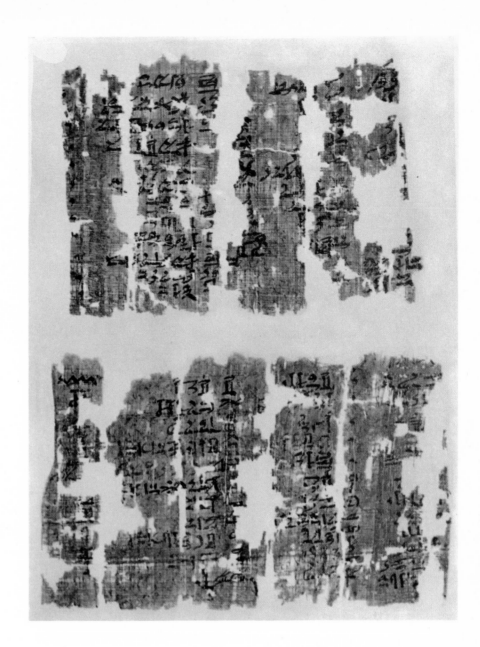

So that Solomon's wisdom surpassed the wisdom of all the people of the east, and all the wisdom of Egypt. (1 Kings 4 : 30)

Under the terms of his treaty with Hiram, king of Tyre, Solomon received cedars and cypresses of Lebanon to provide the timber for the Temple and the royal palace. Solomon availed himself of Tyrian technical knowledge and experience in felling the trees, bringing them down to the coast and transporting them "on rafts by sea to Jaffa" (1 Kings 5 : 9; 2 Chron. 2 : 7,8,16). In this matter, Solomon followed the practice of the kings of Egypt, Assyria and Babylon who used cedars of Lebanon for building purposes. In the scroll of Wenamon (beginning of the 11th cent. B.C.) there is a detailed description of the felling of trees of Lebanon for the Egyptians by the people of Gebal: 300 men and 300 oxen were employed in this work, which lasted for three seasons. In the first, the trees were felled; in the second, the timber was laid out to dry; and in the third, it was brought down to the coast and transported by sea to Egypt.

A relief from Karnak in Egypt, from the reign of Seti I (end of the 14th cent. B.C.), shows the technique of felling wood. Notables of Lebanon are seen cutting down cedars for the Egyptians. One of them is chopping at the base of a tree-trunk, while his companions control the fall of the tree by means of ropes attached to it.

THE house which king Solomon built for the LORD was sixty cubits long, twenty cubits wide, and thirty cubits high.   (1 Kings 6 : 2)

The Temple built by Solomon is described in detail in the Book of Kings. It consisted of three main parts: the vestibule (Heb. *ulam*); the nave (Heb. *hekhal*), in which the priests performed the principal sacrificial rites; and the inner sanctuary (Heb. *debir*) where the Ark and the Cherubim stood. The entrance to the vestibule was flanked by the two great bronze pillars (see the reconstruction below). In front of the whole building stood the bronze "sea" (see p. 216). The centre of the court was occupied by the bronze altar: although not listed amongst the appurtenances of the Solomonic Temple, this altar is mentioned in the description of the inauguration ceremony (1 Kings 8 : 22, 54, 64).

Excavations carried out in Palestine (Beth-Shan, Megiddo, Lachish and elsewhere), in the Lebanon and Syria (Gebal, Qatna, Ugarit and elsewhere), have brought to light the remains of various Canaanite temples. The one that most resembles Solomon's Temple in plan was excavated at Tell Tainat in Syria and is from the 9th cent. B.C. It, too, was divided into three sections, and at its entrance also two pillars were found. A Canaanite temple from the end of the Late Bronze Age, which might be considered as a prototype of the Solomonic temple, has recently been excavated at Hazor. This, too, consisted of three parts; in the third, the "inner sanctuary" (seen in the foreground of the plate above), various ritual implements were found.

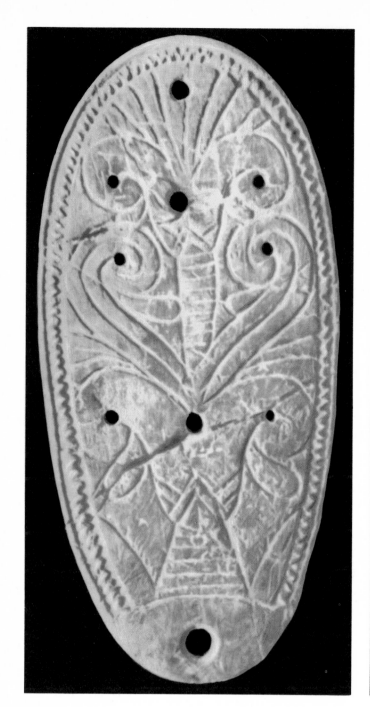

IN the form of gourds and open flowers . . . (1 Kings 6 : 18)

The inner walls of the Temple were inlaid with "boards of cedar" (1 Kings 6 : 15), as was the usage in some Babylonian temples. In Solomon's Temple, the ornamentation consisted of mouldings "in the form of gourds and open flowers". Flower- and plant-shaped patterns were a regular feature of ancient ornament, being particularly common in the ivories found in Palestine and Syria. Their design is usually stylized in the extreme. The origins of the designs are to be found rather in myth and ritual than in artistic feeling.

The left-hand plate above shows the cover of a cosmetic spoon from a Late Bronze Age temple at Lachish: it is engraved with an "open flower" pattern. On the right is an ivory plaque found at Megiddo (also from the Late Bronze Age) with a repeated palm-leaf motif. At the bottom of page 215 is a fragment of ivory from Samaria with a continuous pattern of alternating lotus-flowers and buds.

Now the capitals that were upon the tops of the pillars in the vestibule were of lily-work ... (1 Kings 7 : 19)

The two great pillars of cast bronze, with their capitals, were one of the show-pieces of Solomon's Temple (see p. 213, bottom plate). They apparently remained standing right down to the day of the Temple's destruction. It is not clear what their function was — whether they had some actual architectonic purpose, or were simply ornamental. Some scholars consider them to be reminders of the ritual pillars (Heb. *mazzebah*), while others hold that they commemorated the pillar of smoke and the pillar of fire that went before the Israelites in their exodus from Egypt. In spite of the wealth of detail given in the Bible, the description of the capitals of the pillars does not emerge at all clearly.

The proto-Ionic (or, more precisely, proto-Aeolian) capital from the times of the Kings of Judah, reproduced above, was excavated at Ramat Rahel. In the same excavations another similar capital was found, together with fragments of a third, all three being made of soft limestone. Modified versions of this type of capital have also been discovered at Megiddo, Samaria, Hazor and at Medebiyeh in Trans-Jordan. These archaeological parallels give us an idea of the design of the capitals of the Temple.

THEN he made the molten sea; it was round, ten cubits from brim to brim . . .

(1 Kings 7 : 23)

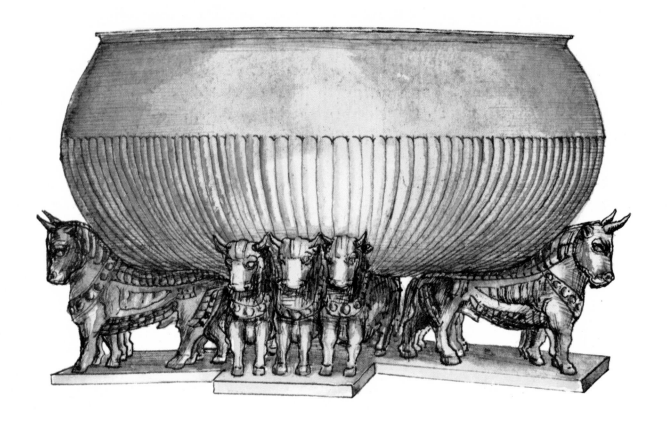

The "sea", and the twelve oxen which supported it, were cast in bronze (see the reconstruction above). The "sea" was ten cubits in diameter, five cubits high, with a circumference of thirty cubits. (The measurements of the diameter and the circumference seem to have been given in round figures). Its volume was two thousand *bath* (1 Kings 7 : 26) and it apparently weighed about thirty tons. According to various calculations made by modern scholars, it could hold from 9,000 to 13,300 gallons of water. Hence, when full, this basin was of no mean weight. It served primarily as a reservoir from which the lavers were filled, the water in it being presumably collected from the cisterns on and around the Temple Mount. The "sea" was of special ritual importance, since the washing of the hands and feet was a necessary preliminary to the priests' officiating in the sanctuary (Ex. 30 : 17—21). Basins for storing water were a common feature of the temples of Babylonia and the other lands of the ancient East as well as southern Arabia. Like Solomon's, they too were sometimes called "seas". Some modern commentators regard the "sea" as a cosmic symbol.

THIS was the construction of the stands: they had panels, and the panels were set in the frames and on the panels that were set in the frames were lions, oxen and cherubim. ... Moreover each stand had four bronze wheels...

(1 Kings 7 : 28-30)

The ten "stands", which, like the "sea", were of bronze (see p. 216), were made to hold the ten lavers (1 Kings 7 : 38—39). The "stands" had wheels, to facilitate the carrying of water from the "sea" to every part of the Temple court. The details in the description of the "stands" and their technical significance (1 Kings 7 : 27—37) are somewhat obscure. Such movable "stands" were common enough in the shrines of the ancient East, as is testified both by archaeological finds and literary evidence. However, the closest parallel to the "stands" in Solomon's Temple comes from Cyprus where miniature "stands" from the 11th-10th cent. B.C. have been discovered. One of them, from a tomb in Cyprus, is in an almost perfect state of preservation (see the reproduction above). Each side of the body of the "stand" is decorated with two winged sphinxes facing each other. The upper part of the "stand" is ring-shaped, with a spiral design round its rim. This ring was evidently intended to hold a laver, as with the "stands" in Solomon's Temple. It is not yet clear for what purpose such "stands" were placed in graves; possibly they are miniature replicas of the "stands" used in temple-courts.

Now as Solomon finished offering all this prayer . . .
he arose from before the altar of the LORD, where he had
knelt with hands outstretched toward heaven . . .

(1 Kings 8 : 54)

King Solomon stood before the altar and raised his hands to heaven (1 Kings 8 : 22); then he knelt down (cf. 2 Chron. 6 : 13) and uttered his prayer (Kings 8 : 23—53). At the close of his prayer he rose and, with his hands still outstretched, stepped forward to bless the people of Israel (ibid. 54—62). Sometimes in the Bible a prayer ends with obeisance before the altar, as in the bringing of the first fruits (Deut. 25 : 5—10) (where the Hebrew word meaning "to kneel down" has been translated "to worship"); or again, on the eighth day of the installation ceremony, we are told that the people "shouted, and fell on their faces" (Lev. 9 : 24). But in Solomon's case, only kneeling is mentioned.

Other nations in the ancient East were also accustomed to kneel before the altar. The plate above is a reproduction of a small altar from the 13th cent. B.C. with a relief depicting Tukulti Ninurta I, king of Assyria, in prayer before the altar. The figure of the king appears twice on the relief, once standing and once kneeling. He holds a sceptre in his left hand, and his right hand is raised towards the altar. The altar represented on the relief is a replica of the altar itself, with the addition of a staff and an oblong shield — the emblems of Nusku, the god of fire.

THEREFORE he said, "What kind of cities are these which you have given me, my brother?" So they are called the land of Cabul to this day.   (1 Kings 9 : 13)

The lavish consumption and multifarious trading of Solomon's reign progressively depleted the country's natural resources. Eventually, the king could no longer supply Hiram with wheat and oil, as in the early days of their alliance (1 Kings 5 : 11). Nor was the Israelite kingdom any longer as strong militarily as it once had been. Solomon was, therefore, obliged to cede to Hiram twenty Galilean cities in payment for the cedar, cypress and gold sent to him from Tyre (1 Kings 9 : 11). The cities in question were apparently in that region of the coast opposite the island of Tyre which had belonged to Israel since David's time. Cabul was probably at the south-eastern end of this region. It is mentioned in the list of Asher's possessions (Josh. 19 : 27); and its name has been preserved to this day in the village of Kabul, situated at the approaches to western Galilee, about nine miles south-east of Acre. These cities, which did not please Hiram, were evidently in the inhospitable mountains. The interpretation of the name "Cabul" is uncertain: according to Josephus, it means "a land of marshes". The plate shows a view of the region round Kabul.

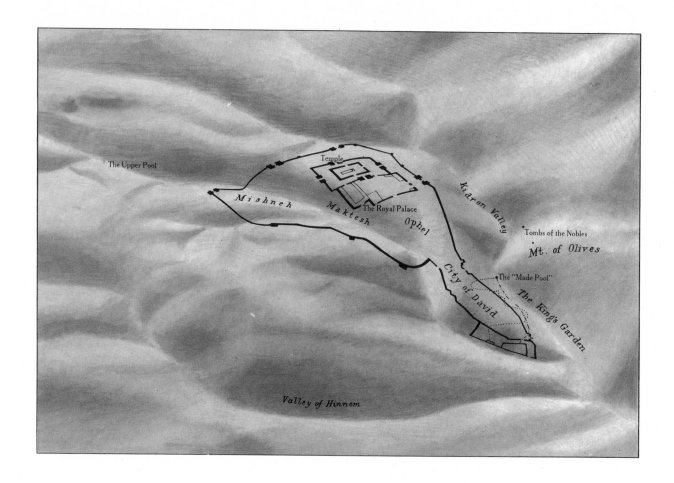

The Upper Pool · Temple · Mishneh · Maktesh · The Royal Palace · Ophel · Kidron Valley · Tombs of the Nobles · Mt. of Olives · The "Made Pool" · City of David · The King's Garden · Valley of Hinnom

Aₙd this is the account of the forced labour which King Solomon levied to build the house of the LORD and his own house and the Millo and the wall of Jerusalem . . .   (1 Kings 9 : 15)

Like all the great monarchs of antiquity, Solomon aspired to invest his capital with the splendour befitting a political and religious centre. This ambition found practical expression in large-scale building activities and in the extension of the city's confines. There is general agreement amongst scholars that the City of David was situated on the ridge where Jebus had stood. The mount, on which Solomon erected the Temple, was connected with the City of David by filling in the intervening area with earth. This filling is called the Millo — a name derived from the Hebrew verb meaning "to fill". Scholarly opinion is divided on the actual extent of the wall of Jerusalem in Solomon's reign, and throughout the period of the First Temple.

Ancient Jerusalem was built upon two spurs of the main ridge of the Judaean watershed, to the north-west of the Old City of our day. Below these two hills there are deep valleys: on the west the Valley of Hinnom, on the east the Kidron Valley. Between them is a third valley which, in the time of the second Temple, was called the Tyropoeon, "the valley of the cheese-makers". There are three different opinions about the extent of the area occupied by the capital in biblical times: One opinion would limit it to the more easterly of the two hills. According to this view the expansion of the city in Hezekiah's reign occurred only along the lower part of the central valley into which the king diverted the waters of the Gihon by the tunnel that he had hewn in the rock (see p. 291). At the other extreme, there are scholars who would enlarge the city's limits to include both the more westerly of the two hills and the valley between them. The third view, which is a compromise between these two extremes, would include in the royal city of Solomon the eastern hill and both the upper and lower parts of the central valley (the Maktesh or "Mortar" in the lower part and the Mishneh or 'second city' above it. The plan here is based on this third theory.

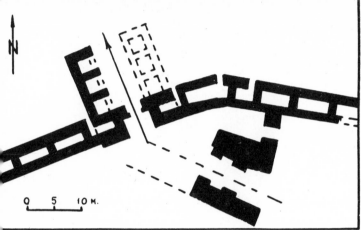

As part of the great building programme executed by Solomon, the Bible mentions the establishment of fortified cities on the main highways of his kingdom. In the excavations carried out on the mounds of the three cities specifically named in the text, remains have been found of walls from Solomon's time, complete with their gates: at Megiddo (see reconstruction at the bottom right), at Hazor (upper view) and at Gezer (see plan). The design of the gateways of all three cities is exactly the same. From this we may deduce that all three were built by royal command on a single masterplan, and possibly by the same architect. The plan of the gateway is as follows: the entrance, protected on either side by a square tower, led into a roofed vestibule, about 60 ft. long, with small chambers running off it, three to the right and three to the left (cf. Ezek 40 : 5—16). These sidechambers, which served as guardrooms, had walls strong enough to carry an upper storey. The gate itself must have been wide enough to take a chariot and its team (see p. 225). In front of the main gate an outer gate was built, to obviate any possibility of a frontal attack on the main gate.

HAZOR and Megiddo and Gezer. (1 Kings 9 : 15)

KING Solomon built a fleet of ships at Ezion-Geber, which is near Elath on the shore of the Red Sea, in the land of Edom. And Hiram sent with the fleet his servants, seamen who were familiar with the sea, together with the servants of Solomon . . . 　　(1 Kings 9 : 26-27)

At Ezion-Geber (Tell el-Kheleifeh), on the gulf of Elath, an ancient settlement has been unearthed. The archaeological finds from the site show that it was once an important industrial centre, with a highly efficient metallurgical furnace for the smelting of copper. It is most likely that this industrial centre was established by Solomon, the ruler who did so much to develop the crafts, industry and foreign trade of Israel. It is conjectured that the ore from the mines of the Arabah, after being smelted and refined at Ezion-Geber, constituted the principal commodity exported thence by ship. Some scholars are of the opinion that the expression "ships of Tarshish" (1 Kings 10 : 22) refers to large vessels designed for the transport of metals across the sea.

Solomon made use of Tyrian ship-builders and also of Tyrian sailors who, together with the king's servants, voyaged to countries rich in gold, spices and precious stones. The ships of Solomon were built on the pattern of Phoenician vessels. A reconstruction of such a vessel, based on reliefs from the 8th cent. B.C., is reproduced here. The Phoenician ship was larger than its Egyptian counterpart. It was flat-bottomed and had an oblong sail, made of sturdy material.

ONCE every three years the fleet of ships of Tarshish used to come bringing gold, silver, ivory, apes, and peacocks.

(1 Kings 10 : 22)

Setting sail from the Gulf of Elath, King Solomon's merchant fleet forged commercial links with Asiatic and African countries, above all with Ophir. The exact location of Ophir is unknown. Possibly it is to be identified with that country in the region of the Red Sea which the Egyptians called Punt, from which they used to import merchandise similar to that imported by Solomon from the lands of the south. The most famous voyage of the Egyptian fleet to Punt was undertaken in the reign of Queen Hatshepsut (first half of the 15th cent B.C.), for the purpose of "bringing back the precious products of the whole land". The picture reproduced above — from the temple of that queen at Deir el-Bahri — shows one of the Egyptian ships anchored on the shores of the Red Sea. The crew are loading their vessel with the riches of Punt: bags of gold and incense, various woods (including ebony), ivory tusks, balsam, antimony and monkeys. In the upper panel, the emissaries of the Queen of Punt are seen on their arrival at Thebes carrying royal gifts. The leading figures are bearing whole trees of frankincense.

The type of monkey imported into Egypt is illustrated in the lower picture from the tomb of the vizier Rekhmire (15th cent. B.C.). Some scholars hold that the Hebrew word *tukki*, which is translated "peacock" above, also designated a kind of monkey. The commoner opinion, however, is that it is a bird belonging to the same class as the peacock or the *Gallus ferrugineus*.

AND Solomon gathered together chariots and horsemen; he had fourteen hundred chariots and twelve thousand horsemen, whom he stationed in the chariot cities . . . (1 Kings 10 : 26)

The excavations at Megiddo throw light on the lay-out of Solomon's "chariot cities". In stratum IVB — the city of Solomon — several groups of stables were unearthed. In the reconstruction of the city in the bottom plate these stables can be seen in the background, to the right of the fortress and to the left of the city gate. All the stables were divided lengthwise into three aisles by means of two rows of square stone pillars, each with a hole in a corner for the tethering of the horse. (One of these posts excavated at Megiddo is shown above). Between the posts there were stone mangers. In the stables of Megiddo there was room altogether for about 450 horses. Since it was usual to allot three horses to a chariot (a team of two and one reserve), it follows that Megiddo was the base of a force numbering 150 chariots. Solomon might thus have had some ten "chariot cities" of similar size to accommodate his 1400 chariots.

NOW King Solomon loved many foreign women: the daughter of Pharaoh, and Moabite, Ammonite, Edomite, Sidonian, and Hittite women.

(1 Kings 11 : 1)

Solomon took wives from the neighbouring countries to the south, east and north of Israel, after the manner of the kings of the ancient East. Such political marriages were an accepted means of strengthening the friendly relations between states. The Bible makes special mention of his marriage with the daughter of Pharaoh, which was considered a particular distinction (see p. 206). Solomon's matrimonial alliances with the peoples of Trans-Jordan were designed to reinforce the dependence of the states conquered by David on the Kingdom of Israel. Those with the Sidonians were intended to ensure the continuation of the Phoenician friendship which had begun in David's reign. The object of the Hittite marriages was apparently to strengthen the political bonds between Israel and the neo-Hittite states in Syria, such as Hamath (see p. 174).

The presence in Israel of this large number of foreign wives inevitably led to an increase in idolatrous practices. In the neighbourhood of Jerusalem, high-places were erected to foreign gods: "And so he did for all his foreign wives, who burned incense and sacrificed to their gods" (1 Kings 11 : 8). The plates show court women and political marriages among the nations of antiquity. On the right is a stele from Abu Simbel in Egypt, showing the Hittite King giving his daughter in marriage to Ramses II (who is not seen in the picture). This marriage was meant to strengthen the peace treaty between the Hittite Empire and Egypt in the first half of the 13th cent. B.C. The middle plate is a painting from Thebes in Egypt which portrays two Egyptian princesses, the daughters of a high official in the reign of Thutmose IV(15th cent. B.C.). The first, who is married and is called "the lady of the house", is holding a scarf, the second a cup. They are accompanied by a harpist. In the reproduction on the left, a queen of Ugarit, from the 13th cent. B.C., is seen presenting an offering to the gods.

My father chastised you with whips, but I will chastise you with scorpions. (1 Kings 12 : 11)

The flogging of tax-evaders was a regular practice in the East, and, as such, is often portrayed in Egyptian art. In a relief (above) from the tomb of Mereruka (third millennium B.C.), a village headman, who had been remiss in the payment of taxes is being beaten by two of the tax-official's minions. This punishment was sometimes made even crueller by the use of spiked and barbed whips; hence the reference to "scorpions". Rehoboam compares Solomon's oppression of the people to ordinary flogging and boasts that he will make their yoke still heavier, till it is like a flogging with "scorpions". Reproduced below is part of an Egyptian stele of the Eighteenth Dynasty which shows that Rehoboam's simile is based on fact. One of the Egyptian workmen is carefully preparing a lash from a branch bent into the shape of a bulrush. This is evidently the ordinary lash. His fellow-worker is putting the finishing touches to a flail which has a sting-like spike at either end. This is presumably a "scorpion"

The immediate cause of the revolt of the ten tribes after Solomon's death (c. 930 B.C.) was the heavy burden of taxes that Solomon had imposed on the people. But the underlying historical reasons are to be found in the deep-rooted antagonism between Judah and the "House of Joseph", signs of which had already appeared in the period of the Judges. This latent antagonism flared up into open rupture after Saul's death, especially in the revolt of Sheba the son of Bichri. Nor did the short period of unity in the reigns of David and Solomon heal the breach. On the contrary, Solomon's system of taxes, with its preferential treatment of Judah, (cf. p. 208) exacerbated the already strained relations between the two sections of the nation. So much so that, while Solomon was still on the throne, an abortive attempt at rebellion was made by Jeroboam the son of Nebat, who was in charge of "all the forced labour of the house of Joseph" (1 Kings 11 : 27—28). After Solomon's death, Jeroboam returned from his voluntary exile and placed himself at the head of the uprising against Solomon's successor, Rehoboam. The rebels established a separate kingdom, ruled by an independent dynasty, with its capital at Shechem. Subsequently, still in Jeroboam's reign, the capital was transferred to Penuel in Trans-Jordan and later to Tirzah, north-east of Shechem. The tribes which remained loyal to David's line were Judah, Simeon (which had in fact been incorporated in Judah, cf. p. 58) and Benjamin, in whose territory Jerusalem lay. The more northerly of the conquered regions of Trans-Jordan—Ammon and Moab—were included in the Kingdom of Israel, while the more southerly Edom remained under Judah (see map).

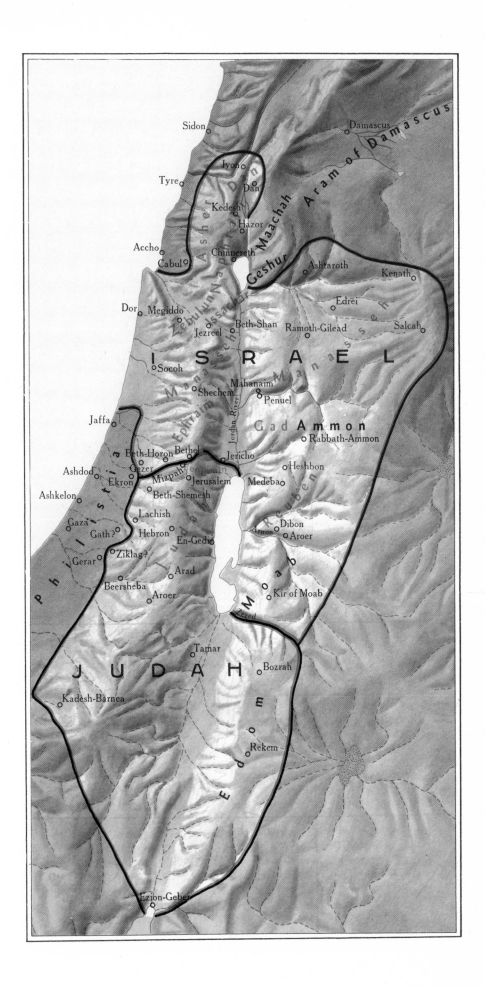

AND he offered sacrifices upon the altar; so he did in Bethel,
sacrificing to the calves that he had made . . . (1 Kings 12 : 32)

The worship of the calf can be traced back to a primitive cult adopted by the Israelites during their wanderings in
the wilderness (Ex. 32—cf. Vol.I, p. 171). This connection is most clearly expressed in Jeroboam's words: "Behold your gods, O Israel, who brought you up out of the land of Egypt" (1 Kings 12 : 28). It has indeed been
maintained that the backsliding Israelites did not actually regard the calf (or bull) as the incarnation of a god,
but rather as the pedestal of an invisible god standing above it. Similarly the cherubim in the Temple were the
visible throne of the Lord ("who sits upon the cherubim") whom no mortal eye might behold. From archaeological evidence it seems that the peoples of the ancient East used sometimes to conceive of their gods as standing
on the back of an animal. Thus, the storm-god, known to us from Mesopotamian and Syrian tradition, is sometimes represented as standing on a bull, while, in other instances, the bull itself is the emblem of the god. Occasionally this bull is depicted as a young steer and this may provide a parallel to the Israelite cult of the calf. The
Bible denounces Jeroboam's innovations and his burning of incense on the altar as heinous sins (1 Kings 12 : 20;
13 : 1—2, 33—34; 2 Chron. 11 : 13—16).
The reproduction above — from Alaça Huyük (15th cent. B.C.) — shows two figures standing before an
altar. The one in front, apparently a priest-king, holds a staff in his left hand and is raising his right towards
the altar. The figure behind is perhaps his wife, the priestess-queen. To the right of the altar, and facing it, there
is a horned bull, evidently the god's emblem, standing on a pedestal.

THE LORD will smite Israel,
as a reed is shaken in the
water . . .   (1 Kings 14 : 15)

Two kinds of reed grow in Palestine: the *Arundo donax L.* and
the *Phragmites communis Trin.* Since the latter is the more
common, it is presumably the one meant in our verse. It grows
in places where there is plenty of moisture, such as the beds
of watercourses and marshes (cf. Isa. 19 : 6; Job 40 : 21). The
lower part of the long, thin stem is often under water. At the
top it terminates in a tail-like flower. The stem, being slender
and flexible, is easily shaken by wind and water. This is the
characteristic referred to in our verse. Just as the slender reed
cannot resist the slightest breeze, so will the people of Israel
be unable to withstand their foes and will be uprooted from
their land: "and root up Israel . . . and scatter them beyond the
Euphrates" (1 Kings 14 : 15). "A reed of a staff" is an expression
used in the Bible to signify a vain, illusory assurance (2 Kings
18 : 21; Isa. 36 : 6; Ezek. 29 : 6).
Reproduced below is a section of a wall-painting from the
northern palace of Amenhotep IV (Akhenaton) at el-Amarna
(middle of the 14th cent. B.C.), showing reeds growing in
a marsh.

IN the fifth year of King Rehoboam, Shishak king of Egypt came up against Jerusalem; he took away the treasures of the house of the LORD and the treasures of the king's house; he took away everything . . .

(1 Kings 14 : 25-26)

The description given in the Bible of the campaign of Pharaoh Shishak (in Egyptian: Sheshonk) against Rehoboam bears the marks of having been taken from a chronicle of names and dates. The date mentioned here is actually the first in the Bible that can be definitely connected with Egyptian records. An inscription of Shishak, from the southern wall of the temple of Amon at Karnak (see the reproduction), records the Pharaoh's conquests in Palestine (in c. 926 B.C.). In the centre of the relief stands Amon holding a rope to which captives are bound in rows. Each one of the captives is the ruler of a conquered city, the name of which is engraved on his body within an oval ring. At the right, other captives are seen on their knees, with their hands raised in submission. Although the inscription says nothing at all about the actual course of the war in Palestine, it is possible to reconstruct the Egyptian monarch's line of advance from the detailed list of captured places (about 180 in all). Shishak's forces overran the Negeb of Judah and the Kingdom of Israel, taking and sacking many settlements as they went. Jerusalem is not mentioned in the list: it was evidently saved from conquest by the heavy tribute that Rehoboam paid to the Pharaoh. The Bible specifically mentions the deliverance of Jerusalem, attributing it to the submission of the king and his ministers to God's will, as expressed in the words that the Lord put into the mouth of Shemaiah, his prophet: "They have humbled themselves; I will not destroy them, but I will grant them some deliverance, and my wrath shall not be poured out upon Jerusalem by the hand of Shishak" (2 Chron. 12 : 7).

ND king Asa sent them to
Ben-Hadad the son of Tabrimmon, the son of Hezion, king
of Aram, who dwelt in Damascus . . .   (1 Kings 15 : 18)

The first half of the 9th cent. B.C. saw the rise of the Aramaean kingdom of Damascus as one of the important
states in Syria. This was in part due to the astuteness of its king, Ben-Hadad the son of Tabrimmon, in taking
advantage of the rift between Judah and Ephraim. First he made a treaty with Baasha, king of Israel. Then he
broke this treaty and joined forces with Asa, king of Judah. While Baasha was mustering his army in southern
Ephraim to do battle with Asa at Ramah, Hadad attacked and destroyed his "store cities" in the north of the
country, from Iyon to Chinnereth (1 Kings 15 : 19—20; 2 Chron. 16 : 3—4). The biblical Ben-Hadad, the son
of Tabrimmon, is apparently the same as the king of Damascus, Ben-Hadad I, who is mentioned on a votive stele
from the 9th cent. B.C. discovered near Aleppo (see the reproduction). In the upper part of the stele the god
Melkart is seen wearing a knee-length cloak. He holds a bow in his right hand and an axe in his left. On the
lower part of the stele are engraved the name of the man who dedicated it and the names of his ancestors: "Bar-
Hadad, son of Tabr(amman so)n of Hazia(n)" (the letters in brackets are missing). If this restoration of the ancestors' names is correct, the names on the monument are identical with those given in the Bible: Bar-Hadad and
Ben-Hadad are simply the Aramaic and Hebrew forms of the same name which means "the son of the god
Hadad". It is conjectured that this name, connecting the king with the city's great god, was borne by all the
rulers of Aram-Damascus. The second half of the name Tabrimmon, in Accadian Ramman, was one of the
appellations of the god Hadad (see 2 Kings 5 : 18; Zech. 12 : 11).

$\mathbf{A}$ND when Baasha heard of it, he stopped buil
ding Ramah, and he dwelt in Tirzah.

(1 Kings 15 : 21)

The military support given to Asa by the king of Aram forced Baasha to abandon his plan of fortifying Ramah which was close to the border between Ephraim and Judah. He therefore withdrew to Tirzah which has already been mentioned as the royal residence of Jeroboam's dynasty (1 Kings 14 : 17). Tirzah remained the capital of the kingdom of Israel during the rule of Baasha's dynasty and for the first six years of Omri's reign. Omri subsequently moved his capital from the city, perhaps because it had been damaged during the revolts of Zimri and Tibni. Tirzah lay in the territory of Manasseh and bore the same name as one of the daughters of Zelophehad, of the tribe of Manasseh (Num. 27 : 1—7; see Vol. I, p. 232). The Book of Joshua mentions the king of Tirzah as one of the thirty-one kings who were defeated by the Israelites (Josh. 12 : 24).
Tirzah is usually identified with Tell el-Farah, about seven miles north-east of Shechem, at the mouth of Wadi Farah (see the map). The site overlooks the junction of two roads, one of which runs north to Beth-Shan and the Jordan Valley, the other eastwards to the fords of the Jordan and Gilead. The site was abundantly supplied with water and the beauty of its scenery had become proverbial: "You are beautiful as Tirzah my love, comely as Jerusalem" (Song of Sol. 6 : 4). The excavations show that the city was founded in the fourth millennium B.C. and that it was well fortified in the second millennium. It reached its apogee at the beginning of the 9th cent. B.C. under the dynasty of Baasha. In the view above are seen the excavated remains of buildings at Tirzah from the time of the Kingdom of Israel, some of them the remains of private houses.

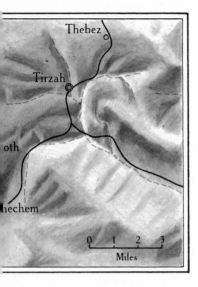

Thebez

Tirzah

Shechem

oth

0   1   2   3
Miles

Aᴺᴰ Baasha struck him down at Gibbethon, which belonged to the Philistines; for Nadab and all Israel were laying siege to Gibbethon.

(1 Kings 15 : 27)

During a war against the Philistines, Baasha the son of Ahijah, of the house of Issachar, seized the opportunity offered by the Israelite army's being engaged in the siege of Gibbethon to exterminate Jeroboam's dynasty and to seize the throne. Zimri's conspiracy and short-lived reign also occurred while the people "were encamped against Gibbethon, which belonged to the Philistines" (1 Kings 16 : 15). Evidently, the battle for this city, one of the key-points on the Israelite-Philistine border, was fierce and protracted. Gibbethon is listed as one of the cities set aside by the tribe of Dan for the Kohathite families of the Levites (Josh. 21 : 23). The paucity of topographical data makes the exact location of the city difficult: it is commonly identified with Tell el-Malat, between Gezer and modern Ekron.

On an Assyrian relief found at Khorsabad, from the reign of Sargon II (721—705 B.C.), there is a portrayal (reproduced below) of the capture of Gibbethon — in cuneiform writing, Gabbutunu — by the Assyrian army in 712/11 B.C. in the course of Sargon's campaign against Ashdod. The Assyrian troops, armed with round shields and bows, are shown attacking the city and firing arrows at its walls.

HE bought the hill of Samaria from Shemer for two talents of silver; and he fortified the hill, and called the name of the city which he built, Samaria, after the name of Shemer, the owner of the hill.　　　　　　　　　　　　　　　　　　　　　　　　　(1 Kings 16 : 24)

The Bible dismisses Omri, one of the greatest kings of Israel, with no more than a brief reference. In fact, it mentions only one undertaking during his reign — the foundation of the city of Samaria. The hill of Samaria, north-west of Shechem, on which the new city was built, commands several highways leading up into the mountains and down into the plain. Samaria also has the additional advantage of fertile valleys at its foot (see the view on p. 236). The name Samaria was, according to the biblical tradition, taken from the name of the previous owner of the hill on which the city was founded. In both the Bible and Assyrian documents the name Samaria was used to designate the whole of the mountains of Ephraim, and sometimes even the whole Kingdom of Israel. Samaria remained the capital of Ephraim until the inhabitants of the Northern Kingdom were taken captive to Assyria. In the heyday of the kingdom it was a byword for its wealth, luxurious living and cosmopolitanism (see for example, Amos 3 : 12, 15; 4 : 1).

The excavations carried out at Samaria — to-day the site of the Arab village of Sebastiyeh — have brought to light the remains of palaces, houses of courtiers, storehouses and granaries from the time of the dynasties of Omri and Jehu. The relics of its walls, with their silent testimony to its ancient might, lend vividness to the description by the prophet Amos of the people of Israel as "those who feel secure on the mountain of Samaria" (Amos 6 : 1). The numerous ivory ornaments found amongst the ruins of the city are evidence of the technical perfection and artistic sophistication achieved there under foreign influence (cf. pp. 250—251).

Photographed above is a section of the wall of Samaria from the time of the first Israelite kings (9th cent. B.C.). It is built of courses of hewn stone placed as stretchers alternating with pairs of headers. Each stone has a narrow margin cut along two or three of its edges. This type of masonry, which was borrowed from the Phoenicians, is characteristic of Israelite walls of that period.

"DEPART from here and turn eastward, and hide yourself by the brook Cherith, that is east of the Jordan." (1 Kings 17 : 3)

The prophet Elijah's first appearance before King Ahab indicates the nature of his mission. Immediately after having prophesied that Israel will be afflicted by a severe drought, he flees from Ahab's wrath. At God's bidding, he hides "by the brook Cherith, that is east of the Jordan". Elijah came from Gilead; according to one conjecture, actually from the city of Yabesh-Gilead (explaining the epithet "Tishbite" as meaning "Yabeshite"). He would, therefore, naturally seek refuge in his homeland. For this reason, scholars have been inclined to identify the brook Cherith — mentioned only here in the Bible — with one of the easterly offshoots of the Wadi Yabis, which begins its course in the Trans-Jordan desert and passes below the city of Yabesh-Gilead. The Bible relates that the prophet flying from Ahab turned eastwards i.e. towards the Jordan, and eventually came to a desolate spot. There food was brought to him miraculously (1 Kings 17 : 6) and water provided by the watercourse, which could not have been perennial since it dried up after a time: "And after a while the brook dried up, because there was no rain in the land" (ibid. 7).
The photograph shows the landscape near Wadi Yabis, where the prophet Elijah grew to manhood.

AND she said, "As the LORD your God lives, I have nothing baked, only a handful of meal in a jar, and a little oil in a cruse . . ."

(1 Kings 17 : 12)

When the brook Cherith dried up and Elijah had no more water to drink, he went, at God's bidding, "to Zarephath, which belongs to Sidon". In the gateway of the city, the prophet came upon a widow who, with her son, was dying of hunger on account of the drought which was afflicting the land, as he had prophesied. A miracle now occurred, and all three of them — the widow, her son and the prophet — found adequate sustenance in a handful of meal in a jar and a little oil in a cruse: "The jar of meal was not spent, neither did the cruse of oil fail" (1 Kings 17 : 16).

The cruse was a kind of jug made to hold oil or wine. The plate is a reproduction of a Phoenician vessel from the time of the Kings of Israel, such as must have been in common use in Zarephath which belonged to Sidon, where the widow of the biblical story lived. Similar vessels have also been found in Palestine. The trefoil-shaped lip was designed to facilitate the pouring out of the liquid. In ancient times, vessels of this kind, filled with oil, honey or balsam, were regularly traded between Palestine and Syria.

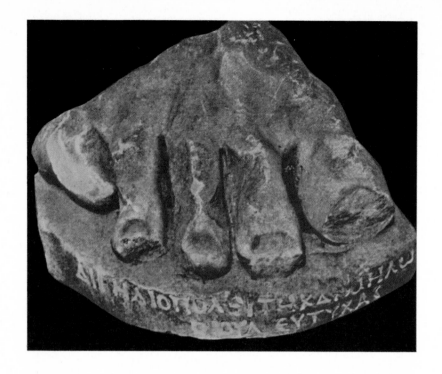

So Ahab sent to all the people of Israel, and gathered the prophets together at Mount Carmel. (1 Kings 18 : 20)

From Zarephath, near Sidon, Elijah returned to Israel in order to fight against the influence of the Sidonian religion which spread throughout the country in the time of Ahab and Jezebel. It would seem that Elijah's choice of Mount Carmel as the scene of his trial of strength with the priests of Baal was deliberate. This mountain was supposed to be sacred to the "Baal of the Heavens", a god worshipped throughout the ancient world, whose cult had spread as far as Carthage. "Baal of the Heavens" was also used as an appellation of Hadad, the life-giving god of the mountains, the lord of the rain and the lightning. From the earliest times, Hadad was identified with the god of the Carmel who commanded the distant horizon from his vantage point and protected seafarers. In the Hellenistic and Roman periods the "Baal of the Carmel" was identified with Zeus, the god of the skies, the clouds and the mountain-tops.

Reproduced above is a fragment of a votive foot which was found on Mount Carmel. Below the toes is a dedicatory inscription in Greek (about the 2nd cent. A.D.) to Heliopolitan Zeus, "(the god) of the Carmel"; the existence of the cult of this god, who is identical with Hadad on Mount Carmel, shows the true identity of the Baal with whom Elijah had to contend. The grandeur of the Carmel, which filled the inhabitants of ancient Israel with religious awe, has left its mark on Hebrew legend.

Below is a view of the western slopes of Mount Carmel.

ᴀɴᴅ they cried aloud, and cut themselves after their custom with swords and lances, until the blood gushed out upon them. (1 Kings 18 : 28)

Self-laceration, like shaving the head and cutting off the beard, was usually an expression of grief. Although the Law of Moses forbade this practice to the Israelites (Lev. 19 : 28; Deut. 14 : 1), and especially to the priests (Lev. 21 : 5), it was occasionally adopted by the people (Jer. 16 : 6; 41 : 5). However, the self-laceration of the priests of Baal in the contest on Mount Carmel has no connection with mourning, but is an act of ritual ecstasy such as finds no echo in Israelite tradition. That is why the Bible stresses that the priests of Baal acted "after their custom", that is to say, in a way foreign to the customs of Israel.

Ritual ecstasy, culminating in self-laceration, was a common feature of several ancient religions, and was practised, among others, by the Phoenicians. In classical sources there is reference to a "dancing Baal", i.e. apparently to Baal regarded as the god of the dance. An ecstatic leaping was actually part of the cult of Osiris at Rome. In the relief reproduced here a troupe of fanatics is seen twisting and swaying in front of the statues of Egyptian gods that were popular in Rome. The purpose of their gyrations is to call forth the resurrection of the god Osiris. Similarly, Jezebel's prophets on Mount Carmel sought, by their wild frenzy, to arouse Baal to a demonstration of his might, after they had called upon him by name "from morning until noon . . . but there was no voice and no one answered" (1 Kings 18 : 26).

BUT he himself went a day's journey into the wilderness, and came and sat down under a broom tree . . .

(1 Kings 19 : 4)

Elijah fled from Jezebel's murderous fury into the desert south of Beersheba. There he at last found rest for his weary body "and he lay down and slept under à broom tree" (1 Kings 19 : 5). This is, no doubt, the shrub still to-day called "the desert broom" *(Retama Roetam Forsk. Webb.)*, which grows in the gullies of the Negeb desert, in Edom and in the Sinai peninsula. The bush is leafless, except in the short rainy season when it produces a few leaves and is covered by white, scented blossoms (see the photograph). The few leaves shrivel up and drop off after the spring and the photosynthetic process is performed by the bare, green shoots. Sometimes the broom grows high enough for its shade to provide protection for a human being. Its thick roots are still to-day, as in ancient times, used for fuel: they are the "glowing coals of the broom tree" mentioned in the Book of Psalms (120 : 4 and cf. Job 30 : 7). Presumably the broom (Heb. *rotem*) gave its name to Rithmah, one of the halting-places on the Israelites' journey through the wilderness (Num. 38 : 18).

AND he arose, and ate and drank, and went in the strength of that food forty days and forty nights to Horeb the mount of God. (1 Kings 19 : 8)

Still harried by Jezebel, Elijah continued his flight southwards "to Horeb the mount of God". Taken literally, these words must refer to Sinai, the mountain which had been hallowed since the time of Moses, the first and greatest of the prophets. None the less, it is possible that the two names are not exactly synonymous, but that one designates a whole mountain range and the other a particular peak. An ancient tradition, going back at least to the Byzantine period, identifies Mount Horeb-Sinai with Jebel Musa (photographed below); but this identification is uncertain (cf. Vol. I, p. 151). Here, on Mount Horeb, God revealed Himself to Elijah in the moment of the prophet's despair. As at the Giving of the Law, God passed across the mountain in the elemental forces of nature, in a wind that "rent the mountains, and broke in pieces the rocks", in an earthquake and in fire, and finally, by contrast, in a still small voice (1 Kings 19 : 11—12).

Archaeological investigations in the Sinai peninsula have shown that, in spite of the great distances and the difficult country, there was communication between Judah and southern Sinai in the period of the Monarchy along tracks through the desert. Pottery vessels of the type in common use in Judah at that time have been discovered at Feiran, the most important oasis in the whole region, about 32 miles north of Jebel Musa (cf. Vol. I, p. 148). Presumably it was along these desert tracks that Elijah made his way from Beersheba (1 Kings 19 : 3) to the mountain of God.

THE people of Israel encamped before them like two little flocks of goats . . .

(1 Kings 20 : 27)

Ben-Hadad, the ruler of the Aramaean kingdom of Damascus, led his army to Aphek, located by most scholars beside the modern Arab village of Fiq to the east of the Sea of Galilee. He came in order to do battle with the Israelites who were advancing upon him through the mountains of Golan. The two hosts were now encamped opposite each other, waiting for a suitable moment to attack. The aim of the Aramaeans was to draw the Israelites out of the hills and have the battle fought out on level ground (1 Kings 20 : 23), where they could exploit the advantage afforded them by their chariots and cavalry. The Israelites, for their part, clung to the hills where they had proved themselves superior to the Aramaeans in a previous engagement (ibid.). For seven whole days, the Aramaeans in the plain and the Israelites on the hill stood facing each other at close quarters, "like two little flocks of goats". The meaning of this simile, which is found nowhere else in the Bible, appears to be that the two armies were like young goats with horns threateningly lowered, about to tussle with each other.

Reproduced below is a fragment of a glazed vessel found at Ashur, from the late Assyrian period, with, painted on it, two rams apparently about to engage in combat and ready to jump at each other.

Now Naboth the Jezreelite had a vineyard in Jezreel.
(1 Kings 21 : 1)

Naboth's vineyard was close to the royal palace in the city of Jezreel, which presumably stood on the site of the modern village of that name (Arab. Zerin). The ancient city lay at the foot of Mount Gilboa beside the spring of Jezreel (see p. 155), whose waters ensured rich yields to the fields to the north of it. The land to the south of the spring, on the other hand, could not be irrigated from it and was therefore dependent on the rainfall which is not heavy in this region (see Hos. 2 : 22—23). The city was built some distance away from the marshes on an eminence in the Valley of Jezreel, to which it gave its name (Josh. 17 : 16; Judg. 6 : 33; Hos. 1 : 5).

Jezreel enjoyed a favourable climate; it was the most fortunately placed of the settlements in the valley on account of its proximity to the international "Sea Road" on the west and to the highway running along the mountains of Ephraim to the east. It was situated on the watershed dividing the westward-flowing Kishon river from the eastward-flowing river of Harod. It was also the link between Judah and Samaria to the south, and Galilee to the north. Archaeological excavations have indicated that there was no permanent settlement on the site before the Israelite period. After the Israelite conquest of Canaan, the city was included in the territory of Issachar (Josh. 19 : 18). It became a place of considerable importance in the time of Saul; and in Solomon's reign it was one of the cities in the fifth administrative district (see p. 208). Because of its strategic importance, excellent climate, beautiful natural surroundings and fertile soil, it was further favoured by the kings of Omri's line, who fortified it and made it their winter capital and royal residence (2 Kings 8 : 29; 9 : 15, 17, 30). Jezreel was the scene of the fulfilment of Elijah's prophecy of retribution: it was there that Jehu meted out punishment to Ahab's line, thus avenging the judicial murder of Naboth (2 Kings 9 : 25—26, 36—37).

The photograph shows the site of Jezreel with Mount Gilboa behind. At the foot of the mountain are the spring of Jezreel and the fields of the Valley of Jezreel.

AND after this Ahab said to Naboth, "Give me your vineyard, that I may have it for a vegetable garden, because it is near my house . . ."   (1 Kings 21 : 2)

Ahab coveted Naboth's vineyard as a vegetable garden, because of its closeness to the royal palace. The biblical word for garden *(gan)*, when used by itself, may designate a vegetable garden, an orchard or a vineyard. Occasionally it is also used for any watered plot (Job 8 : 16; Song of Sol. 4 : 12). The kings of Israel and Judah evidently liked to have such gardens around their residences. Special mention is made in the Bible of "the kings' garden" in Jerusalem close to the city wall (2 Kings 25 : 4; Neh. 3 : 15) and also of the "garden of Uzza" (2 Kings 21 : 18, 26).

Particularly magnificent were the gardens around the palaces of the Egyptian kings and their nobles, with their profusion of fruit-bearing and other trees, of vines and aromatic shrubs, and their bathing-pools and irrigation ponds. The relief reproduced above — from the tomb of Mereruka at Sakkarah (second half of the third millennium B.C.) — depicts a vegetable garden in which labourers are carefully watering the lettuce-plants.

So she wrote letters in Ahab's name and sealed them with his seal.   (1 Kings 21 : 8)

The letters concerning Naboth sent by Jezebel to the elders of Jezreel, being stamped with the king's seal, were taken by the recipients to be a royal decree. The story implies that Jezebel herself, as the king's wife, had no executive authority. Generally speaking, royal prerogatives were accorded to the king's wife only if she ruled in her own right, as in the case of Athaliah in Judah (2 Kings 11). The rulers of the Hittites and of the Syrian kingdoms sometimes followed a different custom. This is indicated by the seal-impression of Suppiluliuma who reigned in the first half of the 14th cent. B.C. On this seal the title of the queen (Tawannanna) appears alongside the king's name (see the plate at the bottom of the opposite page). Royal seal-impressions of this kind were found in the palace archives at Ugarit. So far no royal seal-impressions or actual seals of the kings of Israel and Judah have been found. Seals have occasionally been found belonging to officials or ministers on which appear the names of kings known to us from the Bible, such as Jeroboam II the son of Joash king of Israel, and Uzziah, Ahaz and Jehoiachin, kings of Judah (see p. 278).

AS soon as Jezebel heard that Naboth had been stoned and was dead, Jezebel said to Ahab, "Arise, take possession of the vineyard of Naboth the Jezreelite . . ."

(1 Kings 21 : 15)

In the judicial murder of Naboth, Jezebel punctiliously observed the outward forms of established legal procedure: first, there was the proclamation of a fast, as was customary when a sin had been committed against God (1 Sam. 7 : 6). This was followed by the condemnation of Naboth, on the evidence of two witnesses, as laid down in the Law of Moses (Deut. 17 : 6—7). He was accused of cursing God and the king, for which the Law prescribed the punishment of death by stoning (Lev. 24 : 10—17). The story about Naboth's vineyard implies that the king, by virtue of his royal prerogative, inherited the property of anyone executed for blasphemy or lèse-majesté.

This ruling is already implicit in a legal document (reproduced above) from Alalakh, in northern Syria, which was drawn up in the 15th cent. B.C., The document relates that the plaintiff had betrothed a woman and paid her father the bridal price. The father subsequently committed a crime, was tried, found guilty and executed, and his property passed into the king's possession. The plaintiff thereupon broke off his betrothal, sued the king for the repayment of his bridal price and actually won his case. Here too it is implied that the property of an executed criminal passed to the king.

A section of the "Monolith Inscription" of Shalmaneser III (column 2, lines 90—95).

"I destroyed, tore down and burned down Karkara, his royal residence (i.e. of Irhuleni, the king of Hamath). He brought along to help him 1,200 chariots, 1,200 cavalrymen, 20,000 foot-soldiers of Hadadezer of Damascus, 700 chariots, 700 cavalrymen, 10,000 foot-soldiers of Irhuleni from Hamath, 2,000 chariots, 10,000 foot-soldiers of Ahab the Israelite, 500 soldiers from Que(?), 1,000 soldiers from Musri (Egypt?), 10 chariots, 10,000 soldiers from Irqanata, 200 soldiers of Matinu-balu from Arvad, 200 soldiers from Usanata, 30 chariots, 10,000 soldiers of Adunu-balu from Shiana, 1,000 camel-(rider)s of Gindibu from Arabia, (?)000 soldiers of Basa, son of Ruhubi, from (the mountain) of Amana (all together) these were twelve kings."

FOR three years Aram and Israel continued without war.

(1 Kings 22 : 1)

The Bible refers only in passing to the cessation of hostilities between Aram-Damascus and Israel. No explanation is given of this development and no other events which occurred at that time are mentioned. This omission is partly filled for us by an Assyrian inscription. After Ahab had successfully checked the expansion of the Aramaeans and made a peace treaty with them (1 Kings 20), he joined a large defensive alliance of nations led by the Aramaean king Hadadezer (who is the same as Ben-Hadad), against Shalmaneser III, king of Assyria. In the "Monolith Inscription" found at Kurkh, some 20 miles south of Diarbekir (see plate) from the sixth year of his reign (853 B.C.), a section of which is translated here, Shalmaneser describes his victories in his usual boastful manner. He relates that the opposing armies were drawn up for battle at Karkar, in the territory of Hamath. The inscription contains a detailed list of the allied kings and their forces, including the 2,000 chariots and 10,000 foot-soldiers of "Ahab the Israelite". The size of the chariot force of the Israelite king, which was by far the largest in the army of the allies, indicates the special attention that Ahab had devoted to this arm.

On the stele, Shalmaneser is seen standing before the emblems of the gods — a winged disc, a star, a disc and crescent, and a horned veil. His hand is upraised in a gesture of thanksgiving for his military achievements. After the manner of Assyrian kings, he announces to the gods the magnitude of his victories: "I slew 14,000 of their soldiers with the sword, descending upon them like Adad when he makes a rainstorm". In fact, however, the battle ended in stalemate, with the allied kings successful in halting the south-westwards advance of the Assyrian army.

AND struck the king of Israel between the scale
armour and the breastplate... And the king was
propped up in his chariot... (1 Kings 22 : 34-35)

Under Ahab, the Israelite army was well equipped with chariots (see p. 248) and protective armour. The king
himself, commanding his forces in battle, stood upright in his chariot wearing a coat of mail. He did not relax
his posture even after he had been wounded "between the scale armour and the breastplate". To ensure its wearer
freedom of movement, the coat of mail was made in two main sections — the breast-plate and the sleeves.
The joint between the sleeves and the breast-plate was the weak point of the coat of mail. It is noteworthy that
Joram, King of Judah, was also struck "between his arms", just like Ahab (2 Kings 9 : 24).
The words of the Bible are illustrated by the reproduction above of part of a gilt boss on the leather sides of the
chariot of Thutmose IV (late 15th cent. B.C.). An arrow of the Pharaoh is seen striking home exactly at the joint
of the coat of mail worn by a fleeing Semitic charioteer.

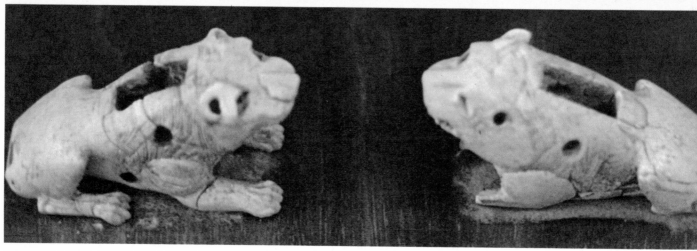

Now the rest of the acts of Ahab, and all that he did, and the ivory house which he built . . . are they not written in the Book of the Chronicles of the Kings of Israel?

(1 Kings 22 : 39)

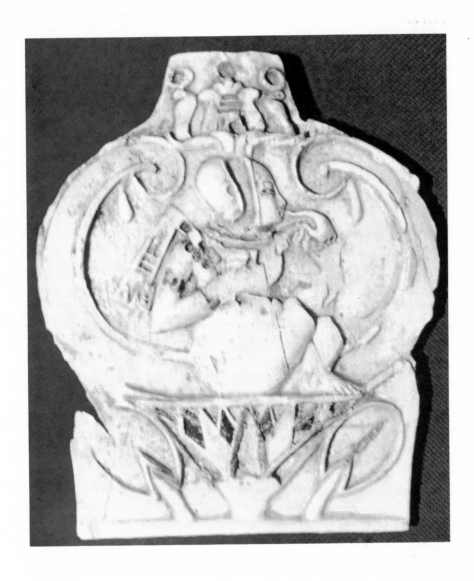

In its summing-up of Ahab's reign, the Bible mentions as one of the king's enterprises "the ivory house" that he had built. By this expression (cf. Amos 3 : 15; Ps. 45 : 8) is meant a palace in which the tables, chairs and beds were adorned with ivory reliefs or inlays after the fashion popular in Phoenicia, Assyria and Babylonia in the first millennium B.C. Ivory ornamentation of this kind has been found in Canaan dating back to an age prior to the Israelite conquest (the Megiddo ivories, cf. p. 45). The fashion evidently spread in the time of the kingdom of Israel as a result of Sidonian influence (1 Kings 10 : 18, 22). The excavations at Samaria have brought to light many exquisitely wrought ivory carvings of the same technique as that practised then in Mesopotamia, Egypt and the Phoenician cities. Scholars are inclined to assign them to Ahab's reign and to consider them part of the remains of "the ivory house". Hundreds of ivory reliefs dating to the 9th cent. B.C., i.e. the time of the dynasty of Omri, have also been found at Arslan Tash in Syria (cf. p. 264).

The upper plate on p. 251 is a reproduction of an image of the god Horus, adorned with beads and armbands, set in a lotus-leaf frame. He has a flail in his right hand and the tip of his left index-finger is held to his lips in a ritual gesture. The relief is inlaid with gold-leaf and various other coloured materials. Like a similar medallion discovered at Nimrud, it may have served to adorn the back of the king's throne (1 Kings 10 : 18). In the upper plate on p. 250, a lion is depicted sinking its teeth into the neck of a bull. In the lower plate, two roaring lions are seen crouching face to face. Lions like these were presumably used in the arm rests of a throne. The motif of this ivory points to northern, Hittite-Assyrian influence; but the delicate workmanship of the manes and hindquarters of the lions indicates an affinity to Egyptian art. The precision of the modelling and the beauty of the coloured and gold inlays show that the technical standard of the ivories found in Israel was fully comparable to that of other countries of the ancient East.

NOW Ahaziah fell through the lattice in his upper chamber in Samaria . . .

(2 Kings 1 : 2)

Most of the dwellings in ancient Israel were single-storied buildings. Only the rich were in the habit of adding an "upper chamber", i.e. a room built on to the flat roof where the air was fresher and cooler, "the cool chamber" (Judg. 3 : 23—25). This upper room was normally reserved for the senior inhabitant of the house, or for the reception of an important guest, such as a prophet (1 Kings 17 : 19; 2 Kings 4 : 10—11; and see p. 259).
There was evidently an upper chamber to the palace of the Israelite kings in Samaria, presumably overlooking the inner courtyard. For the safety of its occupants, it was surrounded with a "lattice", a fencing of trellis-work. The exact form of this "lattice" can perhaps be inferred from the censer-stands in the Phoenician style found both at Megiddo in Palestine and in Cyprus. Reproduced here is a bronze stand from the city of Kurion in Cyprus, dating to the 11th cent. B.C. It is in the form of a house or house-courtyard, in which a musician, seated on a chair, is plucking the strings of a harp. The ceiling of the house, which is also the roof, is supported by a column crowned by a characteristical proto-Aeolian capital. The roof terrace above is surrounded by a criss-cross fencing which may be the same as the biblical "lattice".

THEN he went to the spring of water and threw salt in it ... So the water has been wholesome to this day, according to the word which Elisha spoke.
(2 Kings 2 : 21-22)

The prophet Elisha is portrayed in the Book of Kings as a wonder-working "man of God". He provides food for the hungry, heals the sick, restores the dead to life, helps the unfortunate and turns the land's curse into blessing. One of his miracles was to make sweet the bitter waters of the spring at Jericho, thus turning them into a blessing for the inhabitants.

Since the Middle Ages, it has been customary to identify the spring mentioned in this verse (2 Kings 2 : 21) with Ain es-Sultan close to Jericho, which is also known as "Spring of Elisha". Some scholars hold that this is the location of "the waters of Jericho" which marked the border between Benjamin and the tribes of Joseph (Josh. 16 : 1). The spring has an abundant supply of water, its daily flow in winter amounting to approximately 8,500,000 gallons, and its annual average to about 4,000,000 gallons per day. It still provides water for the gardens and orchards of Jericho. The existence of such plentiful, life-giving waters in the desolation of the Jordan Valley seemed a marvel to the ancients. The palm-girt "Spring of Elisha" is seen in the view above.

A ND two she-bears
came out of the woods
and tore forty-two of
the boys.
(2 Kings 2 : 24)

The story about the "two she-bears" that tore forty-two small boys in pieces, after Elisha had cursed them, is meant to bring home the dire punishment awaiting those who made fun of the prophet. In biblical times, man and beast went in terror of the bears (*Ursus arctus syriacus* — the Syrian bear) that prowled in the forests of Benjamin, in the mountains of Ephraim and elsewhere in Israel (1 Sam. 17 : 34—37; Amos 5 : 19; Lam. 3 : 10). So much so, that "a bear robbed of her cubs" was used as a symbol of great danger (2 Sam. 17 : 8; Hos. 13 : 8; Prov. 17 : 12). To-day, a few surviving wild Syrian bears are to be found only in Persia and Turkey.
In the reproduction above of a relief from the 12th cent. B.C. found at Medinet Habu, a bear is seen attacking a man in the tangled undergrowth of a wood. The victim tries to escape by climbing a tree, but the bear has managed to seize him by his foot. The man's companion is seen ineffectually shooting an arrow at the bear from the tower of a Canaanite city.

The Inscription of King Mesha

1. I (am) Mesha, son of Chemosh ... king of Moab, the Di-
2. bonite — my father (had) reigned over Moab thirty years, and I reig-
3. ned after my father, — (who) made this high place for Chemosh in Qarhoh [...
4. .] because he saved me from all the kings and caused me to triumph over all my adversaries. As for Omri,
5. king of Israel, he humbled Moab many years (lit. days), for Chemosh was angry with his la-
6. nd. And his son followed him and he also said, "I will humble Moab." In my time he spoke [thus],
7. but I have triumphed over him and over his house, while Israel hath perished for ever! (Now) Omri had occupied the la-
8. nd of Medeba, and (Israel) had dwelt there in his time and half the time of his son (Ahab), forty years; but
9. Chemosh dwelt there in my time. And I built Baal-Meon, making a reservoir in it, and I built
10. Qaryaten. Now the men of Gad had always dwelt in the land of Ataroth, and the king of Is-
11. rael had built Ataroth for them; but I fought against the town and took it and slew all the people of
12. the town as satiation for Chemosh and Moab. And I brought back from there Arel (or Ariel), its chieftain, drag-
13. ging him before Chemosh in Qerioth, and I settled there men of Sharon and men of
14. Maharith. And Chemosh said to me, "Go, take Nebo from Israel!"
15. So I went by night and fought against it from the break of dawn until noon, tak-
16. ing it and slaying all, seven thousand men, boys, women, girls
17. and maid-servants, for I had devoted them to destruction for (the god) Ashtar-Chemosh. And I took from there the
18. [...] of Yahweh, dragging them before Chemosh. And the king of Israel had built
19. Jahaz, and he dwelt there while he was fighting against me, but Chemosh drove him out before me. And
20. I took from Moab two hundred men, all first class (warriors) and set them against Jahaz and took it
21. in order to attach it to (the district of) Dibon. It was I (who) built Qarhoh, the wall of the forests and the wall of
22. the citadel; I also built its gates and I built its towers and
23. I built the king's house, and I made both of its reservoirs for water inside
24. the town. And there was no cistern inside the town at Qarhoh, so I said to all the people, "Let each of you make
25. a cistern for himself in his house!" And I cut beams for Qarhoh with Israelite
26. captives. I built Aroer, and I made the highway in the Arnon (valley);
27. I built Beth-Bamoth, for it had been destroyed; I built Bezer — for it lay in
28. ruins — with fifty men of Dibon, for all Dibon is (my) loyal dependency. And I reigned [in peace]
29. over the hundred towns which I had added to the land. And I built
30. [...] Medeba and Beth-Diblathen and Beth-Baal-Meon, and I set there the
31. [...] of the land. And as for Hauronen, there dwelt in it [... And]
32. Chemosh said to me, "Go down, fight against Hauronen. And I went down [and I fought against the town and I took it], and Chemosh dwelt there in my time ...

NOW Mesha king of Moab was a sheep breeder; and he had to deliver annually to the king of Israel a hundred thousand lambs, and the wool of a hundred thousand rams. But when Ahab died, the king of Moab rebelled against the king of Israel.   (2 Kings 3 : 4-5)

After Ahab's death, the kings of Israel lost control of their dominions in Trans-Jordan. When Jehoram succeeded to the throne, Mesha, the Moabite king, threw off the Israelite yoke. A parallel and complementary account to that given in the Bible is found on the memorial stele erected by "Mesha the son of Chemosh ... the Dibonite" to commemorate his mighty deeds. The stele was discovered in 1868 at Dibon in Trans-Jordan. Made of black basalt, it is about 40 in. high and 27 in. wide. The inscription on it is written in Moabite, which is hardly distinguishable from biblical Hebrew. Each word is separated from the next by a dot and the end of every sentence is marked by a vertical line.

It is assumed that the stele was erected between 840 and 820 B.C. On it Mesha first thanks the god Chemosh for delivering him from his foes. Then he goes on to relate the enslavement of Moab to Israel in the reigns of Omri and his son, and its subsequent liberation after a bitter struggle. Mesha boasts of his conquests and of his savagery to his foes. He then glories in the blessings that he has brought upon his land, listing the cities that he has built, the gates and towers he has erected, the cisterns he has dug and the highways he has constructed.

THEN he said, "By which way shall we march?" Joram
answered, "By the way of the wilderness of Edom."

(2 Kings 3 : 8)

Joram, king of Israel and Jehoshaphat, king of Judah, accompanied by the
king of Edom who was a vassal of Judah, went to war with Mesha, king of
Moab, who had thrown off his allegiance to Israel. As the Jordan fords were
blocked by the enemy, the allies advanced upon Moab from the Judaean
desert, by way of the Arabah, south of the Dead Sea.

On the road to Edom, "the way of the wilderness of Edom" (2 Kings 3 : 8),
the allied armies suffered from a severe shortage of water. They were saved
as if by a miracle: in consequence of a sudden flooding the valleys were
filled with water, as Elisha had prophesied (2 Kings 3 : 17).

The line followed by "the way of Edom" (see map) can be reconstructed
from the remains of fortresses still standing along its course. These include
the large fortress of Uzzah in the central hills and a strong watch-tower
east of it, at the point where the road debouches on to the shore of the
Dead Sea. The road descends along Wadi el-Qeini (Valley of the Kenites?),
the upper part of which is shown in the photograph, dominated by Uzzah
(seen as a line on the horizon in the far background).

THEN he said, "Go outside, borrow vessels of all your neighbours, empty vessels and not too few. Then go in, and shut the door upon yourself and your sons, and pour into all these vessels; and when one is full, set it aside."

(2 Kings 4 : 3-4)

Like Elijah before him (1 Kings 17 : 8 ff.), Elisha helped a widow in distress. The contents of the jar of oil in her house (2 Kings 4 : 2) miraculously sufficed to fill all the many vessels that she borrowed from her neighbours. "As she poured they brought the vessels to her", until the oil stopped flowing only because there were no more containers (ibid. 5—6).

On various sites in Israel and Judah, vessels characteristic of the period of the Israelite kingdom have been found which could have been used as oil-containers, like the jar reproduced here. The distinguishing marks of this type of jar are its three handles and the spout close to its rim in place of a fourth handle. This spout has only a narrow orifice and apparently served as a stand for the juglet used to draw the liquid up out of the jar. The drops of liquid left on the sides of the juglet then dripped back into the jar through an orifice in the stand. It may well be that the widow used a juglet of this kind to fill the borrowed vessels with oil.

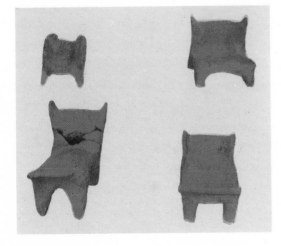

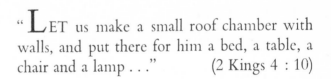
"LET us make a small roof chamber with walls, and put there for him a bed, a table, a chair and a lamp . . ."   (2 Kings 4 : 10)

Whenever he came to Shunem, Elisha stayed in the house of "a wealthy woman", which presumably means the house of one of the rich aristocratic families (2 Kings 4 : 8). In honour of "the man of God" the family erected a "roof chamber with walls", i.e. a special room on the upper floor of the house, (cf. p. 253) which was reached by a flight of steps. In the photograph above, the steps leading to the second floor of a house excavated at Hazor from the period of the Israelite kingdom can be clearly seen.

The woman of Shunem furnished this upper room with articles customary in the houses of Israelite notables at that time. Clay models of such furnishings have been found in a grave at Lachish from the 8th or 7th cent. B.C. Reproduced in the lower plate are: a) a couch; b) a chair with a back; c) a bed with a separate "head of the bed" (cf. Gen. 47 : 31; 1 Sam 19 : 13).

The "lamp" must have been of the usual Iron Age type, with a pinched rim to hold the wick (see middle plate).

ONE of them went out into the field to gather herbs, and
found a wild vine and gathered from it his lap full of wild
gourds . . .   (2 Kings 4 : 39)

During his sojourn at Gilgal with the sons of the prophets, Elisha was not only the spiritual head of the group,
but also its counsellor in practical affairs. Because of the famine in the land (2 Kings 4 : 38), the sons of the
prophets were reduced to picking wild plants for food. One of the company, for instance, tried to prepare a
communal meal from wild gourds *(Citrullus Colocynthis (L.) Schrad.)*. This plant, which grows in the Jordan
Valley, trails along the ground and has leaves and tendrils like those of the vine. Presumably that is why it is
called a "wild vine" in our verse. The ripe fruit is yellow in colour (see the photograph). It contains an extremely
bitter substance which, from ancient times, has been used as a laxative. The sons of the prophets, who were
ignorant of the nature of the fruit, picked it and cooked it: "But while they were eating of the pottage, they
cried out, 'O man of God, there is death in the pot!'" (ibid. v. 40). Indeed, some modern authorities maintain
that the fruit of the wild vine, if eaten in large quantities, may even cause death. Just as the man of God had
previously made the waters of Jericho fit to drink (see p. 254), so now he made the pottage of gourds fit to eat
by throwing meal into the pot. Then he gave the order: "'Pour out for the men, that they may eat'. And there
was no harm in the pot" (ibid. 41).

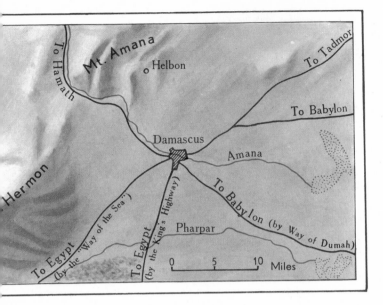

"ARE not Abana and Pharpar, the rivers of Damascus, better than all the waters of Israel? . . ." (2 Kings 5 : 12)

The oasis of Damascus, one of the most fertile and beautiful in the Orient, was famous for the abundance of its waters and the richness of its produce (cf. 2 Kings 8 : 9). When Elisha sent his messenger to tell Naaman, the commander of the Aramaean army, to cleanse away his leprosy by washing in the Jordan, Naaman suggested that the two rivers of Damascus — Amana (in this verse Abana) and Pharpar — far excelled all the rivers of Israel. Amana is the modern Barada which rushes down from Jebel Zabedani. The mountain itself, which is part of the Anti-Lebanon range (cf. Song of Sol. 4 : 8), was also called Amana. The Pharpar is to-day called Awaj; it flows into Damascus from the south (see the map). These two rivers provided irrigation for the lands around Damascus.

The lower plate is an aerial photograph of part of the modern city of Damascus. The houses and gardens receive their water from canals which stem off from the branches of the Amana as it flows through the city. In the background can be seen the gardens with which the city is encircled.

261

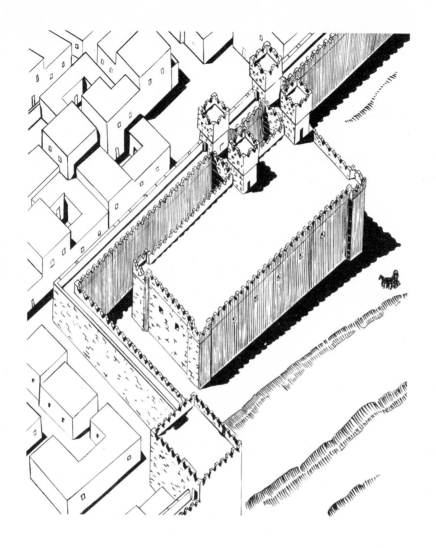

BUT Elisha said, "Hear the word of the LORD: thus says the LORD. To-morrow about this time a measure of fine meal shall be sold for a shekel, and two measures of barley for a shekel, at the gate of Samaria." (2 Kings 7 : 1)

Closely besieged by the Aramaeans, Samaria was reduced to famine. Food prices rose so steeply that the king himself despaired of being able to save his people (2 Kings 6 : 24-28). Nevertheless ,Elisha prophesied that the siege would be raised, the dire conditions eased, and the price of corn lowered "at the gate of Samaria". His words reached the market which, in the cities of Israel, was set up in the square inside the gate (see p. 107). Here the city's inhabitants would gather to buy and sell their wares (Jer. 17 : 21) and to carry on trade with foreign merchants (Neh. 13 : 15-21). Eventually the gateway became the centre of the city's economic life, as it was the most convenient place for the conduct of any public business (see Vol. I, p. 90). Hence, the market in the gateway of the capital city no doubt played an important part in the national economy. In most of the countries of the ancient East, it was the temple, with its adjacent workshops, granaries and treasuries, that was the centre of the city's public life. In Israel, on the contrary, where the temple had no economic role, the administrative and commercial importance of the gateway remained undiminished throughout the period of the Monarchy.

The plate shows a reconstruction of the complex of buildings constituting the eastern gateway of Samaria. The road leading to the city gate passes between the wall (on the left) and a large bastion (on the right), and thus any attackers could be harrassed from either side. The dimensions of the tower are 118 by 53 ft., and its distance from the wall is 26 ft. before the turn in the road and 13 ft. after it. Inside the gate there is an open space which may have been the site of the market.

THEY said to one another, "Behold, the king of Israel has hired against us the kings of the Hittites . . ." (2 Kings 7 : 6)

The Aramaeans were thrown into a panic by "the sound of chariots and of horses" in the Israelite camp (2 Kings 7 : 6). They imagined that the kings of the Hittites and the kings of Egypt had come to the rescue of Samaria. "The kings of the Hittites" at this period were simply the rulers of the petty states, stretching from southern Anatolia to the interior of Syria, that emerged from the disintegration of the Hittite empire in the 12th cent. B.C., and continued to use the Hittite hieroglyphic script. Among these states were Yaadi, Hattin, Carchemish, and Hamath which were at war with the Aramaeans of Syria, on and off, for hundreds of years and were therefore natural allies of Israel. The friendly relations between David and the king of Hamath have already been mentioned on p. 174. Later, Solomon traded with the kings of the Hittites (1 Kings 10 : 29).

Information about the sporadic warfare between Hittites and Aramaeans is provided by an inscription of Zakar, the king of Hamath and Laash, in the first part of the 8th cent. B.C. (see the reproduction on the right). This inscription, cut in the rock about 24 miles south-east of Aleppo, is written in Aramaic and thus bears witness to the ever-increasing Aramaean influence even in the kingdom of Hamath. It relates that "Bar-Hadad, the son of Hazael, king of Aram" marched out at the head of a confederacy of kings of Syria to do battle with the king of Hamath and Laash, but was defeated. It was thus reasonable for the Aramaean king to fear that his long-standing foes, "the Hittites", were coming to the aid of Joram, the son of Ahab.

The reproduction on the left is a relief from Carchemish (9th—8th cent. B.C.) showing a war-chariot characteristic of the late Hittite and Aramaean kingdoms (cf. p. 176).

AND Hazael became king in his stead.
(2 Kings 8 : 15)

Hazael, king of Aram-Damascus, whose name appears in the Bible and in Aramaean and Assyrian inscriptions, was a contemporary of Jehu, king of Israel. Like Jehu, he seized the throne by conspiracy and became the founder of a new dynasty. The Bible recounts that, like Jehu again, he was proclaimed king by an Israelite prophet (1 Kings 19 : 15—16; 2 Kings 8 : 13). It was during Hazael's reign that the Assyrian armies commanded by Shalmaneser III made repeated attempts to conquer Syria and Palestine (in the second half of the 9th cent. B.C.). However, Hazael succeeded in checking their advance and in maintaining his independence. In the latter part of Jehu's reign — about 815 B.C. — Hazael conquered all the parts of Trans-Jordan till then held by Israel. Eventually he reached Gath, whence he prepared "to go up against Jerusalem" (2 Kings 12 : 17). This is the victory over Israel that is referred to in Elisha's prophecy: "You will set on fire their fortresses, and you will slay their young men with the sword, and dash in pieces their little ones, and rip up their women with child" (ibid 8 : 12).

Reproduced below is an ivory inlay from the side of a bed, (second half of the 9th cent. B.C.) which was found at Arslan Tash (Hadathah) on the Euphrates. On it are engraved the following letters: *yzt.h* (on the left-hand fragment) . . . *br'm'. lmr'n. hz'l. bšnt* . . . (i.e. "Bar Ama to our lord Hazael in the year . . ."). Reproduced above is another ivory tablet found nearby, possibly a part of the same bed. It is the relief of a god or king in Phoenician-Aramaean style. The carefully modelled features give the figure an expression of dignity. Some scholars hold that this is actually a portrait of Hazael.

So a man on horse-
back went to meet
him… (2 Kings 9 : 18)

Joram, king of Israel, despatched a horseman from Jezreel to meet Jehu and find out if his intentions were peaceful (2 Kings 9 : 17—20). From this it may be inferred that such horsemen were primarily used as messengers and heralds. Indeed, it was not till long after horses had been harnessed to chariots that they began to be ridden as war-steeds. The reason for this lay in the difficulties involved in handling the horse on the battle-field. The rider's use of his weapons was greatly restricted, since he had to hold the reins while at the same time carrying his weapons and shield, which called for a high standard of training. Archaeological excavations show that only at the end of the second millennium B.C. did horses begin to be ridden, and then not so much for actual fighting as for communications (as in our verse) and guard duty. However, by the time of the Israelite Monarchy, cavalry units had become a regular feature of the armies of Israel and the neighbouring countries.

A good illustration of how horses were ridden in the time of the Monarchy is provided by a relief (see the re-production) from the 10th or 9th cent. B.C. which was discovered at Tell Halaf (Gozan). The rider is mounted on the horse without saddle or spurs. Slung over his shoulder is a round shield, the regular protection of the horseman from the earliest times. The reins are in his left hand, while in his right he holds a weapon.

JEHU said to Bidkar his aide, "Take him up, and cast him on the plot of ground belonging to Naboth the Jezreelite; for remember, when you and I rode side by side behind Ahab his father . . ."

(2 Kings 9 : 25)

Jehu orders that the body of Joram be cast on to the plot of ground that had once belonged to Naboth the Jezreelite. In doing so, he recalls the murder of Naboth and the harsh prophecy of Elijah against the house of Ahab: "The Lord uttered this oracle against him . . . 'I will requite you on this plot of ground'" (2 Kings 9 : 25—26; cf. 1 Kings 21 : 17—26). Jehu also mentions in passing that he and his aide, Bidkar, "rode side by side behind Ahab" when the prophet angrily denounced the king.

A relief from the palace of Ashurbanipal at Calah, reproduced above, illustrates Jehu's words: the king is standing in his chariot, with the charioteer at his right hand, and behind him his aide who is shading his master's head. The chariot is followed by a mounted member of the king's bodyguard, leading a horse without a rider. When the aide was not accompanying the king in his chariot, he and the bodyguard "rode side by side" behind him, i.e. they rode together on a pair of horses behind the chariot.

JEZEBEL heard of it; and she painted her eyes, and adorned her head, and looked out of the window. (2 Kings 9 : 30)

When Jezebel received the news of the killing of Joram at Jezreel, she knew that her own doom was near. Proudly determined to betray no sign of fear, she prepared to confront the usurper, Jehu, in a manner worthy of her royal forefathers. She painted her eyes with antimony to heighten her self-assurance (cf. Jer. 4 : 30), and she adorned her head after the fashion of ladies of noble birth. Then she took her stand at the window, the customary position in the ancient Orient from which to welcome honoured guests (see p. 172). Knowing that her fate was sealed, she greeted Jehu with mocking abuse: "Is it peace, you Zimri, murderer of your master?" (2 Kings 9 : 31).

Below is a reproduction of an Egyptian relief, probably of the Eleventh Dynasty (end of the third millennium B.C.). On it a hairdresser is seen holding a triple strand of curls. The inscription reads: "The hairdresser Inu".

WHEN the messenger came and told him, "They have brought the heads of the king's sons," he said, "Lay them in two heaps at the entrance of the gate until the morning."

(2 Kings 10 : 8)

Like all usurpers, Jehu dealt savagely with the fallen dynasty, its ministers, its great men and its priests (2 Kings 10 : 11). The slaughter at Jehu's bidding of Ahab's seventy sons in Samaria by the royal ministers and elders was made into a public spectacle and justified as being the fulfilment of the Lord's command by His prophet (ibid. 9—12). The decapitation of the king's sons and the piling of their severed heads in two heaps in the gateway are parallelled by the conduct of the Assyrian kings, who used to make a boastful display of their brutalities. Such mutilation of the enemy's dead was intended both to provide the victor with a bloody proof of his valour and to express his contempt for the fallen foe (cf. pp. 72 and 89).

Reproduced below is a wall-relief from Nineveh, one of a series depicting the campaign of the Assyrian king, Sennacherib, in southern Mesopotamia. On the bank of a river, under an avenue of palms, stand Assyrian officers facing a scribe and a quartermaster who are making an inventory of the spoil. Besides weapons and other articles, severed enemy heads can be seen dangling by the hair in the hands of the soldiers who had presumably cut them off. The heads that have already been counted are piled in a heap, as described in the verse above.

THE time that Jehu reigned over Israel in Samaria
was twenty-eight years.   (2 Kings 10 : 36)

Jehu, king of Israel (842—814 B.C.) ascended the throne during the advance of Shalmaneser III, king of Assyria, upon the peoples of Syria. At first, these nations had managed to withstand the Assyrian attack by forming a defensive alliance. However, unlike Ahab who had himself taken part in the battle of Karkar (see p. 248), Jehu held aloof from the Syrian confederacy. Taking advantage of the dynastic upheavals in Damascus and Samaria, Shalmaneser forced his way through the Lebanon down to the coast of the Mediterranean in the vicinity of Tyre. With the Assyrians arrayed on the northern border of the kingdom of Samaria, Jehu hastened to pay tribute to them.

On a black obelisk found at Calah, Jehu is portrayed paying tribute to the King of Assyria, together with gift-bearers from other nations. The Israelite King, escorted by Assyrian soldiers, is seen in obeisance at Shalmaneser's feet. Behind the Assyrian king stand the members of his entourage, one of whom is holding a sun-shade. On the other three sides of the obelisk (for these see Vol. III on Hosea 5 : 13) the members of Jehu's entourage are depicted presenting gifts to the Assyrian king. The inscription on the relief mentions by name "Jehu the son of Omri" (i.e. king "of the house of Omri," the name given by the Assyrians to the kingdom of Israel), and lists the individual items of the gold, silver, and vessels of gold and tin that were brought by Jehu as tribute.

WHILE Athaliah
reigned over the land.
(2 Kings 11 : 3)

Athaliah, the daughter of Ahab, king of Israel, reigned in Judah in the years 842—837 B.C. Taking advantage of the political confusion that followed Jehu's conspiracy, Athaliah made herself queen by wiping out almost all the members of the reigning dynasty. In this violent usurpation of the throne she was helped by the privileged position occupied by the queen-mother in Judah. Athaliah was one of the few female despots of the ancient Orient.

Reproduced above is a relief from Zinjirli (ancient Shamal, the capital of the ancient kingdom of Yaadi-Shamal in northern Syria) portraying a woman, apparently a queen, seated before an offering table. In her right hand she holds a cup and in her left hand a flower-bud. In front of her, on the other side of the table, stands a maidservant who is keeping off the flies with a fly-whisk. The seated woman is wearing a round pointed cap and regal apparel, and is resplendent in beads, necklaces and bangles. Laid out on the table in front of her are various kinds of food. At the top of the relief is the winged emblem of the sun-god. The relief is apparently from the 8th cent. B.C., only a few generations after Athaliah's time.

A<small>ND</small> he took the captains, the Carites, the
guards . . .   (2 Kings 11 : 19)

The popular revolt against Athaliah and the anointing of Jehoash as king of Judah, at the instigation of Jehoiada the priest, were made possible by the co-operation of the royal bodyguard. Under their protection, the young king was escorted from the house of the Lord, through the gate of the guards, to the palace, "and he took his seat on the throne of the kings" (2 Kings 11 : 19). Among the units of the royal bodyguard that of the "runners" (Heb. *raṣim*, here translated "guards") occupied a special place. In time of war they acted as heralds; in peacetime they ran before the king's chariot, clearing a way for it through the narrow streets of the oriental towns and guarding the king's person from any attempted assault (see pp. 141 and 182). This unit, being considered to be one of the most loyal to the king, was allocated special quarters next to his palace. The meaning of the appellation "Carite" (Heb. *ha-kari*), given to this unit, is obscure, and was variously interpreted even in the earliest translations of the Bible. One modern view is that it denotes a force of foreign mercenaries composed of Carians from Asia Minor. Other scholars hold that it refers to the royal market-guards, deriving the word from the Assyrian term *karu* which meant *inter alia* a "market place".

Above is a reproduction of a relief from Carchemish (9th or 8th cent. B.C.) depicting two warriors who apparently belong to the king's bodyguard.

AND whenever they saw that there was much money in the chest, the king's secretary and the high priest came up and they counted and tied up in bags the money that was found in the house of the LORD.

(2 Kings 12 : 10)

The monies brought to the Temple were of two different kinds: first, money that formed part of an obligatory offering (especially "the money from the guilt offerings and the money from the sin offerings", 2 Kings 12 : 16) which was of the utmost sanctity and therefore kept for the sole use of the priests; secondly, money-gifts, which were free-will offerings. This latter money was usually spent on the provision of vessels for the Temple (ibid. 13). However, in Jehoash's time it was decided to use it for the repair of the structure of the Temple itself. Later, in the twenty-third year of the reign of Jehoash it was discovered that the priests had been remiss in allocating the necessary sums for the renovations. It was consequently decided to take the collection of the money out of their hands and instead have it placed directly in a chest beside the altar (ibid. 6—10). Every time the chest was filled, the king's secretary and the high priest would take out the money and, through the overseers, pay it to the stone-cutters and craftsmen employed on the repair of the Temple.

At that time there was still no coinage in the ancient East. Hence, in order to fix a monetary standard, gold or silver was first melted down and poured into standard moulds, where it was formed into bars or rings of uniform size and weight which could be counted. A process of this kind is depicted on a wall-painting from the tomb of Puyemre at Thebes in Egypt, from the 15th cent. B.C. The gold seen in the painting is intended for the temple. It has been brought by the representatives of foreign nations as gift-offerings to the overseer of the temple treasury, who is seen measuring the numbers of rings (lower register). Next, the gold is weighed by another official (upper register) with weights in the form of bulls. At the top right stand the priests waiting to take away the gold, the amount of which is recorded in figures in the upper and lower registers.

THEREFORE the LORD gave Israel a saviour, so that they escaped from the hand of the Aramaeans... (2 Kings 13 : 5)

The reign of Jehoahaz, the son of Jehu (814—798 B.C.), was a period of military disaster, foreign domination and political decline for the kingdom of Israel. The onslaughts of the king of Aram sapped Israel's military strength: "For there was not left to Jehoahaz an army of more than fifty horsemen and ten chariots and ten thousand footmen" (2 Kings 13 : 7). This is evidently the time to which the prophet Amos refers in his denunciation of the atrocities committed by the Aramaeans in the Israelite areas of Trans-Jordan: "Because they have threshed Gilead with threshing sledges of iron" (Amos 1 : 3). The Bible relates that, in Israel's dire straits, the Lord sent them "a saviour". This is taken to be a reference to the Assyrian king, Adadnirari III, who launched a series of campaigns against Damascus in the years 805—802 B.C., repeatedly defeating its forces and finally imposing a heavy tribute upon it, thus bringing relief to Israel. The Aramaeans were obliged to withdraw from Israel "and the people of Israel dwelt in their homes as formerly" (2 Kings 13 :5). The figure of Adadnirari III has been preserved on a stele erected in his honour by one of his governors. The stele was discovered at Saba, in the desert south-west of the Sinjar mountains. On it Adadnirari is seen standing before a winged disc (the emblem of the god Ashur) and a crescent moon (the emblem of the god Sin). The inscription contains an account of Adadnirari's campaign against Damascus and the defeat inflicted by him upon Mari, king of Aram, who is identical with Ben-Hadad the son of Hazael.

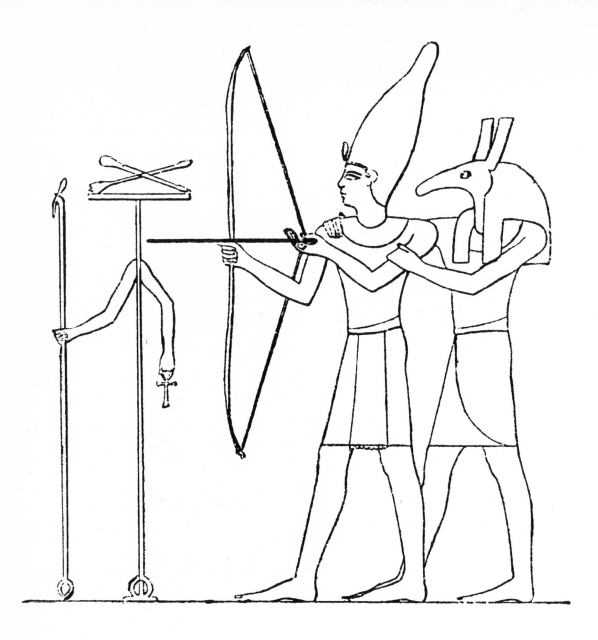

THEN he said to the king of Israel, "Draw the bow"; and he drew it. And Elisha laid his hands upon the king's hands. (2 Kings 13 : 16)

The prophet Elisha took an active part in the political life of the kingdom of Israel and was venerated by its rulers. King Joash called him "My father, my father! The chariots of Israel and its horsemen!"—exactly the words used of Elijah by Elisha himself (2 Kings 2 : 12) — and came to the dying prophet to receive his blessing and counsel. Elisha ordered Joash to shoot an arrow through the window eastwards and called it "the arrow of victory over Aram". As the arrow was shot, the prophet laid his hands on the king's (2 Kings 13 : 16—17), thus imbuing him with something of his own holiness.

A wall-painting from Karnak (15th cent. B.C.) depicts the various ceremonial rites performed at the coronation of Thutmose III. In one of these ceremonies, the Pharaoh is shown shooting arrows to the four points of the compass, while the animal-headed god Seth stands behind him and places his hands on the king's shoulder and arm — a magical assurance of Pharaoh's victories over all his enemies wherever they might be.

HE killed ten thousand Edomites in the Valley of Salt and took Sela by storm . . .
(2 Kings 14 : 7)

Amaziah the son of Joash, king of Judah, (first half of the 8th cent. B.C.), halted the decline of Judah by a victorious campaign against Edom. Presumably, his aim was to gain control of the Arabah through which ran the roads from Judah to Edom, Moab, Elath and to the copper mines near Punon. The Edomites opposed Amaziah's advance in the Arabah itself. The battle was fought out in the Valley of Salt (cf. 2 Sam. 8 : 13—14; 1 Chron. 18 : 12—13; Ps. 60 : 1), identified by some scholars with Ge-Harashim (the "Valley of the Craftsmen") (1 Chron. 4 : 13—14) in the vicinity of the Punon mines. Others would locate it in the barren country of the northern Arabah, west of the Dead Sea (see the photograph below).

After this victory over the Edomites, Amaziah took the fortified city of Sela which guarded the approaches to the mining district. Sela is sometimes identified with the modern es-Sela, a few miles west of Bozrah in northern Edom (see the upper photograph). In ancient times this place was a flourishing agricultural centre with ponds, conduits and cisterns all around it.

HE built Elath and restored it to Judah . . .
(2 Kings 14 : 22)

King Uzziah completed the work of conquest begun by his father Amaziah. He pushed his border with Philistia southwards to the approaches to Egypt and reduced the Ammonites to vassaldom (2 Chron. 26 : 6—8). He extended his control of Edom as far as Elath, thus regaining for Judah an outlet to the Red Sea. This is confirmed by the archaeological finds at Tell el-Kheleifeh, the site of Ezion-Geber or Elath. It is quite likely that Ezion-Geber was the name given to the industrial zone of the revived settlement, which was once more a centre of copper-smelting and metal-working, while Elath designated the residential quarter (see p. 223). Part of Uzziah's town was built on the already existing walls of previous settlements (see the upper illustration) but the design of the entrance-gate was different. The plate below is a reproduction of a seal set into a signet-ring found at Ezion-Geber from the time of Uzziah. The seal is incised with the name of its owner (*lytm* "To Jotham"). The mere existence of such a seal at Ezion-Geber, in the time of Uzziah and his son Jotham, is of special interest, even if it is most unlikely that this was the seal of Jotham, king of Judah.

N OW the rest of the acts of Jeroboam, and all that he did, and his might, how he fought, and how he recovered for Israel Damascus and Hamath, which had belonged to Judah, are they not written in the Book of the Chronicles of the Kings of Israel? (2 Kings 14 : 28)

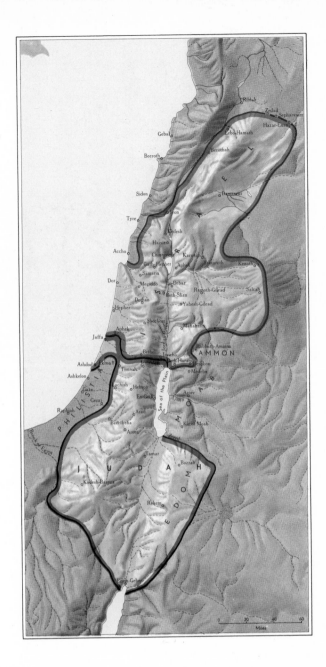

The reigns of Uzziah in Judah and of Jeroboam the son of Joash in Israel (about the middle of the 8th cent. B.C.), were an era of economic prosperity and political revival. They were also a time of territorial expansion (see the map, and the map on p. 208). The Book of Kings gives only the briefest account of the wars and achievements of Jeroboam's reign (784—744 B.C.; 2 Kings 14 : 23—29). It may be inferred that Jeroboam annexed the territories of Damascus and Hamath to his kingdom. By comparison with another verse in the same chapter (ibid. v. 25) and with the Book of Amos (6 : 14), we learn that Jeroboam extended his conquests as far as Lebo Hamath (cf. Vol. I, pp. 243), but not to Hamath itself. (The tell of Hamath, standing in the middle of the modern city of Hama, is seen in the photograph below). Jeroboam furthermore gained control of large areas of Trans-Jordan down to "the Sea of the Arabah" (2 Kings 14 : 25), i.e. the Dead Sea. Altogether, his reign was one of notable achievements: increased Israelite settlement in Trans-Jordan (1 Chron. 5:14—18), close cooperation between Israel and Judah, higher standards of material culture, and the adornment of Samaria with magnificent buildings and palaces. It was marred, however, by grave social injustice. The biblical record places Jeroboam in the category of evil kings (2 Kings 14 : 24), even while admitting that he saved Israel (ibid. v. 27).

IN the twenty-seventh year of Jeroboam king of Israel
Azariah the son of Amaziah, king of Judah, began to reign.

(2 Kings 15 : 1)

On some of the many seals excavated in Palestine, personal names have been found which also occur in the Bible,
among them names identical with those of famous personages. So far, however, no seal actually belonging to a
king of Judah or Israel has come to light, although their names sometimes appear on the seals of ministers and
high officials. The two seals reproduced above are those of royal ministers in the 8th cent B.C. The seal on the
right, which was found at Megiddo, is engraved with the figure of a roaring lion, skilfully executed. The inscription — "to Shema the servant of Jeroboam" — proclaims the name and rank of its owner, one of the ministers
of King Jeroboam II. The word "servant" (Heb. 'ebed), here has the connotation, frequently found also in the
Bible, of minister and high dignitary, as in the title "the servant of the king" which is also engraved on seals of
the same period.

The left-hand seal is inscribed with the words "Abijah the servant of Uzziah", with a slight variation of spelling
that is also found in the Bible. The owner of this seal was one of King Uzziah's ministers.

P̲UL the king of Assyria came against the land; and Menahem gave Pul a thousand talents of silver, that he might help
him to confirm his hold of the royal power. (2 Kings 15 : 19)

Menahem the son of Gadi ruled over Israel during the reign of Tiglath-Pileser III, King of Assyria (745—727
B.C.) also known as Pul. Tiglath-Pileser made a series of military campaigns into Syria and Palestine and
instituted a systematic policy of deporting his conquered enemies to distant lands, turning their countries into
provinces of the Assyrian empire. By such ruthless measures he made Assyria a great world power. In his inscription Tiglath-Pileser lists the tribute paid him by the kings of the West, amongst them "Menahem of Samaria"
and Rezin, king of Aram-Damascus. The heavy tribute paid by Menahem (in 738 B.C.) was exacted mainly
from the owners of agricultural property ("the wealthy men") "fifty shekels of silver from every man" (2 Kings
15 : 20). By this submission to the king of Assyria, Menahem preserved the integrity of his kingdom for the time
being.
Reproduced above is the likeness of Tiglath-Pileser III from a fragment of a relief found at Calah, on the Tigris.

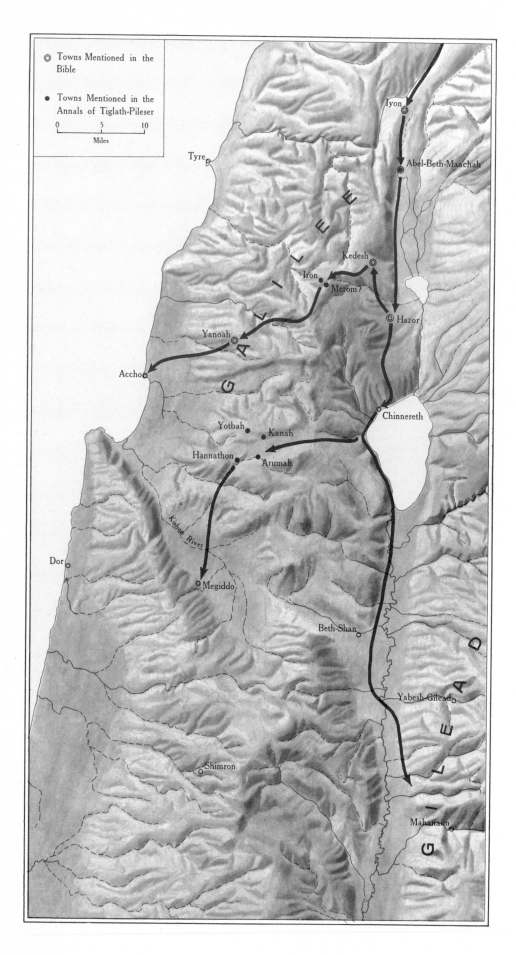

IN the days of Pekah king
Israel Tiglath-Pileser king
Assyria came and captur
Iyon, Abel-Beth-Maachah, Y
noah, Kedesh, Hazor, Gilea
and Galilee, all the land
Naphtali; and he carried t
people captive to Assyria.

(2 Kings 15 : 2

About the year 734 B.C., Rezin, king of Aram-Damascus, and
Pekah the son of Remaliah, king of Israel, rose in revolt
against Tiglath-Pileser III. The Assyrian monarch suppressed
the revolt in a series of campaigns in 733—732 in the course
of which he conquered Aram-Damascus and annexed sub-
stantial parts of the kingdom of Israel. He took the cities
of Galilee, deported most of their inhabitants to Assyria,
imposed a heavy tribute upon the remainder and penetrated
deep into Gilead (cf. 1 Chron. 5 : 25—26). The arrows on the
map (p. 280) indicate the direction of his various campaigns as
reconstructed from biblical and Assyrian sources. Like the
Bible (2 Kings 15 : 30), Tiglath-Pileser relates in his annals that
the people of Israel deposed their king Pekah, and adds that he
appointed Hoshea to rule over them, with his sovereignty
virtually limited to the mountains of Ephraim. The section of
the annals in which these details are given is reproduced at the
bottom right of page 281.
The extent of the devastation of Galilee at that time has been
vividly illustrated by the thick layer of ash and charred embers
found in the citadel and other buildings at Hazor. The various
vessels found still in their places on the floor indicate that the
disaster came suddenly (see the left upper plate). The photograph at the top right is a view of the Valley of Beth-Netophah,
the site of the ancient cities of Kanah, Arumah, Yotbah and
Hannathon which are mentioned in a fragment of Tiglath-
Pileser's annals relating his conquests in Galilee.

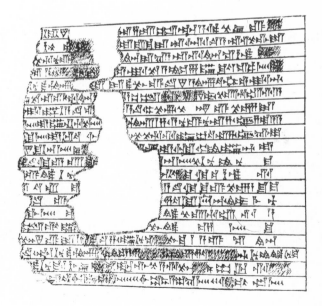

So Ahaz sent messengers to Tiglath-Pileser king of Assyria, saying, "I am your servant and your son. Come up, and rescue me from the hand of the king of Aram and from the hand of the king of Israel, who are attacking me."

(2 Kings 16 : 7)

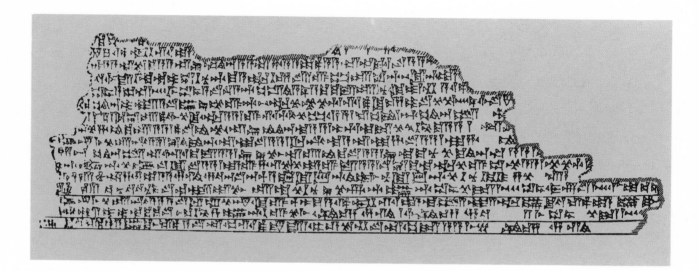

Ahaz, king of Judah, did not join the alliance formed by Rezin, king of Aram-Damascus and Pekah, the king of Israel, against Assyria (see p. 281). Attacked by the two allies (see also Isaiah 7 : 5—6), he appealed to Tiglath-Pileser III for aid, accompanying his request with a gift of silver and gold (2 Kings 16 : 8). In an inscription from Calah, reproduced above, the Assyrian monarch tells of the tribute paid to him by Jehoahaz (i.e. Ahaz) king of Judah and by other Syrian and Palestinian kings who had accepted Assyrian overlordship: "gold, silver, tin, iron, lead . . . gorgeous raiment, the purple apparel of their land . . ."

The plate below is a reproduction of a wall-painting from a palace at Til Barsip from the reign of Tiglath-Pileser III. The king is shown seated on the royal throne, which is held by two of his courtiers, and receiving tribute-bearers. The chief minister is presenting the guests to the king who welcomes them. This no doubt was also the manner in which the "messengers" of Ahaz were received.

IN the ninth year of Hoshea the king of
Assyria captured Samaria, and he carried
the Israelites away to Assyria . . .

(2 Kings 17 : 6)

The final doom of the kingdom of Ephraim was not long delayed. The brief description given in the Bible
of the destruction of Samaria and the deportation of the population of the Northern Kingdom is supplemented
by Assyrian inscriptions. These provide interesting details about the revolts in Samaria, both before and after
the fall of the city, and also about the later deportations in Sargon's reign. Shalmaneser V (727—722 B.C.)
besieged Samaria and took it in 722 B.C., leaving it to his successor, Sargon II, to deport the inhabitants. In the
inscription reproduced here Sargon boasts that he captured 200 Israelite chariots and added them to his own
fighting forces, that he deported 27,900 people from Samaria and that he rebuilt the city as the capital of the
Assyrian province of Samerina.

We can form some idea of the treatment of the exiles from a relief (see bottom plate) depicting the deportation
of the inhabitants of Lachish by the Assyrian King, Sennacherib, which occurred somewhat later (for the whole
relief see p. 287). This particular group of deportees appear to be members of one family. They are led by two
women carrying household utensils in their hands and sacks on their shoulders. Behind them walk two girls who
are also heavily laden. The small children are seated in a cart which would seem to be loaded with corn and
is drawn by a pair of oxen driven by a man, presumably the head of the family.

$\overset{\bullet}{A}$ND he carried the Israelites away to Assyria, and placed them in Halah, and on the Habor, the river of Gozan, and in the cities of the Medes.

(2 Kings 17 : 6)

Mentioned amongst the regions to which the Assyrian king deported the exiles of Samaria (see the thick line on the map on p. 285), is the river Habor, called here also "the river of Gozan" after the principal city on its upper reaches. The Habor flows through a wide plain in north-western Mesopotamia which is thickly dotted with remains of ancient settlements and criss-crossed with roads (see the view above). Gozan (Tell Halaf) was one of the important Aramaean kingdoms at the beginning of the first millennium B.C. At the end of the 9th cent. B.C. the city was captured by the Assyrians (cf. 2 Kings 19 : 12), and subsequently became the capital of the Assyrian province of Gozan. It was to this city that many of the exiles from Samaria were deported.

Fragments of information about the Israelite deportees have come to light in excavations carried out in various parts of Mesopotamia, especially at Tell Halaf. One of the documents from this city, dating to the 7th cent. B.C. (see right below), mentions people bearing names indicative of their Israelite origin: Hoshea, Ishmael and the woman Dayana (Dinah). A potsherd (p. 285, bottom right) from the end of the 8th cent., or beginning of the 7th cent. B.C., discovered at Calah, bears the names, in Aramaic script, of people who must be either Hebrew or Phoenician, e.g.: Hananel, Menahem, Shubael and Elinur. These were probably deportees from Phoenicia or Israel.

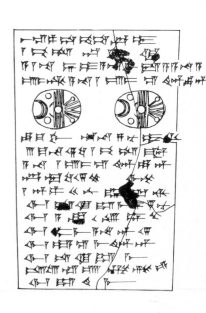

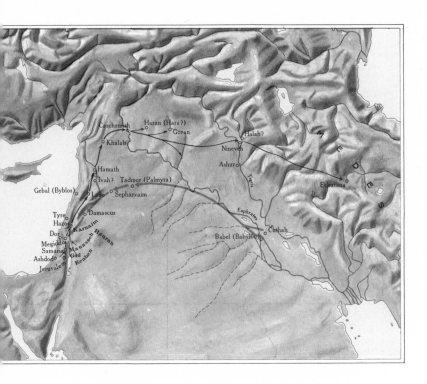

The Assyrian kings, following their policy of deportation, settled the depopulated provinces of Samaria with foreigners from the southern and western parts of their empire. The Bible specifies the places from which these foreign settlers were deported: from Babylon and nearby Cuthah in southern Mesopotamia; and from Hamath and the neighbouring cities of Avva and Sepharvaim in Syria (see the red line of the map). Some scholars, however, hold that Sepharvaim is merely another name for Sippar in southern Mesopotamia. Assyrian documents confirm the Bible's statement that the king of Assyria (Sargon II) repopulated Samaria with deportees from the countries conquered by him. Indeed, Assyrian letters discovered at Samaria refer to people with Babylonian names. The new settlers intermingled with the remnants of the Israelite population and adopted their customs. They worshipped Yahweh, the God of Israel, while at the same time the people of each different city continued to do homage to the gods of their homeland (2 Kings 17 : 30—33). For example, the men of Cuthah kept an idol of their god Nergal (ibid. 30). In the course of time all these different nations blended into a single ethnic and religious entity which apparently emerged as the Samaritan community. In the time of the Second Temple and in the Talmudic period the Samaritans were called "Cuthaeans".

The reproduction of the cylinder seal on the left below (Akkadian period, second half of the third millennium B.C.), which was found at Larsa, shows the god Nergal trampling upon a man who is stretched prostrate on a mountain. The god is holding a sickle-shaped sword in his left hand and a club, in the form of his emblem, in his right. This emblem appears again in the middle plate below, a reproduction from the stele of Esarhaddon at Zinjirli. It consists of a staff topped by two lion's heads facing outwards.

AND the king of Assyria brought people from Babylon, Cuthah, Avva, Hamath, and Sepharvaim, and placed them in the cities of Samaria instead of the people of Israel . . .   (2 Kings 17 : 24)

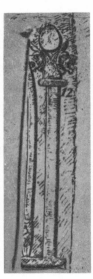

IN the fourteenth year of King Hezekiah Sennacherib king of Assyria came up against all the fortified cities of Judah and took them. And Hezekiah king of Judah sent to the king of Assyria at Lachish, saying, "I have done wrong; withdraw from me . . ." (2 Kings 18 : 13-14)

The biblical account of Sennacherib's attack on Judah (701 B.C.) and of tribute paid by Hezekiah (2 Kings 18 : 13—16) is confirmed by contempo Assyrian sources. On a large four-panelled relief in his palace at Nine Sennacherib had a detailed representation made of the capture of Lach On the first panel (p. 286 top) the infantry, composed of Assyrians mercenaries (without helmets) is shown drawn up in three columns. The is formed by the javelin-throwers wearing hunting-helmets and carr round shields. Behind them stand the bowmen who operate in pairs. Bel the bowmen stand the slingers, whose weapon has the longest range of with a loaded sling in their right hand and a reserve slingstone in their Some of them have piles of additional stones at their feet.

On the second panel (p. 287 top), in the background and on the right is seen

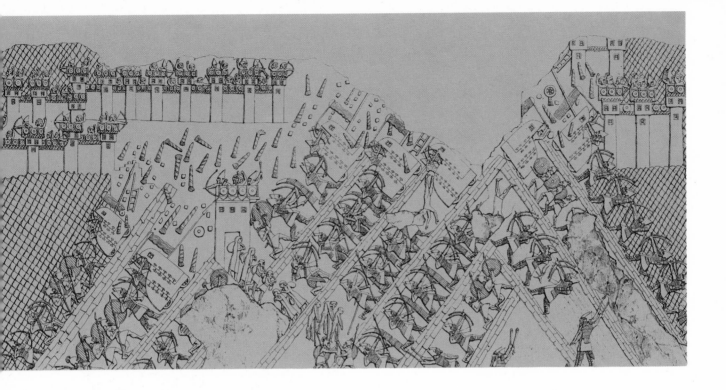

ty of Lachish with its upper and lower walls and the fortifications of the gateway towering above them (the picture corres-
onds exactly to the archaeological remains found on the site). On the turrets and pinnacles stand the men of Lachish, protected
y wooden frames and shields; thanks to these, the defenders can shoot their arrows and sling their stones while standing
pright. In the foreground, the Assyrian army is seen hurling itself into the assault. An attempt is being made to break down the
alls with siege engines, at least seven of which have been placed in position on ramps made of earth reinforced with logs of
ood (cf. p. 192). The defenders throw stones and burning torches at the engines. Their teams are thus obliged to protect the
ngines by pouring water on them from large scoops. The third and fourth panels (lower plates) show the inhabitants being
eported after the surrender of the city. The hilly terrain around Lachish, with its fruit-orchards, vine-plantations and fig-trees,
 clearly seen. The captives are being conducted by Assyrian soldiers past Sennacherib, who is seated on a magnificent throne
 front of the royal tent. Some soldiers are bringing in the spoil — ritual utensils, weapons and a chariot (p. 287 lower plate,
pper register), while others are torturing captives who have been bound to stakes (p.286 bottom register, right). On bo n
ese panels groups of deportees — men, women and children — are depicted in their distinctive dress. (Cf. the detail on p. 283).

AND when the king heard concerning Tirhaka king of Ethiopia, "Behold, he has set out to fight against you . . ." (2 Kings 19 : 9)

While Sennacherib was advancing on the cities of Judah, Tirhaka hastened to Judah's aid, apparently to forestall the approach of the Assyrian armies to within striking distance of the Egyptian border. Tirhaka, in Egyptian Taharka (689—664 B.C.), was the last ruler of the Twenty-fifth, Kushite, Dynasty in Egypt. From the biblical record it transpires that Tirhaka had achieved renown as a military commander as early as the year 701 B.C., even before he ascended the throne; and the Bible anticipates this by calling him "king of Kush" (Ethiopia). In the time of Sennacherib and his successors Esarhaddon and Ashurbanipal, Tirhaka was the most formidable rival of the Assyrians. Even after suffering severe defeats at their hands on the soil of Egypt, he continued to fight on until, in 664 B.C., Ashurbanipal conquered Thebes and put an end to his rule.

The right-hand plate is a black granite head of Tirhaka which was found at Thebes. At the top of the head can be seen the end of a kind of covering which was apparently worn under the metal helmet. On the left is a scarab-seal from Palmyra. The inscription proclaims the king's achievements: "Amen, Taharka, he hath caused to be made living for ever".

"BEHOLD, you have heard what the kings of Assyria have done to all lands, destroying them utterly. And shall you be delivered? Have the gods of the nations delivered them, the nations which my fathers destroyed, Gozan, Haran, Rezeph, and the people of Eden who were in Tel-Assar?"   (2 Kings 19 : 11-12)

In his pronouncement to Hezekiah, the Assyrian official called Rabshakeh, so far from denying the existence of the gods of the nations conquered by the Assyrians, explains that those very gods have themselves delivered up their peoples to the king of Assyria. In the same way he had previously explained Sennacherib's success against Judah: "The Lord said to me, Go up against this land and destroy it" (2 Kings 18 : 25). Shown on the left are three idols standing in the facade of the palace of Kappara, king of Gozan (10th or 9th cent. B.C.), one of the kingdoms conquered by Sennacherib's ancestors (see p. 284). The entrance to the palace is flanked by sphinxes which act as guardians of the threshold. The style of the sculpture is late Hittite. Below is an illustration of the custom in the ancient East, particularly in Assyria, of taking into captivity the gods of the vanquished. In this fragment of a relief from Nineveh, Assyrian soldiers are seen carrying off statues of gods of a captured city, probably of some Syrian people who were taken captive by Sennacherib. It was gods such as these that Sennacherib and his predecessors removed from Hamath, Arpad, Sepharvaim, Hena and Avva (2 Kings 18 : 34).

AT that time Merodach-Baladan the son of Baladan, king of Babylon, sent envoys with letters and a present to Hezekiah ... (2 Kings 20 : 12)

Merodach-Baladan (so in Isa. 39 : 1; here, with a slight change of spelling, Berodach), the Chaldean king of Beth Yakin in southern Babylonia, is famed as one of the most determined and daring enemies of Assyria at the end of the 8th cent. B.C. When Sargon II was enthroned in Assyria, Merodach-Baladan seized Babylon and ruled there, until Sargon deposed him in 710 B.C. When Sargon died and was succeeded by his son Sennacherib, Merodach-Baladan once more managed to make himself master of Babylon, with the assistance of his ally, the king of Elam. However, two years later (703 B.C.), Sennacherib advanced on him and compelled him to flee to Beth Yakin. In the course of this struggle he naturally sought allies, both east and west. His connections with Hezekiah were apparently formed at the beginning of Sennacherib's reign, before the Assyrian campaign against Judah. Isaiah the prophet, as is well known, did not welcome the emissaries of the Chaldean king, because of his opposition to any revolt against Assyria which was for him the appointed rod of God's anger.

In the picture — which is a reproduction of an inscribed boundary-stone *(kudurru)* — Merodach-Baladan (on the left) is seen bestowing a grant of land on a Babylonian official. The king, dressed in a long robe, is holding a small object in his right hand and a staff in his left. The official, whose dress is in the main similar to that of the king, is raising his hand in a gesture of reverence. Above the two figures are the emblems of four Babylonian gods: from left to right Nabu, Ninhursag, Ea and Marduk.

THE rest of the deeds of Hezekiah, and all his might, and how he made the pool and the conduit and brought water into the city, are they not written in the Book of the Chronicles of the Kings of Judah?

(2 Kings 20 : 20)

In its summing-up of Hezekiah's reign (715—687 B.C.) the Bible makes special mention of the measures taken by him to secure Jerusalem's water supply. From the various versions of the account of the installations commissioned by the king (2 Kings 20 : 20; 2 Chron. 32 : 3, 4, 30; Isa. 22 : 9, 11) it can be deduced that, in order to deprive a besieging enemy of water and ensure the besieged inhabitants of an adequate supply, Hezekiah blocked up the springs and an ancient conduit outside the walls, and deflected the waters of the Gihon (see p. 202) into the city by a channel cut through the rock.

The tunnelling work is vividly described in the Siloam Inscription (discovered in 1880) which was engraved on the wall of the completed tunnel. The inscription — reproduced above — is broken and the beginning seems to be missing. It is about 15 in. high and about 29 in. long. It is written in biblical Hebrew; both the contents and the lettering show that it is from the reign of Hezekiah. The cutting of this tunnel was, for those times, a remarkable feat of engineering, calling for accurate planning based on numerous preliminary calculations. The workmen cut through the rock from both ends of the tunnel till they met in the middle, as related in the inscription: "And on the day of the piercing through, the hewers smote each so as to meet his fellow, pick against pick." When the work was completed, "the water flowed from the source to the pool, 1200 cubits."

An echo of the acclamation with which Hezekiah's achievement was received can still be heard in the words of Ben Sira (Eccles. 48 : 17): "Hezekiah fortified his city, in that he brought water into it, and he hewed through the rocks with iron and dammed up the pool with mountains."

"AND I will wipe Jerusalem as one wipes a dish, wiping it and turning it upside down."

(2 Kings 21 : 13)

In proclaiming the coming of God's wrath upon Judah and Jerusalem (2 Kings 21 : 10—16), the prophets in the reign of Manasseh remind their bearers of the fall of Samaria and the kingdom of Israel: "And I will stretch over Jerusalem the measuring line of Samaria, and the plummet of the house of Ahab" (ibid. 13). Jerusalem will be overthrown, like a plate that, having been cleaned and wiped, is turned upside down. The popular parable of the plate is used here in reference to the deportation of the people from their devastated land. A similar parable, that of the overturned bowl, was popular in later generations.

In biblical times the plate (Heb. *salahat*) was used both for cooking and for serving food (Prov. 19 : 24; 26 : 15; 2 Chron. 35 :13). The plate seen in the photograph above is of the type characteristic of the period of the Monarchy, such as has been found in many places in Israel. This particular plate comes from Judah and is distinguished by its red slip which has been well burnished on the potter's wheel (the marks of the burnishing are still visible). It is almost flat and can easily be wiped clean. From the popular parable we learn that, after a dish had been cleaned, it was customary to put it away face downwards.

"AND let them give it to the workmen who are at the house of the LORD, repairing the house, that is, to the carpenters and to the builders, and to the masons . . ."

(2 Kings 22 : 5-6)

The Book of Kings records two renovations of the Temple in Jerusalem: the first in the reign of Jehoash (see p. 272), and the second in the reign of Josiah. In both cases the work of repair was paid for, at the king's command, with the silver which the people were accustomed to bring to the Temple and which was collected in a special box near the altar. Moreover, in both cases it was the king's secretary and the high priest who removed the silver from the box, melted it down and subsequently handed it into the charge of the responsible overseers, "who have the oversight of the house of the Lord." The latter then paid the several kinds of craftsmen employed on the work. No account was demanded of the overseers, since it was known that "they dealt honestly" (2 Kings 12 : 12—16; 22 : 5—7).

In the ancient East it was usual for kings to take the temples under their care and to have them renovated from time to time. The relief reproduced above shows Ashurbanipal, king of Assyria (7th cent. B.C.), holding a basket on his head. This apparently symbolizes the king's personal interest in the renovation of the temple of Esagila in Babylon (cf. Vol. I, p. 44).

AND he deposed the idolatrous priests whom the kings of Judah had ordained . . . those also who burned incense to Baal, to the sun, and the moon, and the constellations, and all the host of the heavens.

(2 Kings 23 : 5)

Josiah's aim in his religious reforms was not only to restore the original worship of God, but at the same time to stamp out all remnants of idolatry — popular and "official" alike. One of these idolatrous rites was the burning of offerings to the heavenly bodies. Again and again in the Bible it is explicitly forbidden to worship the sun, the moon and the heavenly bodies and to bow down to them (Deut. 4 : 19; 17 : 3; Jer. 8 : 2; and elsewhere). The "Baal" in our verse is apparently Baal of the skies, whose rites have already been described in detail in the account of Elijah's contest on Mount Carmel (1 Kings 18 : 20—29; see p. 240). The word translated "constellations" (Heb. *mazalot*) denotes the signs of the Zodiac. Originally an Akkadian word, it appears in a Canaanite inscription of the 4th cent. B.C. (excavated at Larnaka in Cyprus) as *mzl n'm,* meaning "good fortune" as in post-biblical Hebrew *(mazal).*

A bronze model (reproduced above) from the 12th cent. B.C., found at Susa, is considered by many scholars to illustrate the cult of the dawn ("the rising of the sun" in Assyrian terminology). According to a Jewish tradition, this cult was also practised by "the people of Jerusalem". Two naked figures are seen in a kneeling posture. One of them is stretching out his hands in front of him, and the other is holding a basin of water for lustration. At the right stands a building with steps, symbolizing a temple. The surface of the model is covered with altars, ritual pillars, asherah trees, water-containers, libation basins and other ritual appurtenances.

A<small>ND</small> he removed the horses that the kings of Judah had dedicated to the sun, at the entrance to the house of the L<small>ORD</small>, by the chamber of Nathan-Melech the chamberlain, which was in the precincts; and he burned the chariots of the sun with fire.   (2 Kings 23 : 11)

As part of his purification of the Temple from all manifestations of idolatry, King Josiah did away with the horses and chariots (in the Septuagint "chariot") that had been dedicated to the sun. The connection of these horses and chariots with sun-worship is still somewhat obscure. Some scholars connect the chariot with Helios, the sun-god of Greek mythology. There is Roman evidence that, on the island of Rhodes, four horses were sacrificed at the annual sun-festival. Furthermore, one of the titles given in Akkadian to the chief minister of the sun-god was "the rider of the chariot".

It is noteworthy that, in Assyrian tradition, "the chariot of the sun" was attached to a portable shrine which always accompanied the Assyrian kings on their military campaigns. A representation of the scene in such a war-camp is given in the picture reproduced above from one of the reliefs of Sennacherib at Nineveh. Seen in the upper register is a portable shrine at which the priests are burning incense. An incense altar and offering table stand in front of the chariot into which are fixed two upright posts, each bearing an image of the sun, the emblem of the god Shamash. The heads of the beasts of prey on the chariot-shaft, only one of which is seen in the reproduction, symbolize the gods of war, Nergal and Ninurta.

IN his days Pharaoh Neco king of Egypt went up to the king of Assyria to the river Euphrates. King Josiah went to meet him; and Pharaoh Neco slew him at Megiddo, when he saw him.

(2 Kings 23 : 29)

With the capture of Nineveh by the united Babylonian and Median armies in 612 B.C. the total collapse of Assyria appeared imminent. This was Babylonia's opportunity to replace Assyria as the dominant power; but, just at this juncture, Egypt recovered some of its former strength and came to the aid of Assyria, in an effort to check the expansion of Babylon and to gain control of Palestine and Syria. From a Babylonian chronicle it appears probable that the Egyptian king Neco marched to the Euphrates as an ally of Assyria. In the new alignment of political forces, Josiah in 609 B.C. took his stand against Egypt (and therefore on the side of Babylonia), because he regarded Egyptian domination as the greater threat. He therefore attempted to hold up the Egyptian advance along the "sea road" at the vital pass of Megiddo. The ensuing battle was apparently short and ended in an Egyptian victory; Josiah himself was mortally wounded. According to the account in 2 Chron. 35 : 23—24, he was carried by his servants from Megiddo to Jerusalem where he died. Neco continued his advance to the Euphrates from which the Babylonians dislodged him only in 605 B.C.

Above is an aerial photograph of the mound of Megiddo showing how it dominates the surrounding country. A citadel, apparently from the time of Josiah, was found among its ruins.

AND Nebuchadnezzar king of Babylon came to the city, while his servants were besieging it; and Jehoiachin the king of Judah gave himself up to the king of Babylon . . .

(2 Kings 24 : 11-12)

Under Nebuchadnezzar, who ascended the throne in 604 B.C., the Babylonians finally wrested the control of Syria and Palestine from the Egyptians. Jehoiachin had only reigned for three months when Nebuchadnezzar captured Jerusalem and despoiled the treasuries of the Temple and of the royal palace. Jehoiachin was taken into captivity together with the members of his court, the ministers, the craftsmen, the smiths and all the military commanders. A Babylonian chronicle from the time of Nebuchadnezzar (right plate) confirms the biblical account of the surrender of Jerusalem in Jehoiachin's reign and the enthroning of Zedekiah by the Babylonian monarch (2 Kings 24 : 8—17; 2 Chron. 36 : 9—10): "And he (i.e. Nebuchadnezzar) encamped against the city of Judah (i.e. Jerusalem), and in the month of Adar, on the second day, he captured the city and took the king prisoner. A king of his own choice he set up in its midst; its heavy tribute he received and carried it off to Babylon". This inscription provides us with the exact date when Jerusalem fell, viz: the second of Adar (March 16th), at the end of the seventh year of Nebuchadnezzar's reign (597 B.C.; Jer. 52 : 28). However, the deportation of the Judaeans to Babylon took place some time later, in Nebuchadnezzar's eighth year (2 Kings 24 : 12).

Reproduced above is a seal-impression bearing the words: "to Elyaqim, the servant of Jochin." Similar impressions have been found on the handles of pottery vessels excavated at Tell Beit Mirsim and Beth-Shemesh. The owner of this particular seal, Elyaqim, was one of the officials of King Jehoiachin. "Jochin" is one of the many variations of his name.

AND he burned the house of the LORD, and the king's house and all the houses of Jerusalem; every great house he burned down. And . . . broke down the walls around Jerusalem.

(2 Kings 25 : 9-10)

It was the policy of the Assyrian and Babylonian kings to raze and burn the cities that they had taken by assault. Such also was the fate meted out to Jerusalem in Nebuchadnezzar's second campaign against Judah in 586 B.C. The actual work of destruction was entrusted to Nebuzaradan, the captain of the guard, who performed his task with systematic thoroughness. The national leaders and royal ministers were put to death (2 Kings 25: 18—22), the remaining dignitaries were deported (ibid. 11), the Temple treasure was pillaged (ibid. 12—18), and the city walls reduced to rubble (ibid. 10). The conquerors vented their fury on the Temple, on the royal palace, and on "every great house".

The picture on p. 299, reproduced from the palace of Ashurbanipal at Nineveh, illustrates the fate of the city of Hamanu in Elam after its capture by the Assyrian army. Soldiers, specially trained for the purpose, are seen breaking down the outer wall of the city, while the gateway and towers go up in flames. Other Assyrian troops, laden with loot, are making their way out of the city. One of them is driving two of the captured inhabitants in front of him. At the very bottom of the relief captive inhabitants of the city are seen eating, under the supervision of an Assyrian guard.

The destruction of Jerusalem put an end to the political independence of Judah which was turned into a Babylonian province. But the hope of redemption and national revival lived on in the people's hearts.

INDEXES

OBJECTS AND MONUMENTS

REPRODUCTIONS

MAPS (drawn by Eng. Pinhas Yoeli)

RECONSTRUCTIONS

PHOTOGRAPHS